Learn Corona SDK
Game Development

Frank W. Zammetti

Learn Corona SDK Game Development

ISBN 978-1-4302-5068-5

ISBN 978-1-4302-5069-2 (eBook)

President and Publisher: Paul Manning
Lead Editor: Michelle Lowman
Development Editor: Douglas Pundick
Technical Reviewer: Peach Pellen
Editorial Board: Steve Anglin, Mark Beckner, Ewan Buckingham, Gary Cornell, Louise Corrigan, Morgan Ertel, Jonathan Gennick, Jonathan Hassell, Robert Hutchinson, Michelle Lowman, James Markham, Matthew Moodie, Jeff Olson, Jeffrey Pepper, Douglas Pundick, Ben Renow-Clarke, Dominic Shakeshaft, Gwenan Spearing, Matt Wade, Tom Welsh
Coordinating Editor: Christine Ricketts
Copy Editor: James Fraleigh
Compositor: SPi Global
Indexer: SPi Global
Artist: SPi Global
Cover Designer: Anna Ishchenko

Distributed to the book trade worldwide by Springer Science+Business Media New York, 233 Spring Street, 6th Floor, New York, NY 10013. Phone 1-800-SPRINGER, fax (201) 348-4505, e-mail orders-ny@springer-sbm.com, or visit www.springeronline.com. Apress Media, LLC is a California LLC and the sole member (owner) is Springer Science + Business Media Finance Inc (SSBM Finance Inc). SSBM Finance Inc is a Delaware corporation.

For information on translations, please e-mail rights@apress.com, or visit www.apress.com.

Apress and friends of ED books may be purchased in bulk for academic, corporate, or promotional use. eBook versions and licenses are also available for most titles. For more information, reference our Special Bulk Sales–eBook Licensing web page at www.apress.com/bulk-sales.

Any source code or other supplementary materials referenced by the author in this text is available to readers at www.apress.com. For detailed information about how to locate your book's source code, go to www.apress.com/source-code.

You know, after you've written seven books, it gets rather difficult to write something as seemingly simple as a dedication. I've done all the usual dedications already: wife, kids, parents, friends, and acquaintances. I've even dedicated a few to famous figures, dearly departed artists, inanimate objects, fictional characters I dig, universal constants in physics that make life possible and, once, even to myself!

Where do you go from there exactly?!

So, after long, tortured hours of thought on this, it finally came to me.

I dedicate this book to: **this book!**

For, without this book, this book would surely not exist. It is this book that makes this book possible.

Nah, just kidding! Dedicated to my wife, kids, parents, friend, yada yada yada. Thanks and love to all!

Contents at a Glance

Contents

About the Author

Frank W. Zammetti is a servant of the dark lord Sauron but yet is also, paradoxically, one of Daenerys Targaryen's queen's guards and **also** a member of the Q Continuum. Go figure.

In addition, in his spare time, Frank is a longtime developer with around a quarter-century in the IT industry, including over a decade of mobile development experience on a range of platforms using a number of different technologies. He is currently a lead developer/architect for a major US financial firm—but don't hold that against him, the whole "collapse of the financial system and ruin of Western civilization" thing wasn't his fault. Well, **probably** not.

Frank is an occasional speaker at technical conferences and user groups, and an even more frequent eater of free pizza at such events.

Frank is the author of six other books from Apress on a number of topics in the realms of web and mobile development, as well as a number of independent articles for various publications.

Last, Frank may or may not be a ninja assassin. If you ever know for sure, it's too late.

Keep those lights on at night!

About the Technical Reviewer

Peach Pellen has been a mobile application developer since 2009 and worked at Ansca Mobile from 2010 until 2012 as Director of Developer Relations.

She is now an Evangelist at Lanica, creators of the Platino game engine, founded by the former CEO and founder of Ansca Mobile. Lanica is privately held in Mountain View, CA and is currently funded by Appcelerator.

Peach also runs Techority, a website devoted to mobile app development tutorials and other e-learning curriculums.

Acknowledgments

I'd like to thank Peach Pellen for her great work in keeping me honest from a technical standpoint throughout this book. No matter how much experience, knowledge, and skill you **think** you have, nobody's perfect, least of all me, and having a talented person to point out where you blew it is absolutely invaluable!

I also need to thank everyone who had a hand in creating this book on the Apress team, because one thing you learn quickly when writing a book is that you can't do it alone—you need lots of people to help make you look good and get a project like this done! So, to Steve Anglin, Mark Beckner, Ewan Buckingham, Gary Cornell, Louise Corrigan, Morgan Ertel, Jonathan Gennick, Jonathan Hassell, Robert Hutchinson, Michelle Lowman, James Markham, Matthew Moodie, Jeff Olson, Jeffrey Pepper, Douglas Pundick, Ben Renow-Clarke, Dominic Shakeshaft, Gwenan Spearing, Matt Wade, Tom Welsh, Christine Ricketts, James Fraleigh, Anna Ishchenko, and anyone I may have quite inadvertently left out: **thank you, thank you, thank you!**

Last but not least, thank you to Corona Labs for creating a product I actually **wanted** to write about!

Introduction

Writing mobile apps is hard. Writing mobile **games** is even more so.

Why is that? Well, there are probably lots of reasons I could state, but one jumps to the forefront almost immediately: variety. The variety of platforms available today is staggering when you consider developing an application that runs everywhere. From iOS to Android, from BlackBerry to Windows Mobile, not to mention a number of lesser platforms, there are lots of places your app could run.

Even if you simply concern yourself with the two market-share leaders, iOS and Android, it's still a daunting task to develop for both. Sure, you could always develop two versions of the same application targeted for each platform, and plenty of times that's exactly what is done. That approach, however, has the significant downside of requiring substantially different skill sets and tools, which means you generally need two sets of developers to maintain two completely (or nearly completely, anyway) code bases.

You can, of course, go with a web-based approach and let HTML, JavaScript, and CSS be the common platform you develop to. While that works in many cases, for things like games it tends not to work as well. You're giving up much of the capabilities, power, and performance of the native platforms in that model, something most developers would prefer not to do. It's a trade-off to consider, though: maintaining a single, potentially less feature-rich and performant code base versus maintaining multiple "ideal" code bases.

Thankfully, there's another option. There are a number of cross-platform tools that let you develop a single code base that can run on multiple platforms while still maintaining most, if not all, of the native capabilities you'd have if you'd done true native development.

Of them, the Corona SDK is one of the best.

In this book, we'll explore the Corona SDK together, see what it has to offer, and learn how to use it to develop high-performance applications that can run equally well on iOS and Android. We'll focus our attention on game development, since that's what Corona is focused on. However, we'll also see how it's not **exclusively** for that—you can in fact develop **any** type of application you want with Corona!

The Book: An Overview

We'll break up the experience over the course of 11 chapters in which we'll build a game, Astro Rescue, that will demonstrate a significant chunk of Corona functionality. The contents of those 11 chapters will break down thusly:

1. What is Corona? Why use it? The functionality it provides, how to get it, licensing and a first small example running in the simulator on your desktop PC.

2. The basics of Lua, the language that underpins Corona.

3. The overall structure of a typical Corona game, including things like code modules, the Storyboard API, basic event processing, object-oriented game design, program flow, and configuration files.

4. Getting started with graphics. Getting things on the screen, moving them around, memory management, transitions, UI widgets, and more.

5. The core Astro Rescue game code. We'll get deeper into graphics, get going with some audio, and of course the underlying logic behind the game. Things like the main loop, core events, and the beginning of input handling. We'll get into sprites and animation in more depth and get a first look at physics.

6. Deeper into the core game code we go! We'll walk through the main loop in detail and look closer at graphics, transitions and animation, drawing techniques, and so on.

7. Various forms of input events such as touch, accelerometer, and gyroscope control will be looked at here.

8. Collision events, a core concept of most games. Here we'll also get into some "special effects" like masking and gradients.

9. We'll complete walking through the game code here and finish up any odds and ends that remain to be seen.

10. Some advanced topics such as ads, SQLite, in-app purchases, and game network integration.

11. How to take the now-completed Astro Rescue project and build it for Android and iOS devices, how to get it onto those devices, and test and debugging techniques. We'll also look at the app store models available to us and how to get your app published in them.

By the end, you'll have a solid foundation on which to build. You'll have a good picture of what Corona provides and a better understanding of how to put it to good use. You'll be able to quickly and easily create the next great Angry Birds–level hit, at which point I hope you remember your favorite author. ☺

Saving Your Fingers

Are you the sort that likes to type in every bit of code you see in a book? If so, have at it and enjoy!

For the rest of us, you can obtain the source code for this book by visiting www.apress.com/source-code and save yourself a lot of time and energy.

Perfection Is Relative

This book is certified 100% flawless.

Not a single mistake will be found anywhere within it.

On the off chance that proves to not be **entirely** accurate, errata will be posted on the Apress web site.

But, as I said, its not a real concern anyway.

;)

If You Want to Yap at Me

Have a comment to fire at me? A compliment to pay? A complaint to lodge? I'm all ears—virtually of course! Feel free to fling e-mails my way at fzammetti@omnytex.com. I'm also on "the Twitter" at the not very creative username of @fzammetti.

Part 1

Get Ready . . . Get Set . . .

Walking on water and developing software from a specification are easy . . . if both are frozen!

—Edward V. Berard

On two occasions I have been asked, "Pray, Mr. Babbage, if you put into the machine wrong figures, will the right answers come out?" I am not able rightly to apprehend the kind of confusion of ideas that could provoke such a question.

—Charles Babbage

I have always wished for my computer to be as easy to use as my telephone. My wish has come true because I can no longer figure out how to use my telephone.

—Bjarne Stroustrup

Einstein argued that there must be simplified explanations of nature, because God is not capricious or arbitrary. No such faith comforts the software engineer.

—Fred Brooks

Say Hello to My Little Friend: The Corona SDK

When did you start programming? What first piqued your interest? If it became a lifelong passion, as it has with me, then you almost certainly have an interesting story to tell when answering that question.

My own story is in many ways unique in that I was most definitely in the right place at the right time at a special point in human history when personal computers were just coming into existence and, more importantly, just starting to enter the public consciousness. Through a bit of luck, coupled with a drive to do something I found enthralling, I was propelled down a very specific road in life that I am happily still traveling.

You see, as David said in **Prometheus,** "Big things have small beginnings." (Your opinion of that movie will determine whether you find that line the best thing about it or just one of many cool things!)

The Corona SDK is in a sense this same concept in microcosm: when you look at what it is, and especially at how easy it makes a great many otherwise complex things, it's really kind of surprising, perhaps even shocking, that you can do such incredible things with it with so little effort.

This book, I hope, will provide you with the foundation you need to take your idea—however small the kernel of the idea may be—and, combined with the Corona SDK, grow it into something huge.

Before I get to the Corona SDK itself though, allow me to be a bit self-centered and talk a little bit about myself!

A Long Time Ago In a School (Perhaps) Far, Far Away . . .

When I was around nine years old, my school district introduced a new curriculum dealing with computers. It was only a trial program and they didn't know if it would get any traction, so they asked six of the top students in the school if they'd like to participate. As you can guess, I was one of those students (my grades subsequently sank down to much more, umm, let's go with **modest** levels . . . but at the time I was near the top). I had heard about computers on **Star Trek** and other television shows, but I had never seen one in person to that point in my life and I didn't really have an appreciation for what they were and what they could really do. In any case, being a science and electronics geek even at that age I of course said, "Absolutely I want in!"

So, for about an hour once a week I got to leave my regular class and head down to a small room with a couple of computers and learn how to program (after learning what they really were and could do, of course). We six initial students did this for a few weeks, but seemingly with each class the number of students that showed up shrank (it was completely voluntary and we could quit at any time). Eventually, it was just me left.

One day, I had gone to the computer lab after school and I discovered to my surprise that I wasn't alone, as had always been the case before. On this day, another student (also named Frank, coincidentally) was there. It turns out this other Frank was quite a bit more advanced than I was at programming. He had written a program that at the time amazed me beyond words. What it did was draw a man, like so:

```
\ 0 /
 \#/
  #
 / \
/   \
```

I know, that barely looks like a man! However, you have to understand that until that point all I had seen in person on a computer screen was plain old text. I mean, I thought it was extremely cool that I could have text that asked for two numbers and text that told me what they were when multiplied by each other—that on its own was cool! An actual graphical man, though? That was a whole other level of cool!

The program that alter-Frank made also drew the man in another slightly different way:

```
  0
 /#\
/ # \
 | |
 | |
```

It would draw that first version of the man, wait maybe a quarter second, then clear the screen and draw the other version. The program did this repeatedly and the effect, for anyone that has ever drawn some pictures in a notebook and then rapidly flipped the pages, was animation!

Believe me: I realize just how silly all of this sounds when compared to our modern Xbox games. However, you have to try to understand what it was like for me: this was just astounding! He had essentially replicated what you do with a notebook and some drawing **on a computer screen!** He took a very simple, basic technique and wrote a program to do it, yielding something that, really, most people at that point hadn't seen computers do.

Now, it didn't take long at all before I realized that this conceptually simple technique leads quite naturally to something much greater: video games! The basic notion of drawing something on the screen, clearing the screen, and then drawing it slightly differently is, to this day, the core concept behind how a video game works in terms of what you see on the screen. It's all a much more complex affair now naturally, but the basic foundation is identical to what my doppelganger showed me that day.

Before that week was out, I had written my first very simple video game that had graphics. As I recall, it was nothing but a simple Pong-type game, but that was enough. I knew I would be programming games for the rest of my life.

Back to the Future

A big part of working in information technology, where I make my living, is keeping your skills sharp. As a longtime developer and author, others recognize me as someone who strives to keep his skill set current and his abilities honed. As such, I frequently am asked by less-experienced developers for advice on what they can and should do to improve their skills.

My answer for a great many years has been three simple words: **write video games!**

There are a number of key benefits to writing video games, some less obvious than others.

First, writing video games requires you to tackle problems that you wouldn't otherwise encounter in typical "business" programming, and while the solutions to those problems aren't necessarily applicable directly on the job, the mental processes that go into solving those problems are.

Second, some of what you have to deal with when writing video games **is** in fact directly applicable! AI, data structures, performance tuning, and much more—these are things that come into play all the time in the business world just as often as in game development.

A third important benefit is that writing games is **fun!** This matters and shouldn't be discounted, because programming for a living in nearly any environment—unless you happen to have the **perfect** job, I suppose—isn't always as fun as you'd like it to be. Sure, for most of us developers, simply solving problems brings us joy, so we can derive happiness in our jobs where others sometimes can't in theirs. Nevertheless, there are always periods that drag, always projects that you'd rather not be doing. Of course, it's your job, so you do them anyway. Sometimes it's also just **very hard** work that can be very stressful.

Writing video games is different, though, the very nature of what you're programming is **intended** to be **fun!** The process of creating it is similarly fun!

Ultimately though, writing video games is a challenge, one that sharpens your skills and makes you a better overall programmer, and that's why I always counsel developers to write games in their spare time.

The point of course being that whatever your goals for the games you write, whether it's to make a million bucks or just to hone your skills, it's one of the very best programming exercises you can do for yourself.

Hey, Wait, Isn't This Book about the Corona SDK?!

All of that being said, programming games can also be **hard.** Especially when we're talking about mobile game development, that can be very true. In the mobile space, you have an additional challenge of dealing with the multitude of platforms out there in consumers' hands. Do you write your game for iOS? Do you write it for Android? What about Windows Phone? Or BlackBerry? Or webOS? And on and on and on in this ever-changing environment.

Of course, if you want to try to sell your work you'll want to hit as many of those platforms as you possibly can to give yourself as much of a chance as possible at success, so now you're talking about cross-platform development. That's where it gets **really** hard! They all have different technological underpinnings, different ways of writing code, different languages, integrated development environment (IDEs), deployment models, et cetera. How do you pull that trick off?

There's definitely multiple ways to go about it, some better than others. One way that has become very popular these days, and the way this book focuses on, is to find some third-party cross-platform library that solves the multiplatform problem for you. When you do that, in a sense you take a virtual-machine approach: the library presents an application programming interface (API) to you that it guarantees will work the same (mostly, anyway, as we'll see in later chapters) across all the platforms it supports. You write your application to that API, which represents a virtualized machine, instead of targeting the physical platform natively. The library acts as an abstraction layer for you, keeping all the platform differences hidden for the most part. It's not a true virtual machine in the case of Java, for example, but conceptually from your programmer's point of view, it's very similar.

That's precisely what the Corona SDK is, or simply Corona for short from here on out.

Corona: History at a Glance

Corona is a product of Corona Labs, Inc., formerly Ansca Mobile. It was originally created by Walter Luh and Carlos Icaza, former employees of Adobe. Corona saw its first release in December 2009 supporting a single platform: Apple's iOS, the iPhone more specifically, since this was before the iPad arrived (and the iPod Touch, for the purposes of this discussion, isn't really any different than the iPhone). New versions with new features came fairly quickly following the initial release.

In April 2010 the 2.0 version of Corona was released, and this is when things really started to pick up as this was the first cross-platform release, now supporting not only the iPhone but now the iPad and, more importantly in a sense, Android. I don't say "more importantly" in any way to belittle iOS but only to say that Android represents the first true cross-platform release (after all, the iPad still runs iOS).

January 2011 saw another big feature released: the ability to develop on Windows. Up until that point only Unix-based platforms, MacOS more specifically, could run the Corona toolset (which I'll get to shortly).

April 2011 introduced another new target platform to Corona: Barnes and Noble's NOOK Color tablet.

Over this whole timeline, Corona's popularity began to grow. Many apps and games atop the charts of all the popular app stores were created with Corona, among them Bubble Ball (see Figure 1-1), the product of eighth-grader Robert Nay, which managed to reach the very top of the free-game chart in the iTunes Store!

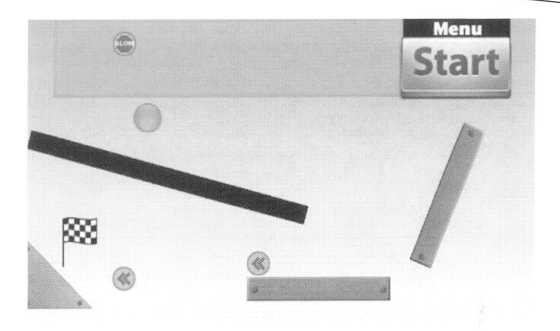

Figure 1-1. *Bubble Ball screenshot*

Many other games have ridden Corona to high places on the charts and have brought in good money for their developers, and this is on all platforms Corona supports. Some other great examples of Corona include Engineer by Etherient, as seen in Figure 1-2.

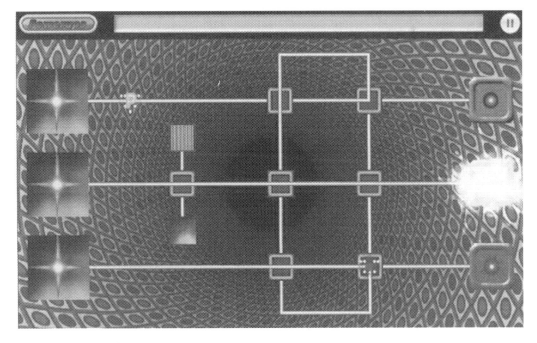

Figure 1-2. *Engineer screenshot*

In the interest of full disclosure, Engineer is actually my own game. However, another one that isn't is The Secret of Grisly Manor, from developer Fire Maple Games, as seen in Figure 1-3.

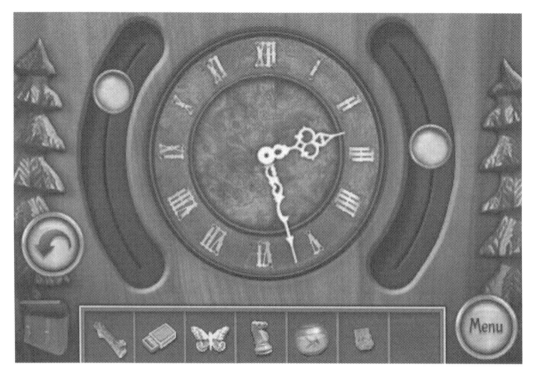

Figure 1-3. The Secret of Grisly Manor screenshot

As you can see, Corona is a horse you can most definitely ride to a win in mobile application development, most especially if you're developing games. But, none of this really answers what Corona is and what it can really do, so let's get into those details now.

A Tool That Works for You

Corona is a software development kit (SDK) that uses the Lua scripting language layered on top of C++ and OpenGL. It uses a proprietary OpenGL ES rendering engine that provides applications written with it automatic hardware acceleration. This includes sprites, a concept that we'll get into starting in chapter 5, which are animated using the device's graphics processing unit, or GPU. What this means in short is that without doing very much optimization on your part, the games (and nongame apps) that you build with Corona should be quite fast on most devices.

> **Note** As with virtually any discussion of performance in programming, it's generally accepted that Corona apps can be as fast as those written with most other libraries. It's also not hard to write your code in such a way that you kill performance. I'll discuss optimizations and the things to watch out for as you go through the chapters of this book. The point stands though: so long as you don't go out of your way to hurt performance, and you don't do anything truly boneheaded, performance shouldn't be a concern for most projects.

Corona also includes a transition library that allows you to do tween-based animations on sprites and other objects with a single line of code in most cases. If you've ever hand-coded animations before, then you realize how fantastic something like the following actually is:

```
transition.to(player, {
  time = 500, delay = 1000, alpha = 0,
  onComplete = function()
    print("Done");
  end
});
```

That's a single line of code (albeit formatted across a couple of physical lines in a text editor) that fades an object referenced by the variable player after waiting one second after its execution over the course of half a second, and then displays a message in the console window (which you can open alongside the simulator for debugging purposes). The best part is that this goes off and happens without any intervention on your part. You don't need to continually update the alpha property of the object over time, don't need to update anything on the screen manually, none of that sort of stuff that is typical in most graphics-related programming. You can animate a great many properties of an object, all at once or separately, yielding some impressively complex animations—again, with very little code, and no ongoing work on your part.

In fact, it's this notion of doing the complex with simple code that is a key concept of Corona, and you'll be seeing plenty of that as you progress through this book. But for now, let's get back to describing Corona at a fairly high level.

The Corona API is rich and extensive and provides a great many capabilities. As I've mentioned, sprites and tween-based animations are a big part of it. You also get native UI integration; audio API functions; the ability to interact with native device components such as camera, GPS, various sensors, and multimedia playback; fonts and text functions; and a highly robust built-in physics engine. You also get things like integration with online scorekeeping systems, database functionality, direct file system I/O, and analytics. You of course also get some of the more primitive types of APIs you'd expect such as math utilities, collections, cryptographical functions, and network access.

In other words, virtually everything you might need to build any type of application is almost certainly present in Corona, and if they're not you can roll in any of a number of third-party libraries to augment your needs (I'll talk about third-party add-ons in chapter 10).

You can run Corona on either Windows or OS X machines to do your development work, and it installs like any other application you've ever installed for either platform. You can download a completely 100% functional SDK from the Corona web site at http://coronalabs.com. In fact, now would be as good a time as any to go ahead and do that if you haven't already. Go ahead, I'll wait patiently for you!

> **Note**   Although you can download the SDK for free, develop your application, and test as for as long as you want, Corona is not actually free. To be able to release apps written with Corona to one of the stores, you'll need to purchase a yearly subscription. The prices aren't too bad, even for a small independent developer such as myself (at the time of this writing it's $349 for the all-inclusive option, or $199 for either iOS support only or Android support only). There are a number of other benefits that come with this cost: access to subscriber-only forums for support, faster build times (we'll talk about building apps in chapter 11 and why this matters), and access to the latest versions of Corona before the public releases (which are updated only two or three times a year on average).

The Corona SDK includes the usual SDK components including the API libraries, documentation, and examples.

More important, though, it also includes the Corona Simulator. The simulator is a cross-platform application that, as the name implies, allows you to simulate a target platform. It doesn't simulate an iOS device or an Android device; what it does essentially is simulate an idealized device that supports the Corona API. You write your application to that API, **not** to the underlying platform you intend to target. The simulator then runs your code at more or less full speed. What this means to you as a developer is that what you see in the simulator is, 9 times out of 10, what you'll see on a real device. As with all simulator/emulator applications, there's sometimes some imperfection that sneaks through, but by and large you should run into very few differences between simulator and real device.

The simulator is actually a very simple application to use and looks like what you see in Figure 1-4.

Figure 1-4 *The Corona simulator*

You can run the simulator in portrait or landscape mode, whichever is appropriate to the application you're building, and you can select from a number of different skins to give the simulator the appearance of a physical device. In the screenshot in Figure 1-4 I'm using the Android Nexus One skin. Selecting a skin not only changes the outwards appearance of the simulated device, but also changes the virtual screen size, allowing you to test your application across a range of screen variants.

You also have the ability to zoom the simulator to let you see details a bit closer. This can be especially useful when you're doing your final round or two of tweaks to make sure everything is lining up exactly right. In addition to zooming, you also have the ability with the simulator to rotate the device various ways and to shake the device to exercise gyroscope functionality.

The very first time you start the simulator you will actually be greeted with the Welcome screen, as seen in Figure 1-5. From here you can do a number of interesting things. First, you can create a new project. This will create a template for you with all the basic files you need to have a working Corona application. You can do that and immediately run the application in the simulator. Naturally, you can launch the simulator itself and run an application you select in it. You can also access a collection of demos and examples that show you how to do all sorts of things with Corona. Interestingly, I had never noticed the Demos section before writing this very paragraph! Just goes to show that even when you've been using Corona a while you'll still find new, interesting things that it can do that you didn't know before, even aside from the new features that show up frequently.

Figure 1-5 Corona simulator welcome screen

Last, assuming you've ponied up the subscription cost, you can also access your online dashboard. Here you can get all sorts of useful information about Corona and the applications you've published. This uses the analytics capabilities in Corona to tell you things like how many people are playing a game you've published. You can also get information about programs from third parties that have partnered with Corona Labs to provide you with additional services for things like promoting your game.

Another feature that definitely needs to be mentioned is Corona's build system. In short, when you build an application for distribution, whether that's to an app store or to your own device for testing, that happens in the cloud, meaning on Corona Labs' own servers. For example, for Android builds you **do not** need to have the Android SDK installed at all! You initiate a build from the simulator and it packages up your application code and assets, ships it all off the Corona Labs' servers, and in a few seconds (normally) you get back a packaged application (an .apk file in the case of Android) that you can load up on a real device immediately. For iOS builds, the story is only marginally more complex; you **do** need Apple's SDK installed in that case, and you **must** do the build on a Mac, because Windows machines cannot do iOS builds at this time. There's also a little bit more involved when you're doing a build for real distribution, as opposed to development, but that's a story for chapter 11. For now it's enough to know that Corona Labs has taken most of the pain out of device-specific application building, and that's a Wonderful Thing™.

Note   Only your Lua script, in the form of precompiled bytecode stripped of all comments and debugging information, is ever sent to the Corona servers. Your images, sounds and other assets are not sent to the server.

Although not directly supplied by Corona Labs, there are a number of add-ons available that extend Corona in exciting ways. Three of the most popular come from the same company, X-Pressive. They are Particle Candy, Widget Candy, and Text Candy. Particle Candy adds amazing particle effects such as smoke, explosions, electrical sparks, and fire. These are real-time rendered effects with all sorts of manipulations possible. Using Particle Candy can give your game that extra professional look. Text Candy provides a host of text rendering options including animations. Ever see a game title screen with the name of the game bouncing around, spinning, growing, and shrinking, that sort of thing? Well, Text Candy lets you do that sort of thing with ease! Last, Widget Candy provides a collection of graphical user interface (GUI) widgets to use in your apps such as buttons, sliders, progress bars, and grids.

Aside from these sorts of add-on libraries there are all sorts of tools, some free and some not, to make developing with Corona easier. From tools to create physics bodies from your graphical assets to tools for creating tile-based levels and tools for creating sprites from Flash assets, there's always something available for virtually any need you may have that isn't covered by Corona itself.

So now that you have at least a baseline concept of what Corona is and what it can do, how about you jump right in and put together a simple application, just to get your feet wet a little bit?

Baby-Steppin' It

From here on out, I will assume that you have done the following:

- Downloaded and installed Corona on your chosen development platform
- Run it to confirm it works and have registered your copy (you'll need to do that the first time you run it)
- Acquired at least **some** programming experience

While you do not need to be an expert programmer by any stretch to read this book, and I will be making an effort to assume as little preexisting knowledge as possible as I go on, you really **do** need to have a grasp of the basics of programming before going much further. You may be able to work your way through it by spending a lot of time with Google to get up to speed on the fly, but I'm making the assumption that you don't need to do this and are good to go with the basics.

I'll also assume you have a text editor to use throughout the book. You don't need a proper IDE to do Corona work, a plain old text editor of your choice will suffice just fine, although at least finding one that specifically has Lua support, such as Notepad++ on Windows, is a better option, so you at least have basic syntax highlighting. That is in fact another benefit of Corona: there's a very low barrier to entry. A text editor and the SDK is all it takes, initially at least; while you don't **need** a proper IDE, it's certainly not a **bad** thing!

MORE ON IDE SUPPORT

There are a number of Corona-specific IDEs that are now available including Corona Complete (http://coronacomplete.com) and Lua Glider IDE (www.mydevelopersgames.com/Glider). While you don't need an IDE I certainly would encourage you to check these out.

I have yet to find proper support for Corona in any major IDE, such as Eclipse. What you can get for nearly all of them, however, is Lua support, and for the most part that's all you need. Yes, a proper debugger would be nice, but in my experience that is not a requirement for getting work done.

If you don't already have an IDE I'd suggest taking a look at IntelliJ IDEA (www.intellij.com). While IDEA is ostensibly Java focused, it's general-purpose enough to work great for Lua work. There is a Lua plug-in for it to give you the usual syntax highlighting, error checking, and code completion facilities. IntelliJ offers a free community edition of IDEA, so it's a perfectly no-cost option. I prefer it to Eclipse on the basis of performance alone (although I use Eclipse for other work as well and have no big complaints about it generally).

In any case, as mentioned, throughout this book I'll be assuming you have nothing but a plain old text editor to work with. That will be more than enough for what we'll be doing.

To get started, simply create a directory somewhere convenient on your local file system. Just so you're on the same page, call it corona_book. Under it, create a ch_01 directory. Then, open your text editor and in that file, paste or type the following content:

```
display.newRect(
  0, 0, display.contentWidth, display.contentHeight
):setFillColor(
  graphics.newGradient( { 255, 0, 0 }, { 0, 0, 0 } )
);

circle = display.newCircle(
  display.contentWidth / 2, display.contentHeight / 2, 32
);

function moveCircle()
  transition.to(circle, {
    x = math.random(32, display.contentWidth - 32),
    y = math.random(32, display.contentHeight - 32),
    onComplete = function()
      moveCircle();
    end
  });
end

moveCircle();
```

USE THE SOURCE, LUKE!

This is as good a time as any to tell you that the all the source code for this book is available for you to download from the Source Code/Download area of the Apress web site. If you are around my age then you almost certainly remember the olden days, when magazines like **Run** and **Compute** included page after page of hex numbers that you could enter using a special program and have a working game or some other program at the end. If you know what I mean then I'm sure you look back nostalgically on those times. Note, however, that I did not call them the good old days! Hey, I like to reminisce as much as the next guy, but even I don't want to go back to doing all that typing by hand, nor should you want to do it now! So grab the source code from the web site and save yourself from having a similar tale of days gone by to tell people when you write your own book at some point in the future!

Save the file in the directory you created and then launch the Corona simulator. On the File menu select Open Project, navigate to the corona_book/ch_01 directory, and select that main.lua file. Your application should start up and you should see in the simulator what is shown in Figure 1-6.

Figure 1-6 My first Corona application

Yes, I agree, it isn't much to look at, but think about it: that's a complete, working Corona app, in just a few short lines (four, technically) of code! You didn't need any fancy tools to create it and, I suspect, the code was pretty self-explanatory on top of it all, even without your having seen Corona code before (presumably not in any great depth anyway).

What's going on in the code? Well, I'll briefly walk you through it. Naturally, there are many things that you will not know at this point, so rather than repeating, "you'll get to this later" a bunch of times, I'll just say it once here at the start: you'll get to all the details later, and much more! Nevertheless, for now, just a quick, basic rundown will give you a nice flavor for Corona code.

The first line of code you see does two things.

```
display.newRect(
  0, 0, display.contentWidth, display.contentHeight
):setFillColor(
  graphics.newGradient( { 255, 0, 0 }, { 0, 0, 0 } )
);
```

First, it creates a rectangle. This rectangle covers the entire screen. This is simple to achieve by defining the upper left-hand corner at x/y coordinates (0,0) and by defining the width and height of the rectangle as equal to the width and height of the screen, respectively—two values that Corona supplies to us as properties of the display object, which you'll be seeing a lot of throughout this book. This also means that no matter what device you run it on, it'll always cover the entire screen (go ahead, change the view in the simulator to another device—say, iPad—and notice that it still works exactly as you'd expect it to).

Now, this line of code does something else: it fills that rectangle with a gradient that goes from pure red (RGB 255, 0, 0) to black (RGB 0, 0, 0). More precisely, it is creating a gradient object via the call to graphics.newGradient(), which Corona knows how to use to fill another object. By passing this object to the setFillColor() method of the rectangle object created by display.newRect(), you get what you see on the screen in the simulator.

At the risk of jumping ahead a bit I'll tell you that the display.newRect() method isn't actually returning any sort of special "rectangle" object but is in fact returning something called a DisplayObject. Virtually everything you do on the screen with Corona is a DisplayObject. A DisplayObject has a known set of methods and properties that you can manipulate. What this means is that almost anything you can put on the screen in a Corona app you can fill with a gradient like this, or manipulate in a host of other ways. It's a very consistent and flexible API that provides you with a lot of power!

But, back to the program at hand . . . here is the next line of code.

```
circle = display.newCircle(
  display.contentWidth / 2, display.contentHeight / 2, 32
);
```

You can now probably figure out for yourself: it creates a circle, which again is a DisplayObject. This circle is centered on the screen by taking the width and height of the screen, dividing each in half, and passing them as the first two arguments. The last argument is the radius of the circle. Note in this instance the reference to this circle is stored in the rather uncreatively named variable circle. In the case of the rectangle earlier, there was no need to do this because the program does not manipulate the rectangle after it's created, but the circle is a different story so you need a reference to it.

Next, you get to the real meat of the program with line 3.

```
function moveCircle()
  transition.to(circle, {
    x = math.random(32, display.contentWidth - 32),
    y = math.random(32, display.contentHeight - 32),
    onComplete = function()
      moveCircle();
    end
  });
end
```

This may look somewhat complex if you have never seen syntax like this before, but it's actually quite straightforward. A function named moveCircle() is defined. Within it you can make use of Corona's transition library by calling the transition.to() method. This is an exceedingly powerful method that lets you tween almost any property of a DisplayObject. In this case, you are tweening a property of our circle object, so you pass that as the first argument. The second argument is an object that defines the tween parameters. In this case, you are manipulating the x and y coordinates of the circle (which are properties of a DisplayObject). It's a simple random number somewhere on the screen, subtracting the radius of the circle so it never winds up partially or entirely off an edge of the screen.

The other property of this object that defines the tween is onComplete. This is a reference to a function to execute when the tween is finished. Here, I've defined that function inline. This is entirely a style choice, however; you can (and I'd say in many cases should) define this outside the call to transition.to(). But, since I specifically wanted to show you how much you can accomplish in as few lines of code as possible, I did it this way. (I'll acknowledge that some of these lines of code are longer than how you might typically write them, but still, it's technically true!)

> **Note**   In this instance it really would have been easier to just write onComplete=moveCircle because there's no real need to define the inline function and then have it do nothing but call moveCircle() anyway. Making onComplete reference moveCircle() does the same job with less code; of course, by doing that I wouldn't have been able to show you inline functions properly!

The function that executes onComplete just calls our moveCircle() function again, so that every time the circle reaches its randomly chosen destination it moves somewhere else. The result is not a perfect bouncing ball, but is more of a circle that drank too much coffee and is going a little bananas!

The final line of code is a simple call to moveCircle(), which kicks the whole thing off. Without that, all we'd see on the screen is the gradient-filled rectangle with a white circle in the middle, but there would be no motion.

One thing that you may have noticed is that there is no special entry point to the program, no special functions you have to implement. Simply stated, Corona starts executing the Lua script file you name at the top, and you can begin drawing immediately! There is no special setup to do, either; you're good to go right from the start. Notice too that the circle is on top of the rectangle. This isn't by accident: the z-index of elements is determined (initially at least) by the order in which they are drawn. Reverse the first two lines of code and you won't see the circle because it will be obscured by the rectangle. It sometimes takes planning to make sure things are layered properly on the screen, but those are details we'll get to a bit later.

As I hope you will agree, Corona is very powerful, allowing you to do a lot with a little bit of code. There's plenty more to come in this department, but hopefully this little program has whetted your appetite.

Summary

In this chapter, you were introduced to the Corona SDK. You learned that it is a tremendously powerful cross-platform development kit for mobile applications, especially games. It provides a supersolid foundation to build upon and gives you all the tools you need to create great things.

You got your first taste, albeit a small one, of what you can accomplish with just a little bit of code. In doing so, you got Corona installed, got the simulator up and running, and saw some of its capabilities.

In the next chapter, you will begin to look at Lua, the scripting language that underpins Corona. You will learn the basics of using it so that you can move on in later chapters to building an honest-to-goodness game and learn about many facets of Corona in the process.

Buckle up; it's going to be a fun ride!

Chapter 2

The Pillar of Creation: Lua

In Chapter 1, you looked at Corona at a high level and began to get a feel for what it offers. Corona provides the APIs you need to develop great cross-platform mobile apps, but an API is only half of the equation. If all you had was the API, you'd be a carpenter with a stack of wood but no hammer and nails to build anything with.

Fortunately, the other half of the equation—the hammer if you will—is provided to you in the form of Lua.

In this chapter, you'll dive into Lua and start to get familiar and comfortable with it. As I mentioned in Chapter 1, I assume that you have had at least some programming experience; however, I will assume a very low baseline of knowledge. If you're a very experienced programmer, you can zip through this chapter in no time, or quite possibly even skip it entirely and just pick up the syntax as you go. If that's not you, then you should get a good foundation to build on in this chapter, and you'll build upon that knowledge in the chapters to come.

A Jack of All Trades

Lua is a free (released under the developer-friendly MIT open-source license) extension language, which means that it isn't a language you write stand-alone executable programs in à la Java or C/C++. Instead, Lua is always embedded within a host program. The host program is then able to execute a piece of Lua code and manipulate the variables within that piece of code. The host can also register functions written in Standard C that can then be called from the Lua code, which is where a lot of the power and performance associated with Lua comes from (and is a big part of the reason Lua works so well for Corona).

Lua is designed to be used as a scripting language to support the needs of any program that embeds it. The ability of Lua to be embedded, along with the fact that it allows usage of C functions, permits Lua to be used to create meta-languages or so-called domain-specific language (DSL), meaning a scripting language suitable for the specific task its host program provides.

Lua offers support for such common concepts as object-oriented programming, functional programming, and data-driven programming. It is a relatively simple language on its own that, through its extension and embedding capabilities, provides nearly unlimited power to its host. Based on this description it should be obvious that Corona acts in effect as the host program for the Lua scripting language. If you've ever used Visual Basic for Applications (VBA) in an Excel file, or written a module for World of Warcraft, you will understand the basic concept (and in the case of World of Warcraft, you'll know about Lua already since that's what it uses). You use the relatively simple Lua language written against the Corona API to create your application.

Lua is an automatic garbage-collection language that uses an incremental mark-and-sweep collector (although the collector type could be different based on Lua implementation). Which collector it uses isn't terribly important in any case, but the fact that it is a garbage-collecting language is. This means that you as the programmer never have to worry about allocating and deallocating memory; Lua handles it for you. Lua periodically will collect dead objects; that is, objects that are no longer referenced from your code. As you'll see later, this means that while you don't have to worry about deallocating memory, you **do** need to worry about getting rid of references to objects you no longer need. Otherwise you can get in the way of the garbage collector and cause yourself problems, especially on resource-constrained mobile devices.

So, with the 10,000-foot overview of Lua in mind, you can take a look at some of the basics of the language.

The Bare Necessities: Lexicology

Lexicology refers to the study of words: their nature, meaning, and relationship with other words. In programming that means talking about things like keywords and syntax.

Yes, you caught me—I just wanted to use a fancy word to describe a basic concept!

Lua, lexicographically speaking (there, I did it again!) is free-form, meaning it doesn't care about spaces, not unlike many other modern programming languages. How you choose to format your code is entirely up to you. Of course, good conventions are good in **any** language and Lua is no different. Whatever style you choose, simply be consistent with it and you'll be fine. As you progress through this book, you'll see a consistent coding style in my code because it's something I'm hyperaware of and vigilant about. You may or may not agree with every style choice I make, and that is perfectly fine, but you **will** see a consistency to it.

In any case, Lua will accommodate you just fine!

Lua is one of the C-inspired (more or less) languages syntactically, which means, among other things, that it is case sensitive. So, `myspaceshipsprite` is different from `MySpaceshipSprite`.

Statements in Lua can end with a semicolon; however, that is optional.

```
AN INTERESTING NOTE ON SEMICOLONS
```

If you have an interest in language construction as I do, then you might be interested to know that Lua, at least the interpreter used in Corona, doesn't seem to suffer from so-called semicolon insertion, as some other languages such as JavaScript do.

Not sure what I mean? Consider this:

```
return { p : "yes" };
```

In JavaScript, that returns an object with a single property p with a string value of "yes". Simple enough, right? Now, consider this:

```
return
{ p : "yes" };
```

What happens there? Well, you may think it works the same because semicolons are optional in JavaScript; however, you'd be wrong, at least in some JavaScript engines. JavaScript tends to insert semicolons for you at runtime, and one is inserted at the end of the return statement. The section in braces then becomes an anonymous block that does nothing. So, any code calling a function with this code in it will always get null back. It's a subtle little gotcha that'll drive you nuts if it bites you!

But, as I said, Lua doesn't seem to do this, in Corona anyway (perhaps other interpreters do it, I'm frankly unsure). In any case, this is just an interesting (to me at least) aside; the bottom line is that semicolons are truly optional in Lua under Corona and I'm not aware of any gotchas such as this that can crawl out of the woodwork regardless of whether you use them or not. I use them constantly out of habit since I do a great deal of JavaScript work, but it is entirely your choice.

Names in Lua, be they for variables, functions, or anything else that can be named, can be any combination of letters, digits, and underscores of any length. They cannot however, begin with a digit.

Note that underscore is the **only** punctuation-type character that can be used in a name. For example, while this:

```
My$Variable1
```

would be perfectly valid in most other languages, in Lua it isn't. Changing the dollar sign to an underscore, however, would make it valid.

In addition, by convention, elements beginning with an underscore indicate elements supplied by Lua itself. Therefore, while you **can** start a name with an underscore, you probably **shouldn't,** just to avoid the possibility of conflicts.

Blocks in Lua are collections of statements executed as a unit and that share an execution context. The most common block you'll encounter is probably the function:

```
function MyFunction()
end
```

Everything between those lines is a block. Other blocks you'll see frequently are if statements and loops.

```
if a == true then
end
for i = 1, 10, 2 do
end
```

You can also define an anonymous block this way.

```
do
-- Some code
tnd
```

The concept of blocks is important to the discussion of scope, which I discuss later in the "A Place for Your Stuff: Variables, Values, and Types" section. You should also be aware that the term **chunk** is often seen in discussions of Lua. It's really just a synonym for block, and both simply refer to a collection of statements that share some scope.

The Keys to Success: Keywords

A programming language wouldn't be a programming language without keywords: the list of words that have special, specific meanings to the interpreter and that you can't use yourself (outside of string values, of course). Lua's keywords are as follows:

- and
- break
- do
- else
- elseif
- end
- false
- for
- function
- goto
- if
- in
- local
- nil
- not

- or
- repeat
- return
- then
- true
- until
- while

That's actually a remarkably short list of keywords—just 22 in total! Compared to other languages, JavaScript is close with about 29, but then something like Java has around 50! It's amazing what you can actually accomplish with a language with so few keywords, which should probably be a clue that most of Lua's power, and by extension Corona's, comes from an extensive function library, as you'll see throughout this book.

In the same vein as keywords are tokens: those special characters or combinations of characters that have specific meaning when building up expressions. Lua recognizes the following tokens:

- +
- -
- *
- /
- %
- ^
- #
- ==
- ~=
- <=
- >=
- <
- >
- =
- (
-)
- {
- }
- [
-]

- ;
- :
- ,
- .
- ..
- ...

Most of those will be familiar as they have the same meaning as in any other language that uses them. However, a few are less common or unique to Lua, so I'd like to call those out now:

- ~= Not equals (!= in many other languages)

- .. String concatenation (+ or & in many other languages). Note that + in Lua is purely mathematical and is not overload from concatenation as it is in many other languages.

- ... Varargs, meaning a function that can accept a variable number of arguments

Making a Statement: Commenting

Commenting your code is always a good thing and Lua gives you two forms of comments to choose from. The first is termed a short comment and looks like this:

```
-- I am a short comment
a = 5;
b = 6; -- Or at the end of a statement is fine too
```

A short comment can be on its own line or at the end of a line, whichever you prefer, but always starts with a double hyphen (except when it appears inside a string). A short comment runs until the end of the line in either case.

If you guessed there's such a thing as a long comment as well, then pat yourself on the back because there is! It looks like this:

```
--[[ I
Am
a long
comment
]]--
```

--[[and]]-- denote the start and end of a long comment, respectively, which can span multiple lines (but of course doesn't have to). Long comments are frequently used to temporarily deactivate a section of code, but can also be seen for function and program headers or other comments that require more text.

Which you choose is entirely up to you. Personally, I nearly always use short comments, even if I'm writing a long comment that spans multiple lines; I'll just have many lines of short comments in that case. I prefer this because to my eyes it stands out more in the code. Likewise, even if I'm commenting out a section of code during development, I'll usually do it with short comments (albeit automatically using an IDE commenting tool). Especially when you have an editor that does syntax highlighting, which oftentimes means comments show up in a duller color, it helps to quickly identify what code is live and what code is disabled. This is all entirely personal choice, though.

A Place for Your Stuff: Variables, Values, and Types

Lua is a dynamically typed language, which means that variables can point to values of any type, and can point to values of different types at various times. For example:

```
myVar = 123;
```

The type of value myVar points to is a number here, but note that there is no type declared for myVar (assume this is the first statement in the program and I'm not being sly and hiding something!). If the next line of code is:

```
myVar = "123";
```

That's perfectly valid; now, myVar points to a string.

All types of values are first-class citizens in Lua, meaning they can be stored in variables. This means that in Lua, a variable can hold a reference to things like numbers and strings, just like any other languages, but they can **also** hold a reference to things like functions and something called tables, which I'll get to shortly. This means that you can pass around references to all these things, and return them from functions, as you would any "primitive" data types.

Speaking of data types, Lua supports six types of data:

- **nil:** This is usually called null in other languages and indicates a variable that hasn't yet been assigned a value

- **Boolean:** A value of true or false. Note that true and false versus 0 and 1 in Lua is a bit tricky. Consider the following example:

  ```
  a = 1;
  if a == true then
    print("y");
  else
    print("n");
  end
  ```

  What is printed here? In many languages, it would be "y", but in Lua it's "n" because 1 doesn't equal true.

  However, consider this code:

  ```
  a = 1;
  if a then
    print("y");
  else
    print("n");
  end
  ```

You'd expect to see "n" there too, wouldn't you? Contrary to logic, "y" gets printed!

The point I'm trying to make here is simply this: **if you're talking about a true or false value, use true and false!** Don't try and use 0 and 1 as aliases for them. That will ensure you don't run into any unexpected problems.

- **number:** All numbers in Lua are real, double-precision floating-point numbers, plain and simple.

- **string:** The usual array of characters. Note that unlike C you **do not** have to worry about termination characters.

- **function:** A named, callable block of code, pretty much like any other language out there. Note that in Lua a function is considered an object like a table is. Speaking of which . . .

- **table:** The table is pretty much the fundamental data structure in Lua and can be thought of like objects in most other object-oriented languages (although, naturally, they have their own specific characteristics). Tables get their own section coming up shortly so we'll hold off on any more specifics until then.

Variables can be declared anywhere at any time by simply assigning a value to them (and, as mentioned before, the type of that value can change at any time). If you simply write this:

```
a = 5;
```

then you've created a global variable that will live as long as your program executes. The scope of this variable is anywhere within the program; it can be accessed (and changed) from anywhere. The only way to get rid of that variable would be to do:

```
a = nil;
```

Then, the garbage collector will deallocate its memory during its next sweep.

The other scope that Lua understand is block scope, which means that a variable is declared, used, and deallocated within the context of a block of code. The most common place to see this is in a function:

```
function MyFunction()
  local myVar = 6;
end
```

Here, the variable myVar existing only within MyFunction(), as denoted by the local keyword, and when the function exits myVar will be garbage-collected, even if you don't assign nil to it.

> **Note** Because of scope resolution—that is, the procedure Lua uses to locate a variable—declaring things using `local` whenever you can is a good practice in terms of performance.
>
> For example, if you have in a function and in it you write:
>
> ```
> a = a + 1;
> ```
>
> Lua will first look to see if there's a `local` variable named a. If it can't find it, which of course it won't here since there's no local keyword before it, it'll start going up the scope chain. It'll ask: is the variable maybe in a containing block? This will continue until, finally, Lua looks in global scope, where it finds the variable you're incrementing (assuming it was declared in global scope of course, which for the sake of this conversation, it was). All of that work impacts performance (albeit only a small amount if this isn't happening thousands of times a second).
>
> So, unless you actually need (or for some reason want) a variable to be global, declare it locally in some limited scope, and preferably as close to its usage as possible, and shorten the scope chain lookup that has to occur, to keep your app humming along.

Note that this can lead to some interesting situations:

```
myVar = 6;
function MyFunction()
  print(myVar);
  local myVar = 5;
  print(myVar);
end
MyFunction();
print(myVar);
```

What gets printed here? Three values: 6, then 5, then 6. The first `print()` inside `MyFunction()` prints the value of the global `myVar`. Then, we create a new `myVar` scoped to `MyFunction()`, which essentially masks the global `myVar`. Then, once we print `myVar` after returning from `MyFunction()` we're again printing the value of the global `myVar`, which wasn't changed by anything done in `MyFunction()`.

What if you want to access the global `myVar` inside `MyFunction()` after creating the local version of `myVar`? Well, there is a way:

```
myVar = 6;
function MyFunction()
  print(myVar);
  local myVar = 5;
  print(myVar);
  print(_G.myVar);
end
MyFunction();
print(myVar);
```

Try this code and you'll see four values printed: 6, then 5, then 6, then 6. This works because in Lua, all global variables are automatically added to an object _G, which represents global scope. So, you can always disambiguate when you have masked variables, no problem.

That being said, you'll save yourself **a lot** of hassle by avoiding masking like that anyway!

Also, note that while I showed how this works in the context of a function, the rules are the same inside any block. So, if you have an if statement, or a loop, and declare some local variables within it, they will be automatically cleaned up after the block completes.

One exception to that rule is if you do something like this:

```lua
myVar = nil;
function MyFunction()
  local lVar = 1;
  myVar = lVar;
end
MyFunction();
```

Here, after the call to MyFunction(), the variable lVar **will not** be garbage-collected because myVar references it, and it is global-scoped so it won't itself be garbage-collected. The bottom line is you have to be careful not to retain references to anything you don't **really** need to, or you'll quickly run into memory leaks, meaning memory that can't be garbage-collected. For a variable that holds a number of a small string, that's probably not going to cause you any problems in the long run (unless you're creating such variables a lot in a tight loop). However, when I later get to creating graphics and audio, which can take up a lot of memory, it can quickly lead to out-of-memory errors, especially on resource-constrained mobile devices, so better to always be thinking about it and avoid these scenarios entirely.

Lua also offers a multiple assignment form, allowing you to do things like:

```lua
local x, y = 3, 5;
```

This leads to a neat trick to swap the values of two variables:

```lua
x, y = y, x;
```

That's all it takes!

Lastly, simple arrays are defined using braces like so:

```lua
local myArray = { "1", "2", "3" };
```

You can then access the elements using brackets such as myArray[2]. Note that arrays are one-based, so the element "1" is retrieved with myArray[1].

Expressing Yourself: Expressions and Operators

Expressions in Lua aren't much different than in other languages. The usual mathematical tokens operators such as addition (+), subtraction (- or negation if used unwarily), multiplication (*), and division (/) are supported, along with modulo (%) for getting remainders of divisions and exponentiation (^).

Lua also supports the usual suspects of relational comparison operators: equals (==), not equals (~=), less than (<), greater than (>), less than or equal to (<=) and greater than or equal to (>=). Each of those returns true or false as you'd expect. Note that == will first compare the types of the variables and will return false if they aren't the same. In other words:

```
local varA = 5;
local varB = "5";
print(varA == varB);
```

That will print false since varA is a number and varB is a string, even though their values appear to be the same.

> **Note**   It doesn't matter to anything at all, but it always makes me chuckle when I see < and > because as a child I had a friend who would explain those symbols by holding up his hand in the same position and say, "Alligator go that way." Pointless, I know, but it brings a smile to my face thinking about it!

In fact, the previous code **would** return true if it weren't for that rule because, being a dynamically typed language, Lua has another benefit: conversions between numerics and strings usually will happen without your intervention and without any difficulties (it also helps that there's only one numeric type to deal with). Therefore, you can do things like:

```
local a = 5;
local b = "6";
print(a + b);
```

That will print "11", not "56" as in some other languages (or, worse still, produce an error of some kind).

Objects, such as those fabled tables that I've yet to delve into, are compared based on references. So this:

```
local tableA = { prop = "123" };
local tableB = { prop = "123" };
print(tableA == tableB);
```

will print false because we've created two different objects there, and even though they contain the same internal structure and data they are still two completely independent objects.

Lua supports the usual logical operators and, or, and not. For these, nil is considered false and any other value is considered true. Because of this, the negation operator (not) will always return true or false regardless of the type being negated. In all cases, conjunction (and) and disjunction (or) operators will use short-circuit evaluation. This means that the second operand will not be evaluated unless it needs to be (if the first operand is false in the case of conjunction, or true in the case of disjunction, then the second operand does not need to be evaluated since the first is enough to determine the outcome of the evaluation).

As briefly mentioned earlier, the concatenation operator (..) is used to combine values. Note that I was careful not to say "string" there because it works just as well for numerics, and you can mix and match just fine. So, for example:

```
local varA = 5;
local varB = 6;
local varC = "6";
print(varA .. varB);
print(varA .. varC);
```

In the first `print()` statement we're concatenating two numbers, but the result is to print out "56" because they aren't being added. The second `print()` statement likewise displays "56" because here we have a number and a string, so the number is converted to a string and the two strings concatenated. While in other languages the + operator serves both purposes, that isn't the case in Lua; so clearly you have to be aware that + and .. are distinctly different in Lua and use them appropriately.

The last operator worth mentioning is the length operator (#). This can give you the length of things like strings or arrays. So, if you have:

```
local myString = "Testing";
local myArray = { 1, 2, 3 };
print(#myString);
print(#myArray);
```

that will print "7" and "3" because there are seven characters in myString and three elements in myArray.

> **Note**   In Lua there is no ternary operator, so you can't do things like a:b?c like you can in many other languages. The equivalent in Lua would be "a and b or c". Note however that if b is false then this idiom breaks down and doesn't work as expected. To save yourself headache it's better to simply forget all that you know about ternary expressions and just write them out long-form with an if statement.

This also works for tables—speaking of which . . .

Let's Table This Discussion: The Mythical "Table"

So, these table things that I've mentioned a few times, what are they all about? Well, in simplest terms, they are objects. More precisely, they are associative arrays; that is, arrays of elements that can be accessed using an identifier (and as you'll see, the identifier, called a key, can be a numeric index value or something nonnumeric). Tables aren't all that dissimilar from dictionaries in other languages, but they actually share qualities of arrays **and** dictionaries in Lua, making them that much more flexible and powerful.

You saw an array just a little while back:

```
local myArray = { 1, 2, 3 };
```

You can access the elements in the array using bracket notation:

```
myArray[2]
```

This retrieves the second value in the array, 2 in this case. This is sometimes referred to as a plain old array. However, **it is in fact a table!** To make that more explicit, change the code a bit:

```
local myTable = { one = 1, two = 2, three = 3 };
```

You'll notice that you used braces in either case, but now, what you've done is given each element in the table a specific key name that you can use to look up the value. So, to get the value of the element identified by the key "two", use:

```
myTable["two"]
```

This returns 2 again, as before.

You actually have a choice here: because the key name "two" becomes what we term a **property** of the table, you can instead use dot notation:

```
myTable.two
```

This returns 2 as well. Which you use is mostly a style choice, although the general convention most people follow is to use dot notation. However, the bracket notation can come into play when you want to access the properties dynamically:

```
local myTable = { one = 1, two = 2, three = 3 };
local whichProperty = "two";
print(myTable[whichProperty]);
```

Which property is printed is dependent on the value of whichProperty, so in this case we have to use bracket notation because trying to do:

```
print(myTable.whichProperty);
```

would **actually** mean: "print the value of the property named whichProperty" when what we **really** mean is "print the value of the property named by whichProperty".

You may be asking yourself, "Self, doesn't that mean that an array is really just a table?" The answer is yes, it is! When you define an array, what you're really doing is defining a table that just **happens** to use numbers as key values. To illustrate this further, look at this code:

```
local myTable = { };
myTable[1] = "Corona";
myTable[2] = "SDK";
myTable[3] = "Rocks!";
print(myTable[2]);
```

This prints "SDK" since that's the element defined by the number 2 (or at index 2 you could say, even though it should be apparent now that saying that isn't **technically** accurate).

The other thing to notice is that you can indeed create an empty table, as is done in the previous code, and then add properties to it later, and it doesn't matter if they are numerically keyed or not. That means you can do things like:

```
local myTable = { };
myTable.prop1 = "abc";
myTable["prop2"] = "def";
myTable[3] = "ghi";
```

You can now access prop1 by using:

```
myTable.prop1
```

or

```
myTable["prop1"]
```

The same holds true for prop2. However:

```
myTable[3]
```

is the **only** way you can get the value "ghi". Trying to do:

```
myTable.3
```

is **not** valid and results in an error.

Do you remember that length operator (#) from earlier? An important point to remember is that it will only work for tables that have purely numeric keys. For the previous code, if you do:

```
print(#myTable)
```

you'll get 0 because we've mixed and matched numeric and nonnumeric keys, so the length operator can't determine the length. More to the point, talking about the length of a table with both numeric and nonnumeric key values doesn't really make sense. You could argue that length in this context means "how many elements does the table contain," and that's not unreasonable, but it's just not the way it works.

That's why, in most cases, using either numeric keys or nonnumeric keys exclusively in a given table is the way to go, if for no other reason than not confusing yourself when your length operator doesn't work as you expect!

Last, there are no limitations to the types of data a table's properties can reference. Numbers and strings naturally are fine, as we've seen, as are other tables:

```
local myTable = {
  innerTable = {
    propA = "abc";
  }
}
```

Here, `myTable.innerTable.propA` retrieves the value "abc". Plain old arrays work fine as well (i.e., `innerTable` could be a plain old array).

Table properties can also reference functions. I haven't really discussed functions specifically yet, although you've seen them a bit (I'll get into functions next), but for the sake of completing the discussion on tables, here's an example of how that looks:

```
function myFunction()
end
local myTable = {
  funcA = function()
  end,
  funcB = myFunction
};
```

This shows two different approaches: you can define a function inline in the table (`funcA`) or you can set a property of the table to reference an existing function (`funcB` referencing `myFunction()`).

> **Note** One quick point: if you define an array using `a={x,y,z}`, then the first element is index 1. However, there's nothing to stop you from later on doing `a[0]=w` and then accessing the elements of the array starting with index 0. However, all Corona API functions, and most Lua functions, assume an array begins with index 1, so unless you have a really good reason for doing otherwise, always treat arrays as beginning with index 1.

Getting Functional: All about Functions

Functions in Lua are quick and easy to define:

```
function add (num1, num2)
  return num1 + num2;
end
```

This will define a function called `add()` in global scope (assuming this isn't itself inside a function) that accepts two arguments named `num1` and `num2`, adds them together, and returns the result. Note that the arguments have no type specified, so they can be of any type at runtime, allowing quite a bit of flexibility in designing your functions. Of course, since this function adds two numbers you'd expect to only ever pass numbers to it, and in fact you'd have to add some logic to ensure that's the case if there was a possibility of other types being passed in. For example, maybe you want to allow passing **either** two numbers **or** two tables, each with a `number` property, and your function adds the properties together and then returns a new object with the result as a property. You could do this if you wrote the function to tell the difference between a plain number and a table as arguments and act accordingly.

Also, note that there is no return specified in the function definition. You simply either return a value or not (the caller will get `nil` back if you don't explicitly return a value).

A function can also be a property of a table:

```lua
local myTable = {
  add = function(num1, num2)
    return num1 + num2;
  end
};
```

Now you can do:

```lua
function add(num1, num2)
  return num1, num2, num1 + num2;
end
```

A function can also return multiple results:

```lua
local n1, n2, result = add(1, 2);
print(n1, n2, result);
```

This will print "1 2 3", echoing back the input as well as returning the result. This capability isn't used all that often, but it certainly is used and you are free to do so when appropriate.

Not only can a function return multiple values, but also it can accept a variable number of arguments:

```lua
function va(...)
  print(arg[1], arg[2], arg[3]);
end
va(1, 2);
```

Here, the output would be "1 2 nil" because we're passing in two arguments. The function is defined to take a variable number of arguments, as denoted by the three dots in the argument list. Inside the function, we access the arguments by means of the intrinsic arg variable. Since we only passed two arguments the third one, arg[3], is nil. You can also do:

```lua
function va(arg1, arg2, ...)
  print(arg1, arg2, arg[1], arg[2], arg[3]);
end
```

This way, if you know you always have two arguments, followed by some number of additional arguments, you can write the function accordingly. The only rule is that the three dots must be at the end of the argument list.

> **Note**   As a general rule, I suggest nearly always write your functions as properties of a table. This effectively uses the table as a namespacing mechanism, which tends to help avoid naming conflicts (your table names might still conflict of course, but it's usually functions that wind up with conflicts). In fact, much (maybe even most) of the Corona API is written this way.

As with properties, you can add functions to an existing table:

```
local myTable = { };
myTable.add = function(num1, num2)
  return num1 + num2;
end;
```

Now, if you've done some object-oriented programming you may have noticed that I haven't used the term **method** to this point to describe functions that are properties of a table. That's because **technically** what I've defined so far **aren't** methods. The difference has to do with a special reference that is available in a function known as self.

When you call myTable.add() with the code shown earlier, the add() function has no notion of context. That is, it doesn't really know that it's a property of myTable. This is contrary to the object-oriented concept of encapsulation and may seem a bit odd at first. To make it seem more like what we would typically expect and give it context, you have to use a slightly different notation to define and call it:

```
local myTable = { };
function myTable:add(num1, num2)
  return num1 + num2;
end;
```

The difference, of course, is the use of colon instead of dot when adding the function to the table. Now, when you want to call add() you use:

```
myTable:add(1, 2);
```

The difference, aside from the simple syntax swap of colon for dot, is what happens inside the add() function (which is now properly termed a method). You now have access to the intrinsic variable self, which is a reference to myTable. This allows you to do this:

```
local myTable = {
  n1 = 5,
  n2 = 6
};
function myTable:add(num1, num2)
  return self.n1 + self.n2 + num1 + num2;
end;
print(myTable:add(1, 2));
```

Now, the result printed is "14" because add() adds not only the two arguments passed in to it but also the values of the properties n1 and n2 of myTable, which we can access via the self reference variable.

Using the colon when calling a method is in fact just a shortcut. You could still call add() using dot notation like so:

```
myTable.add(1, 2);
```

However, if you were to execute that you'd get an error. You would find that the value of self is 1, the value of num1 is 2 and the value of num2 is nil. The reason is that when you use colon to call a method, the self reference is automatically passed, but when using the dot notation it isn't. To fix this you would have to manually pass a value for the self reference:

```
myTable.add(myTable, 1, 2);
```

Now you would have a valid reference to myTable as self, and num1 and num2 would have the values 1 and 2 respectively as expected. However, from a syntactic perspective, using colon makes the code a lot clearer and less verbose and is therefore the preferred idiom.

> **Note**   This also raises the possibility that you could pass a reference to another object than the one a
> method belongs to, allowing for a kind of polymorphism (not to mention some convoluted code that'll
> likely give you problems down the road). I don't recall ever seeing this done, frankly, but as a technical
> matter, it **is** in fact possible.

In Lua, and therefore Corona, there are a handful of global functions available for your use. Many of them are infrequently used, but a few are used more often. I'll go over a few of them now.

First is ipairs(). This accepts as an argument a table and returns an iterator function, the table, and zero. This allows you to iterate over the pairs or keys and values in the table like so:

```
for i, j in ipairs(t) do
  -- Do something
end
```

The trick here is that the array must be numerically indexed and not have so-called holes—that is, nil elements—because ipairs() will stop with the first one it hits. But if you know your array has holes, or if you want to iterate over all the elements of a table regardless of key type, you can use the related pairs() function, which works essentially the same but will continue until there are no more elements in the table.

Note that with either you should not modify the structure of the table during iteration; that is, add or remove elements. You can of course change elements, although even there you should take care not to nil something that you haven't iterated over yet and thereby stop your iteration sooner than planned in the case of ipairs().

Next is print(). You've seen this a bunch of times so far and it is used simply to echo some string to the console window. You can pass it multiple arguments and they will be separated by a tab, and you can usually pass any sort of type to it and get some sort of result, even if it isn't particularly helpful (a table, for example, will be shown as a reference number).

After that there is tostring(). This converts its argument, which can be any type, to a reasonable string representation. This might not be quite as helpful as it otherwise is if it weren't for the fact that when passed a table that has a __tostring field in its metatable, it will call the function it points to.

Err, wait, what's a metatable you ask? Well, every table has a metatable attached to it, which literally is just another table embedded in it. This table has specific keys in it that, when populated, can change the behavior of the table in some way. Say you have a table:

```lua
local t = {
  prop1 = "frank"
};
```

Now say you want to be able to control what tostring() spits out when passed this table. The first step is defining a function that will do the work for you:

```lua
function t:ts()
  return "t = [ prop1 : " .. self.prop1 .. " ]";
end;
```

The format of the string you return is of course entirely up to you. Now, we could certainly just call t:ts() any time we want. However, to use tostring() we need to attach a metatable to this table and provide a value for the __tostring key:

```lua
setmetatable(t, {
  __tostring = t.ts
});
```

The setmetatable() is another of the useful global functions that does precisely what its name implies. Now, we can do:

```lua
print(tostring(t));
```

This will return a string "t = [prop1 : Frank]" and print it to the console. But, as it happens, calling tostring() like that is actually redundant! As long as you set the metatable __tostring key value appropriately, you can simply do:

```lua
print(t);
```

Your ts() function will be called and you'll get the output expected.

There are a number of other metatable keys that are of some use, however, in my experience they are not used all that often. As such, I'll leave them for your own exploration, although, who knows, you may encounter one or two of them later in this book in the course of building a game!

Another useful global function is type(), which returns the type of the argument passed to it. This can be number, string, Boolean, table, function, thread or userdata. This is how you can implement polymorphism as I alluded to earlier, since you can determine the type of an argument to a function and act accordingly.

The final function I want to mention is pcall(). Normally, when an error occurs in Lua, it gets propagated upwards, normally to the host program to handle. Lua doesn't have the notion of try/catch, but it does have pcall(), which serves a somewhat similar purpose. You pass it a reference to a function (along with a list of arguments) and it executes the function in protected mode and catches the error if one occurs. If the called function executes without error than you get back true plus the returned value. If an error occurs then you get back false plus the error. By way of example:

```
function goodFunction()
  return "goodFunction() done";
end
function badFunction()
  tolowercase(a);
end
print(pcall(goodFunction));
print("Now calling badFunction()");
print(pcall(badFunction));
print("Continuing");
badFunction();
print("Shouldn't see me");
```

The output here is:

```
true    goodfunction() done
Now calling badFunction()
false    attempt to call global 'tolowercase' (a nil value)
Continuing
```

The final print("Shouldn't see me"); doesn't execute because a runtime error occurs as a result of calling badFunction() the second time without wrapping it in pcall(). The first time we call it with pcall() the error is effectively handled and the interpreter doesn't stop. The second time, though, the error stops the program cold.

PCALL(), XPCALL(), AND PERFORMANCE

There's also an xpcall() function that is slightly different than pcall(). With xpcall() you pass as the second argument an error-handler function that will be called. This allows you to have a standardized error-handling mechanism that is attached to all your protected function calls.

Note that both pcall() and xpcall() do indeed introduce a performance overhead to your function calls. Therefore, you really only want to use them during development, or in production code for functions that aren't called in time-sensitive areas of your code, or where you're calling a function that you know could result in an error. (Of course, if you already know that, how about just avoiding the error in the first place?!)

Taking Control: Control Structures

You can control the flow of control in your Lua code using a handful of statements, beginning with the well-known if statement, which takes the general form:

```
if XXX then
  -- Do something when XXX is true
elseif YYY then
  -- Do something with YYY is true
```

```
else
   -- Do something in all other cases
end
```

XXX and YYY are any expression that evaluates to a Boolean. Both false and nil are considered false, while all other values are considered true. Note that the number zero and an empty string are therefore considered true, which can be tricky if you forget!

Of course, all elseif clauses and the else clause are optional. Note that Lua does not have the common switch/case construct. The way to simulate that in Lua is simply a block of if/elseif statements.

Knocked for a Loop: The for, while, and repeat Constructs

Lua supports a handful of iterative statements including the well-known for loop, while loop, and repeat.

A for loop takes this general form:

```
for variable = start value, end value, step do
   -- Some code to repeat
End
```

So, a valid for loop that prints the numbers from 2 to 17 by 3 using the variable i as a counter would be:

```
for i = 2, 17, 3 do
  print(i);
end
```

The while loop takes the form:

```
while expression do
   -- Some code to repeat
End
```

As usual, the code inside the while loop will only execute if expression is true, so if it starts out false the code inside the loop will not execute even once.

Note that unlike other languages, there is no do/while construct to ensure your block executes at least once. There is, however, a way to simulate it, and that's by using the repeat construct:

```
i = 0;
repeat
  print(i);
   i = i + 1;
until i > 0;
```

This ensures that the code inside the `repeat`/`until` block executes at least once, even if the value of the expression, `i > 0` in this case, is `false` the first time through (e.g., if you set `i = 25` to start).

In all cases, the `break` statement is available to break out of the innermost-enclosing loop unconditionally. You can also terminate any loop by returning it from it explicitly.

Compartmentalizing: Modules

When you write a Corona app, it all starts with `main.lua`. You could, if you wanted, write an entire game in just that file! There's no real limitations, other than your sanity and the performance of your IDE, that would stop you from doing this. However, from an architectural standpoint it's not generally a great idea to do this in anything but very trivial cases.

Lua provides the notion of modules to help you better organize your code. A module really is nothing more than other Lua source code files that you include into your `main.lua` file by way of the `require()` statement. So, say you have `main.lua` and you also have `myFunctions.lua`. You would write in `main.lua`:

```
require("myFunctions");
```

Note that we do not need to include the file extension here. The interpreter knows you mean a Lua source file after all!

Now, let's say that `myFunctions.lua` contains the following:

```
function testMe()
  print("hello!");
end
```

In `main.lua` we can call `testMe()` and have it print its greeting to the console as expected.

Now, since clogging up global scope is generally a bad idea (and in point of fact can lead to performance degradation owing to scope chain lookup), the more common thing to do in `myFunctions.lua` is this:

```
return {
  testMe = function()
    print("hello!");
  end
};
```

Now, in `main.lua` we do:

```
myFuncs = require("myFunctions");
myFuncs.testMe();
```

Returning a table is said by many to be what makes `myFunctions.lua` a "proper" module in Lua. If it just contains global functions, it isn't generally thought of as a module. Whatever terminology you choose to use, the point is that `require()` allows you to bring in external code into your Lua program—that's the important concept. Most of the time, however, you'll see in the Corona API that you do in fact get a table back from its execution, and you generally should follow this pattern in your own code if for no other reason than to pollute the global namespace as little as possible.

Two other important notes about modules is that, first, anything not declared in global scope in a module is scoped to the module itself. So, if `myFunctions.lua` includes this line:

```
local myVar = "test";
```

then that variable `myVar` will only be accessible from code inside that module.

This is important in light of the second fact, which is that modules are only loaded once per program execution (unless you go out of your way to defeat this mechanism).

So, let's say you write yourself a `utils.lua` module to include some general utility functions you've written. Being a good module, it returns a table. In `main.lua` you require `module1.lua`, which requires `utils.lua` and assigns the table it returns to a local `utils` variable. This `utils` variable is only accessible to the code in `module1.lua` since it is declared as `local`.

Now, let's say you add `module2.lua` later on. It too needs access to the utility functions. At this point, you have a choice. Your first option is to move the `require("utils")` from `module1.lua` into `main.lua`, which makes it global (assuming you don't define it with `local`, which would then scope it to the code in `main.lua`). The other option, and generally the better one because it avoids extended scope chain lookup, is to also require `utils.lua` in `module2.lua` and assign it to a local `utils` variable there too. Remember, `module1.lua` and `module2.lua` are two separate scopes, two separate namespaces if you will, so there is no conflict with having two `utils` variables defined.

However, the important fact is that `utils.lua` will not be loaded a second time when required in `module2.lua`. The Lua interpreter recognizes that `utils.lua` has already been loaded and so returns the existing reference. This can have consequences if there is, for example, some setup code in a module that may need to be different when it is included from two separate modules.

The easy answer is that your modules shouldn't execute any code when loaded. Since Lua will interpret the included Lua source file top to bottom, if all you have is a table definition with properties and methods defined then nothing will execute per se at load time, other than the return statement sending the table back to the caller. That way, there is no side effect to loading a module, and you can include it as many times as you want without worrying about anything breaking.

Variations on a Theme: Changes Made to Lua in Corona

The version of Lua in Corona has had some fairly minor alterations made to it to work better with the SDK for improved function on mobile devices. The big difference is that you are unable to load Lua code dynamically and execute it. I suspect this has a lot to do with the restrictions Apple places on apps on iOS devices, but regardless of the reason, this means that the following four Lua functions which otherwise would be available to you are not: `dofile()`, `load()`, `loadfile()`, and `loadstring()`.

As a consequence of those functions not being available, you will not be able to use Lua code as a configuration file, as is a common practice in Lua development. You'll either have to store your Lua configuration in an existing Lua file or in some other format.

Summary

In this chapter, you made a new friend: Lua! You saw how this relatively simple language (from a syntax perspective) provides the semantic framework you'll need to make use of Corona. You saw how the usual constructs of programming languages such as variables, data types, loops, control statements, and objects are dealt with. You've built the foundation you need to continue on into the brave new world of Corona itself.

In Chapter 3, you'll be taking your first steps into that world and toward building an actual game with Corona, using the tools gained here and in Chapter 1.

In brief: the setting of the stage is now complete and it's time for the fun to begin!

Part 2

Go!

I love deadlines. I like the whooshing sound they make as they fly by.

—Douglas Adams

It always takes longer than you expect, even when you take into account Hofstadter's Law.

—Douglas Hofstadter

I don't care if it works on your machine! We are not shipping your machine!

—Ovidiu Platon

Perl: the only language that looks the same before and after RSA encryption.

—Keith Bostic

Chapter **3**

Basic Application Structure

As with any software project you can name, building a game starts with building a good, solid foundation. Of course Corona sets you on good footing from the word go, but how you architect the code is at least as important as what the library you use provides.

Many considerations must be taken into account. How do you move from screen to screen? How do you organize your graphics and audio resources? How do you structure the code so that it's logical and at least somewhat extensible in the future, should you decide to enhance the game for your customers?

All of this, and more, is what this chapter is all about. Before I even get to questions of architecture, though, you probably should get an idea of what you're building, shouldn't you?!

The Year Is 2258 . . . The Name of the Place . . . err, Game . . .

Quick: how many sci-fi movies and television shows have you seen, how many books have you read, in which colonists on some faraway planet need to be rescued? I don't know what it is about colonists that makes them so needy, but it sure seems like they're always in trouble and someone always has to go get them out of harm's way! Furthermore, at least in video games, that person always winds up being you, doesn't it?

Well, welcome to Astro Rescue!

You are the pilot of a rescue ship; call it the **U.S.S. Colonist Saver.** You have to fly a distant solar system to rescue some colonists under attack from aliens. Your job is simple: when a colonist materializes near a landing platform and signals SOS to you, you fly down, land on the pad, wait for them to board, and then take off again. Once you have rescued all the colonists, you fly back into the landing bay of your mothership and move on to the next planet. All the while, you have to avoid the aliens that occasionally fly by and shoot plasma balls at you, and refuel when fuel canisters appear . . . because that's what fuel canisters do in space, I guess, just magically appear in the middle of nowhere! (Hey, I've never been in space, have you? It **could** be true!)

As far as game concepts go, I'll admit this isn't going to go head to head with Angry Birds on the sales charts. However, what it **will** do **very** well is allow us to explore a large chunk of Corona functionality. It will demonstrate all of the most important core concepts in the world of Corona development that you would need to build nearly any game you can imagine—perhaps one that **will** topple those angry avians!

Mapping out the Astro Rescue Game

The first step in developing a game, or any piece of software for that matter, is to conceptualize at a high level what the thing will look like, what the parts of the project will be. For this game, at the highest level, we have these parts:

- Title screen
- Main menu screen
- A settings screen for adjusting a few settings the game will support
- The game itself
- An ending scene when the player finishes the game

It may not look like much, but it actually brings us to the first concept in Corona that in all probability you'll use very often as you write your games: the Storyboard API.

A DISCLAIMER OR TWO

Writing a game, or any piece of software really, is largely an art form, regardless of what your boss at work wants to think! We professional developers are of course constantly striving to make it as much of an engineering discipline as possible, and obviously it largely is. However, there will always a portion that is far less rigid than any engineering discipline, such as architecture or electrical engineering.

The result of this is that it is common to find two talented developers have solved the same problem in two very different ways. There's nothing wrong with that; it's to be expected, really, and is probably even truer for game development (until you get to large-scale projects at least, where you have to introduce more rigidity to get things done). The point is only that as you progress through the book, you may not always agree with every choice I've made. However, I'll do my best to always give you the reasons why I've done things certain ways, and even discuss alternatives that I considered along the way.

It's also worth pointing out that since this book is obviously a learning exercise, and Astro Rescue was written for that express purpose, I've sometimes done things in it that I probably wouldn't do normally, just to give you examples of varied approaches to things and to open the discussion of as many parts of Corona as possible. Again, I'll do my best to point those places out to you, so you understand what's really a "best practice" and what's more for educational purposes only.

Last, this book isn't meant to be an exhaustive Corona reference. It would take killing a lot more trees than this to cover everything! I've endeavored to cover the things that you are most likely to need the most when writing a game, those that in my estimation you will use most commonly. I've attempted to give you a good, solid foundation on which to build your house, not detailed blueprints for every single room you might want to build. I highly encourage you to peruse the Corona documentation itself after reading this book, since it goes into much more depth and covers a few topics in detail that are only touched upon in this book.

You're Sceneing Things: The Storyboard API

When you fire up Astro Rescue, the first thing you see is the title screen, as seen in Figure 3-1. Obviously you can't tell from the printed page (yet—but that technology is coming!), but the background is a subtly moving "color tunnel," and the whole thing appears from the center of the screen and expands outward; it doesn't just show up on the screen unannounced. This screen represents the first "scene" in your game.

Figure 3-1. The Astro Rescue title scene

What is a scene? Simply put, it's an individual screen in a game (well, **usually** an individual screen, it doesn't **have** to be). Corona provides an API specifically for managing scenes called the Storyboard API. This API provides a well-defined code structure for your scenes, defines lifecycle events that a scene needs, and exposes functions for managing scenes in various ways.

> **Note**   A given scene does not necessarily have to be a single physical screen, although that's nearly always the case. If you have a menu scene, for example, you may decide that you want your settings screen to be a part of the menu scene in terms of code structure. You can do this, but what you are forced to do then is essentially to write code that, to a large degree, does what the Storyboard API does for you anyway. So, unless you have a really good reason to do otherwise, a single screen should correspond to a single scene.

The basic code structure when interacting with this API is called a scene object, which is a fancy way of saying a Lua table with specified methods attached to it representing the various events in the life of a scene. What does such a scene object look like? The basic outline of a scene object is as you see in Listing 3-1.

Listing 3-1. The Basic Structure of a Storyboard Scene

```lua
local storyboard = require( "storyboard" )
local scene = storyboard.newScene()

-- Called when the scene's view does not exist.
function scene:createScene(inEvent)
end

-- Called BEFORE scene has moved on screen.
function scene:willEnterScene(inEvent)
end

-- Called AFTER scene has moved on screen.
function scene:enterScene(inEvent)
end

-- Called BEFORE scene moves off screen.
function scene:exitScene(inEvent)
end

-- Called AFTER scene has moved off screen.
function scene:didExitScene(inEvent)
end

-- Called prior to the removal of scene's "view" (display group).
function scene:destroyScene(inEvent)
end

-- Add scene lifecycle event handlers.
scene:addEventListener("createScene", scene);
scene:addEventListener("willEnterScene", scene);
scene:addEventListener("enterScene", scene);
scene:addEventListener("exitScene", scene);
scene:addEventListener("didExitScene", scene);
scene:addEventListener("destroyScene", scene);

return scene;
```

Typically, each scene is in its own Lua source file named after the scene. Therefore, in Astro Rescue, since the title scene is rather uncreatively named `titleScene`, the code for it is found in the file `titleScene.lua`.

> **Note**   While that is most typical, and is what I've done in Astro Rescue, another approach is to use the `storyboard.createScene()` function, which returns to you a scene object to which you can then add your event listeners. That way, you can have a single Lua file that defines multiple scenes if you wish, and you can even dynamically create scenes (although trying to come up with a reasonable use case for that gave me a headache!). My experience is this is not done often though, and it's not a pattern I'd suggest using in any case, as it leads to much larger source files than is comfortable to navigate.

To activate a scene only requires a single line of code:

```
storyboard.gotoScene("titleScene", "flip", 500);
```

That triggers Corona to load up `titleScene.lua` and begin to run through the event listeners of the scene object, which are:

- createScene
- willEnterScene
- enterScene
- exitScene
- didExitScene
- destroyScene

This list represents the order in which the lifecycle event listeners will be called as well. Now, this is the complete list of events that a scene can respond to, but it doesn't **have** to respond to all of them. You can handle only the events that make sense for your use case.

Every Event Needs a Handler

Don't worry, I'm going to discuss what each of these is used for shortly, but before I do that there are some other points to touch on. Did you notice this batch of statements at the end of the scene template in Listing 3-1?

```
scene:addEventListener("createScene", scene);
scene:addEventListener("willEnterScene", scene);
scene:addEventListener("enterScene", scene);
scene:addEventListener("exitScene", scene);
scene:addEventListener("didExitScene", scene);
scene:addEventListener("destroyScene", scene);
```

These statements are what activate, so to speak, the event listeners. Here's the basic rundown. Every object in Corona has the ability to respond to various events that can occur. Many different events are generated over the course of a Corona app running. Some are related to user input (screen touches, accelerometer movements, etc.); some are related to generic lifecycle events, like your application starting up or a new frame being drawn to the screen; some are related to physics simulations; and so on. You'll meet many different events throughout this book but for now I'm only interested in the six already listed that are related to scenes.

Each of those `addEventListener()` calls tells Corona that the scene object (since that's what we're calling the method on) wants to be notified when one of these events occurs. For each call, we specify the string name of the event we're interested in as well as the function to call in response. Now, in this case, we are not specifying a function directly but instead passing a reference to the scene object itself. When you pass an object reference (remember that **object** in Corona means table), then when the event occurs Corona looks for a method on the object named after the event. If it finds one, it calls the function; otherwise the event is essentially ignored. This is sometimes referred to as a **table listener,** as opposed to a **function listener,** which is when you pass a reference to a plain old function to `addEventListener()`.

Now, look at that scene template again. Notice that each of the methods added to it match one of our scene events. Those won't actually be called unless we register them as event listeners, but once we do that, it means that the lifecycle events for the scene will be handled by our scene object's methods.

The Life (and Death) of a Scene

What are the scene lifecycle events actually for, you ask? It's pretty straightforward.

- `createScene`: This occurs once per scene and is where you will do most of your setup tasks that should only occur once per scene. For example, typically you would load graphics and audio resources here. This event won't fire, however, if the scene's view display group already exists (a display group is something I'll get into in chapter 4, but for now it's enough to say it's a container for your graphics).

- `willEnterScene`: When you tell Corona to go to a scene, you can do so with various transition effects. Those transitions take some amount of time. This event occurs before the transition begins. It can fire multiple times—every time you go to the scene, in fact. Typically this event is not used quite as often as most others, `enterScene` specifically. When this event fires, nothing for the new scene is visible to the user.

- `enterScene`: This event occurs after any transition effect finishes and is typically where you start any animations that need to start and hook up any event listeners for dealing with user input.

- `exitScene`: This event fires when a you transition from the current scene to a new scene, before any specified transition effect begins, and applies to the current scene. Here is where you typically would do any cleanup tasks, including stopping animations and stopping event listeners for user input. You might also clean up graphic and audio resources, but as I'll discuss in a moment you might not!

- `didExitScene`: This fires after the transition effect on the current scene finishes. Like `willEnterScene`, you tend to use this event less than the other events, but it can be used for cleanup tasks if you need to. For example, maybe you want your game character to continue walking even as the current scene transitions off screen. If you stop the animation in `exitScene`, you won't get what you want because the animation won't be running as the scene transitions off screen. Stopping it in `didExitScene` will let the animation continue until the scene transition completes.

▒ `destroyScene`: When a scene is purged, this event fires. More specifically, any time the scene's view display group is removed, this event fires just prior to that removal. This is where you should do any real cleanup tasks such as destroying graphics and audio resources.

Making the Transition: Transition Effects

So, let me talk about a few things that I glossed over a bit. First, whenever you transition to a new scene you have the option of doing so with a transition effect. The Storyboard API provides a number of built-in transitions to choose from:

▒	`fade`	▒	`zoomOutIn`
▒	`zoomOutInFade`	▒	`zoomInOut`
▒	`zoomInOutFade`	▒	`flip`
▒	`flipFadeOutIn`	▒	`zoomOutInRotate`
▒	`zoomOutInFadeRotate`	▒	`zoomInOutRotate`
▒	`zoomInOutFadeRotate`	▒	`fromRight`
▒	`fromLeft`	▒	`fromTop`
▒	`fromBottom`	▒	`slideLeft`
▒	`slideRight`	▒	`slideDown`
▒	`slideUp`	▒	`crossFade`

Most of these are self-explanatory, but since you should have the Astro Rescue source code already, you can simply change the last line in `main.lua` (which you'll be exploring shortly), the `storyboard.gotoScene()` call, and specify any of these in place of `"flip"` to see them in action for yourself.

Scene Purging for Fun and Profit

The next thing to discuss is when and how scenes get removed from memory. The short and simple answer is that they don't! Once you go to a scene and the Storyboard API loads its source file, the scene object defined in it doesn't go away unless you tell it to.

The long and more complex answer is that isn't **quite** true!

First, I need to be a little more specific: your **view object** is, under normal circumstances, never removed from memory, period. You can pretty well assume that's always true. What I'm really talking about is the view's **display group** getting removed, which for my purposes here means the graphics related to your scene. This can be removed either automatically or manually. When memory is running low, the Storyboard API may choose to purge scenes (never the current scene) to free up memory. It does this intelligently, purging the least-recently used scene. It can also happen manually if you call storyboard.purgeScene(), which purges a specific named scene, or storyboard.purgeAll(), which, as I'm sure you can guess, purges all loaded scenes (again, except the current scene).

There are two other methods that can result in a purge: storyboard.removeScene() and storyboard.removeAll(). The difference between these and the purge methods is that the remove methods actually **do** remove the view object as well! Therefore, while it's true that Corona won't ever purge your **scene objects** automatically, you are free to do so yourself if you wish. It is somewhat unusual to use the remove methods in my experience, but you certainly can if you need to.

There is also a property you can set, storyboard.purgeOnSceneChange. When true, the scene you're leaving will be purged automatically whenever you transition to a new scene.

Lastly, you can disable even the auto-purging of scenes during low memory conditions by setting storyboard.disableAutoPage to true. I would caution against this, though, as you may find your game doesn't play well on low-end devices if you do.

There's a bit of a balancing act here: purging with every scene transition avoids low memory conditions, but it can also negatively impact performance, since a scene's resources are completely loaded and destroyed every time you transition between scenes. For example, not purging the menu scene (Figure 3-2) might make sense so you can move in and out of it as quickly as possible. By default, the Storyboard API won't automatically purge unless low memory conditions occur, but if your game is particularly memory-hungry you may want to set storyboard.purgeOnSceneChange to true.

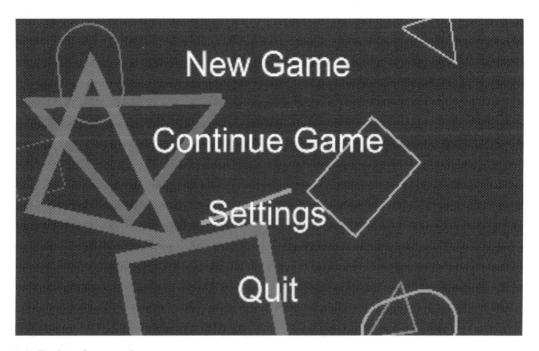

Figure 3-2. The Astro Rescue main menu scene

In the case of Astro Rescue, it being a relatively simple game, you can get away with purging every scene every time. I prefer to do this when I can get away with it because it keeps the game's runtime memory requirements lean-and-mean. The bottom line, though, is you have to make this decision on a case-by-case basis, and in either case you need to understand what happens by default.

Back to the Beginning: The `main.lua` file

Now, I kind of had you jump into the deep end of the pool here by talking about scenes and events and all that, but it was a reasonable place to start after talking about the overall flow of screens in the game. Now that I have done that, you really do need to swim back to the wading area a bit and see where it all truly starts, which is in the `main.lua` file.

Since this is the starting point for the game, both logically and in practice when it's run, I'll just tear through this file bit by bit to show you what's going on in it.

Global Imports

The first few lines that start things off are:

```
json = require("json");
utils = require("utils");
storyboard = require("storyboard");
storyboard.purgeOnSceneChange = true;
```

There are a couple of modules that you need throughout the game, so importing them into global scope makes sense. These are:

- `json`: This provides JSON (JavaScript Object Notation) support for encoding and decoding Lua objects. It may seem odd to use JSON in Lua, but as you'll see, this is a quick and easy way to save objects in a format that is universal and therefore easier to work with in external tooling.

- `utils`: This is a collection of custom utility functions that I wrote. You'll be looking at this after `main.lua` and some configuration files.

- `storyboard`: This is, of course, the Corona Storyboard API that you looked at earlier.

At this point, you also tell the Storyboard API that you want to purge your scenes whenever the game transitions away from them. As mentioned earlier, this is fine for a small game like this, where the scenes load quickly even on pokey devices, but it's something you most likely wouldn't want to do in a larger game unless you had specific memory concerns. In that case, you're probably more likely to want to purge individual scenes specifically, but again, this is something you need to determine in your specific instance).

Global Variables

As discussed in Chapter 2, you generally want to try and avoid putting too much in global scope. That being said, there's nearly always a few things that belong there . . . or if **belong** is too strong a word, there's things that are certainly made simpler by being global. The first two are:

```
titleMusic = nil;
titleMusicChannel = nil;
```

No game would be complete without some sounds, and Astro Rescue is no exception! You certainly will have some sound effects during gameplay of course, and you have two pieces of music (composed by yours truly!) to choose from. One plays during the title scene (as well as the main menu and settings scenes; see Figure 3-3) and one during the ending scene (Figure 3-4) when the player finishes the game (you'll notice I didn't do so well in that particular game!).

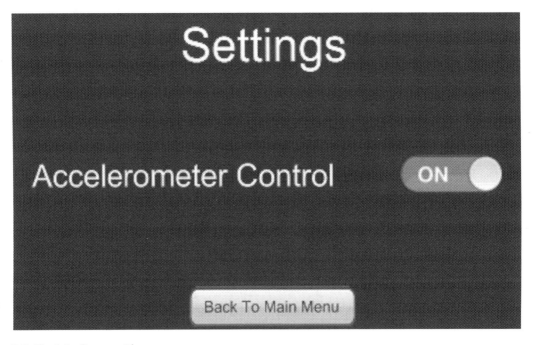

Figure 3-3. The Astro Rescue settings scene

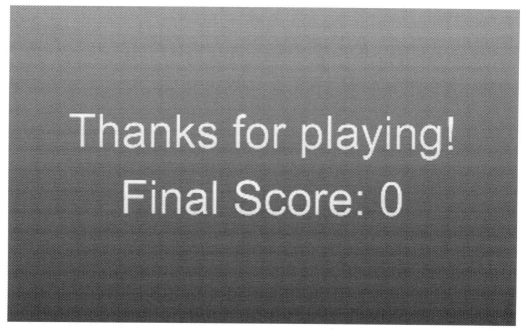

Figure 3-4. The Astro Rescue ending scene

While audio is something you'll look at in depth later on, for now I'll tell you that when you load a sound, whether a sound effect or a music file, you'll get a reference to an object that is the audio resource you loaded. When you want to play it, Corona will hand a channel number back to you. Any device has a certain number of audio channels on which sounds can be played, and each audio resource playing at any given time is assigned a channel to play on. You can manipulate a playing sound by manipulating the channel via various functions Corona provides (e.g., things like stopping or restarting a piece of music). That's why you have two variables: `titleMusic` is the reference to the loaded music file; and `titleMusicChannel` is the channel it's currently playing on, if any. You'll see this same pattern throughout the code and you'll likely follow this pattern too in your own games. The only exception is if you don't intend to manipulate a sound later on, then you probably don't need to keep track of what channel it's being played on.

After those variables, you have one that deals with player control:

```
usingAccelerometer = false;
```

In Astro Rescue, you have the ability to control your ship via touch screen or accelerometer (i.e., tilting your phone or tablet). To be more precise, you in fact control the ship's horizontal motion with the accelerometer (if you decide to), but you still handle vertical thrust via touch events. In either case, the code needs to know which mode of control is being used, and that's what `usingAccelerometer` is for. By default, the game uses touch controls only, so it is `false`, but the user can set it to `true` in the settings scene that you will explore in Chapter 4.

Last, we have an object:

```
gameData = {
  level = 1,
  score = 0
};
```

This is a basic Lua table where the state of the game that we need to persist between program executions resides, so the player can continue the game where it was left off. Only the level the game is currently on and the score are important to record. Things like how much fuel the player has is acceptable to reset every time they play. This also means that if she stops playing in the middle of a level, any progress on that level will **not** be saved. It's of course a judgment call whether that's acceptable or not. Creating a positive experience for the player dictates that you should save any progress **that matters** frequently. What matters, of course, is a matter of perspective. Given the simple nature of this game, and given that it's for learning purposes and not something I'm looking to sell, I see no problem saving just the current level and forcing the player to restart the level when she continues a game. However, as they say on the Interwebs: YMMV (your mileage may vary)!

Dealing with Game State: File I/O Operations

You saw the gameData object a moment ago; now I'm going to show you the three functions that deal with it. You may have been asking yourself why that was done as a table and not just plain old variables. There's actually a method to that madness, and it harkens back to that JSON library you imported. First, look at how gameData is saved:

```
function saveGameData()
  local path = system.pathForFile("gameData.json", system.DocumentsDirectory);
  if path ~= nil then
    local fh = io.open(path, "w+");
    fh:write(json.encode(gameData));
    io.close(fh);
  end
end
```

The functions in the io.* namespace of the Corona API provide the functionality you need to work with files, but before doing that you need to get a full, absolute path to the file you want to work with. For that you have the system.pathForFile() function, which takes care of all the tricky cross-platform issues for you.

This function takes two arguments: the name of the file you want to work with and the base directory it's in. In almost all cases, you'll use one of the constants defined in the system.* namespace:

- system.CachesDirectory gets you a path to a location meant for you to store data that is to persist across application executions.

- system.DocumentsDirectory is similar in that files stored there are meant to be persistent. The primary difference is that on iOS devices, files stored in system.DocumentsDirectory are backed up by synchronizing whereas system.CachesDirectory is not.

- The system.ResourcesDirectory constant gets you a path to the location where your application resources (e.g., things like your sound and image files) are stored. However, due to security restrictions, you can only read files using this path, never write them.

- system.TemporaryDirectory is where you can place files that only need to exist for the current run of the program.

> **Note**   In the simulator, you can view the files in system.DocumentsDirectory and system.TemporaryDirectory by using the Show Project Sandbox option on the File menu. Anything stored in the other two directories is not visible this way.

Therefore, for your purposes, you would want to use either system.CachesDirectory or system.DocumentsDirectory. Since there's no good reason not to have the game state backed up on iOS devices, go with system.CachesDirectory.

The next step is to ensure that you get a full, absolute path to the file from the call to system.pathForFile(). Assuming you do, you can then open the file by calling io.open(). This function accepts the path you got and the mode to open the file in. Here you use "w+", which means write mode where all previous data will be overridden. The other modes are

- "r": Read mode (the default). The file pointer is placed at the beginning of the file.

- "w": Write-only mode. Overwrites the file if the file exists. If the file does not exist, creates a new file for writing.

- "a": Append mode (write only). The file pointer is at the end of the file if the file exists. That is, the file is in the append mode. If the file does not exist, it creates a new file for writing.

- "r+": Update mode (read/write). All previous data is preserved. The file pointer will be at the beginning of the file. If the file exists, it will only be overwritten if you explicitly write to it.

- "w+": Update mode (read/write). All previous data is erased. Overwrites the existing file if the file exists. If the file does not exist, creates a new file for reading and writing.

- "a+": Append update mode (read/write). Previous data is preserved, writing is only allowed at the end of file. The file pointer is at the end of the file if the file exists. The file opens in the append mode. If the file does not exist, it creates a new file for reading and writing.

You get a handle to the file in the variable fh, which you can then call methods on to perform various I/O operations. The write() method is used in this case, which accepts a variable-length list of arguments that can be strings or numbers. In this case, the json.encode() method , which is part of the JSON library that was imported at the start, is used to convert the gameData object to a string of JSON. It probably would have been easier to do something like:

```
fh:write(gameData.level, gameData.score);
```

However, I wanted to show usage of the JSON functionality Corona provides. It may not be very important for this use case, but when you are reading and writing things like level data, it's helpful if it's in a common format like JSON so external tooling can edit it easily.

Last, you need to close the file with a call to io.close(), passing the handle to the file, and you're done.

Reading in saved game state is a little more involved, but not much:

```
function loadGameData()
  local path = system.pathForFile("gameData.json", system.DocumentsDirectory);
  if path ~= nil then
    local fh = io.open(path, "r");
    if fh == nil then
      clearGameData();
    else
      gameData = json.decode(fh:read("*a"));
      io.close(fh);
    end
  end
end
```

The code begins identically to saving state but starts to differ once you determine you have a path to the file. In this case the call to io.open() specified the "r" method for reading, and then you check if the file was actually opened. The io.open() method will return nil if the file couldn't be opened (plus an error message as part of a multivalue return, but for your purposes here the error message is ignored). If the file can't be opened, then a call to clearGameData() is made (which I'll show you next), which effectively resets the game state so a new game can begin.

If the file **is** opened, though, that's where the read from the file is done via the call to the read() method on the fh variable, your file handle. The argument passed to this method is one of three values:

- "*l": Reads the next line (skipping the end of line), returning nil on end of file (EOF). This is the default format.

- "*n": Reads a number. This is the only format that returns a number instead of a string.

- "*a": Reads the whole file, starting at the current position (which is where you start at this point in the code). On end of file, it returns the empty string.

The string that is read in from the file is passed to json.decode(), which takes the string of JSON and translates it to a Lua table, which then becomes the value of gameData. The file is then closed and your work is done.

The clearGameData() method is very simple.

```
function clearGameData()
  gameData.level = 1;
  gameData.score = 0;
  saveGameData();
end
```

The two pieces of actual game state are reset to what they should be for a new game, and the state is saved so that next time through there is a saved file to read in.

Where It All Begins: Initial Execution

The three methods just examined aren't the first executable code hit, though; that distinction goes to this line of code:

```
display.setStatusBar(display.HiddenStatusBar);
```

The display.* namespace is where nearly all the graphics-related functionality in Corona lives, and as such you'll be getting very familiar with it. This first encounter with it is used to hide the status bar that most modern mobile OSs have at the top of the screen. Note that not all devices support a status bar, but since most games are meant to run full screen with none of the typical OS chrome around them, it's a good idea to attempt to hide it like this regardless (and in any case, no harm is done if this doesn't apply to the current device). You can also use the display.DefaultStatusBar to show it, make it translucent with display.TranslucentBar, or make it black using display.DarkStatusBar (again, all subject to device support).

After that I like to do some initial logging, like so:

```
os.execute("cls");
utils:log("main", "ASTRO RESCUE STARTING...");
utils:log("main", "Environment: " .. system.getInfo("environment"));
utils:log("main", "Model: " .. system.getInfo("model"));
utils:log("main", "Device ID: " .. system.getInfo("deviceID"));
utils:log("main", "Platform Name: " .. system.getInfo("platformName"));
utils:log("main", "Platform Version: " .. system.getInfo("version"));
utils:log("main", "Corona Version: " .. system.getInfo("version"));
utils:log("main", "Corona Build: " .. system.getInfo("build"));
utils:log("main", "display.contentWidth: " .. display.contentWidth);
utils:log("main", "display.contentHeight: " .. display.contentHeight);
utils:log("main", "display.fps: " .. display.fps);
utils:log("main", "audio.totalChannels: " .. audio.totalChannels);
```

The first line of code uses the execute() method of the os.* namespace. This namespace houses functions that allow you to interact with the OS at a more native level. It's also where date and time functionality lives. Here, the execute() method accepts a string command to run. The command is entirely dependent on what the OS allows you to do. For example, passing "ls" on an Android device will generate a directory listing (subject to security restrictions). Here, the "cls" command clears the console window in the simulator so that each execution starts the console display fresh.

Otherwise, each execution would append to what is already in the console window, which can get messy quickly.

Following that are a series of `utils:log()` calls. This is a method of the `utils` object that was required earlier that simply logs messages (and objects) to the console. I'll get into that method near the end of this chapter, but for now just think of it as an extended `print()` function, which is a global function that is the basic Corona function for outputting text to the console window.

The `system.getInfo()` method allows you to get the values of various environment variables and properties, including things like

- The environment we're running in (simulator or not)
- What model the device is (e.g., `"Nexus One"`)
- The unique ID of the device
- The platform name (e.g., `"win"` in the Windows simulator)
- Platform version
- Corona version and build number
- The width and height of the screen (the `display.contentWidth` and `display.contentHeight` properties, respectively)
- The frame rate the game runs at (`display.fps`, 30 in the case of Astro Rescue)
- The total number of audio channels available on the device (32 in the Windows simulator).

Once that logging is done, you have to perform a typical task in games:

```
math.randomseed(os.time());
```

The `math.*` namespace is, unsurprisingly, where you find all sorts of mathematical functions, things like calculating square roots; rounding, trigonometric, and logarithm functions; and `randomseed()`, which seeds the random number generator. To get a different sequence of numbers each time the program executes (roughly different, and assuming enough time between invocations) you pass to it the number returned by `os.time()`, which is the current system time in milliseconds.

Next, you have to deal with an audio issue:

```
audio.reserveChannels(2);
```

Naturally, the `audio.*` namespace contains all the audio-related functionality, one of which is the `reserveChannels()` method. As touched upon earlier, normally when you play a sound it gets assigned a channel. If you play a bunch of sounds consecutively, there's every chance it will get assigned the same channel each time. Normally this is fine, but sometimes you want to have a little more control and know exactly what channel will be used by what sound. Moreover, sometimes you want to ensure that you always have free channels available for specific purposes. That's precisely what this line of code does: it reserves two channels (1 and 2, specifically) that will never be auto-assigned when a new sound is played. These channels are what the game will use to play music later, but I'll get to that in the next chapter.

Last, we have two more lines of code to close out `main.lua`:

```
utils:log("appInit", "Going to titleScene");
storyboard.gotoScene("titleScene", "flip", 500);
```

This is a quick log message to let you know via the console window that the game is about to show the first scene, and then the same sort of `storyboard.gotoScene()` call already discussed. This is what truly kicks off Astro Rescue and puts the title scene on the screen.

Utilities

I've mentioned the `utils.lua` file, and now it's time to see what's in it. This is a small collection of utility-type functions that I've written over time, and my suggestion is to always have such a file that is 100% portable from project to project. It'll save you a lot of time.

My version, which in fact is only a subset of the one I use in my real Corona projects (you have to make **some** editorial decisions when writing a book!) begins like so:

```
local utils = {
  isSimulator = false,
  isIOS = false,
  isAndroid = false,
  isWin = false,
  isMac = false
};
```

While 99% of the time you don't need to be concerned with what environment you're app is running in, there are occasions where it comes into play. So, I have these flags that I can check to tell me if I'm running in the simulator, or on an iOS device versus an Android device, or whether it's the Windows versus the Mac version of the simulator.

Of course, flags are no good unless you actually set them, and fortunately Corona provides a way to get the information you'll need to set them properly:

```
if string.lower(system.getInfo("environment")) == "simulator" then
  utils.isSimulator = true;
end
if string.lower(system.getInfo("platformName")) == "iphone os" then
  utils.isIOS = true;
end
if string.lower(system.getInfo("platformName")) == "android" then
  utils.isAndroid = true;
end
if string.lower(system.getInfo("platformName")) == "win" then
  utils.isWin = true;
end
if string.lower(system.getInfo("platformName")) == "mac os x" then
  utils.isMac = true;
end
```

The `environment` variable tells you whether you're running in the simulator or not, and the `platformName` gives you the rest of the information for the other flags.

Talking to Yourself: Log Messages

Earlier I showed you a call to the `utils:log()` function, and I talked about the `print()` function there, which is a global function Corona provides (Lua more specifically, but that's just a bit of trivia for all intents and purposes). That function is actually good most of the time, but it has some problems. Namely, when you try to print a table, most of the time you'll simply get something like this:

```
table: 025C6528
```

That is what you will see if, for example, you use

```
print(gameData);
```

as the last line in `main.lua` (the number may change each time but you get the idea). That's not very helpful! So, the `utils:log()` function deals with tables and provides a more useful output of them. It also allows the log message to be even more useful by allowing you to log a location (meant to be a filename but in no way enforced as such), a message, and optionally an object.

```
function utils:log(inFilename, inMessage, inObject)
  if inObject == nil then
    inObject = " ";
  else
    inObject = " - " .. json.encode(inObject);
  end

  local logMessage = inFilename .. " - " .. inMessage .. inObject;
  print(logMessage);
end
```

First, if the `inObject` argument is `nil`, then it will be outputted as a single space, just to keep the final outputted text looking right. If it's not `nil`, however, then the `json.encode()` function (which you already know about) is used to provide an actual dump of the object. Then the actual output message is constructed and your friendly neighborhood `print()` function is used to actually output it.

The upshot of all of this is that you get a consistent log message format, so, for example, if you execute:

```
utils:log("main.lua", "Here's gameData:", gameData);
```

then what gets printed is:

```
main.lua - Here's gameData: - {"score":0,"level":1}
```

That's a much more helpful bit of logging than what `print()` alone gives you, and without having to do all that formatting every time you want to log something.

You could of course extend this function in a number of ways, perhaps outputting the current time so you can have a rudimentary profiling capability. It's really up to you, but having a function like this is a very helpful thing to have.

Audio Mish-Mosh: Handling Cross-Platform Audio Concerns

The last function in `utils.lua` deals with a slightly sticky situation around audio. Essentially, this is one of those situations where you **do** have to take what device the app is running on into account. You see, for music, Mac (the simulator) and iOS devices use the .m4a format, whereas Android and the simulator under Windows uses the .ogg format. At least at present, there is no common format, aside from .wav, which isn't typically appropriate for music since .ogg and .m4a tend to be a lot smaller due to compression.

```lua
function utils:getAudioFilename(inAudioName)
  if utils.isIOS == true then
    return inAudioName .. ".m4a";
  elseif utils.isAndroid == true then
    return inAudioName .. ".ogg";
  elseif utils.isWin == true then
    return inAudioName .. ".ogg";
  elseif utils.isMac == true then
    return inAudioName .. ".m4a";
  else
    return inAudioName .. ".ogg";
  end
end
```

So, any time you want to play some music, you're of course going to (spoiler alert!) tell the Corona Audio API the name of the file you want to play. Do so by calling this function and passing it the name of the file sans extension. This function will then determine what environment it's running in and return the full filename with the appropriate extension so that you get the .ogg or .m4a versions as appropriate. Just like with the `utils:log()` function, it's **much** better to have this bit of common code in one place rather than have a bunch of `if` statements strewn throughout the code.

Then, the Closer Comes in to Finish the Ninth Inning

At the top of `utils.lua` you create the `utils` object, including a few flags. Then you add the methods to it. Since Lua will execute this file top to bottom, at the end you have a complete `utils` object with all the fields and methods you want. Therefore, to make this a proper module, the last step is to return that object:

```lua
return utils;
```

In `main.lua`, recall you did:

```lua
utils = require("utils");
```

Now it should be apparent why: the `utils` object built up in `utils.lua` is local to it and therefore not accessible to code anywhere else. By returning it at the end and holding the reference to it in that global `utils` variable, you now have a single instance of the `utils` object that you can access from anywhere, which is the general pattern of a Lua module.

Even Further Back: `build.settings` and `config.lua`

In a sense you've moved through this opening volley of code in reverse order, starting with scenes, then `main.lua`, then `utils.lua`. In a strange twist, it actually works to explain it that way! However, there's one more piece of the puzzle that actually comes even before all of that, and that's the `build.settings` and `config.lua` files, both of which come in the form of a Lua object.

The `build.settings` File

The `build.settings` file defines build-time properties and meta information that is (mostly) platform specific. The three most common elements that you'll use are the `androidPermissions` element, the `plist` element under the `iphone` element, and the orientation element, all of which are present in the `build.settings` file for Astro Rescue:

```lua
settings = {

  orientation = {
    default = "landscape"
  },

  androidPermissions = {
    "android.permission.VIBRATE"
  },

  iphone = {
    plist = {
      UIStatusBarHidden = true,
      UIApplicationExitsOnSuspend = true,
      CFBundleIconFile = "Icon.png",
      CFBundleIconFiles = {
        "Icon.png",
        "Icon@2x.png",
        "Icon-72.png",
        "Icon-72@2x.png",
        "Icon-Small.png",
        "Icon-Small-50.png",
        "Icon-Small@2x.png"
      }
    }
  }

}
```

The orientation element is the simplest one: it tells Corona what orientation the game is to be played in. As you'll see in the "`config.lua` File" section, all graphical coding in Corona is done against a virtual screen, independent of the physical screen of the device the game is running on. By configuring it as landscape, that virtual screen acts like a screen on a device that is (typically) wider than it is tall, like most smartphones when turned on their side.

Notice that here you're defining the default orientation, but there's more you can do within the orientation element. You can also handle how the screen will auto-rotate when the player turns the device. For example, when you're playing Astro Rescue as it's meant to be played, it looks like Figure 3-5.

Figure 3-5. Astro Rescue played as it's meant to be played

What happens if the player rotates the screen 180 degrees, though? What they get is what you see in Figure 3-6.

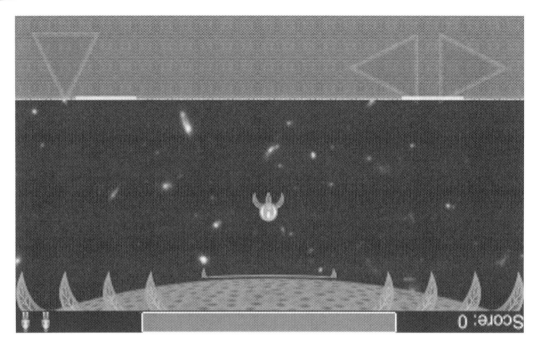

Figure 3-6. I daresay it's going to be a lot harder to play this way!

As you can see, that's not quite what we want because, after all, shouldn't it be the player's choice which way to hold the device? To allow for this, add one more thing to the orientation element:

```
supported = {
  "landscapeLeft", "landscapeRight"
}
```

Now Astro Rescue supports landscape orientation both ways and will effectively rotate that virtual screen I mentioned to match the physical screen and keep right side up all the time.

In addition to landscapeLeft and landscapeRight you can also explicitly support portrait and portraitUpsideDown. For Astro Rescue, though, only the landscape orientations are needed since the game isn't meant to be played in portrait under any circumstances.

Next is the androidPermissions element. This is where you define what permissions the Android build of the game will need. These are the permissions the user is shown when he installs the game. In the case of Astro Rescue we only need to specify the permission allowing the application to vibrate the device (assuming it supports vibration) when an explosion of the ship occurs during the game. The permissions here are numerous and of course Android specific, so I won't describe all the possible permissions here. The Android developer documentation that Google supplies will list all the possible permissions; you simply add the values you need to the list in this element, and Corona and Android take care of the rest.

> **Note**   It's good practice only to add permissions your application actually needs. Don't take the lazy approach and just list everything you think you **might** need someday, as the intention of the Android permission system is that users can intelligently decide if an application is taking too many liberties with their device and data.

Last is the `iphone.plist` element, which is where we can set iOS-specific metadata that winds up in the `Info.plist` file built into every iOS application bundle. Since this element, like `androidPermissions`, is a platform-specific setting, and this book is focused on a library designed to make cross-platform development easier, I won't go into too much detail here. Apple's documentation provides all the possible values you can place here, but it's only right to describe the values you see in the Astro Rescue `build.settings` file:

- `UIStatusBarHidden`: Specifies whether the status bar is initially hidden when the app launches.
- `UIApplicationExitsOnSuspend`: Specifies whether the app terminates instead of running in the background.
- `CFBundleIconFile`: A string with the name of the 57×57-pixel icon.
- `CFBundleIconFiles`: An array of strings containing the filenames of various application icons of various sizes for different iOS device screen resolutions and usages. My advice here is to create a single 512×512 application icon and simply resize it down as necessary.
- `CFBundleDisplayName`: A string that provides the display name of the bundle; that is, the text under the application's icon.

> **Note**   In the Astro Rescue code download, you'll also find an iTunesArtwork file, which is actually a PNG without the extension. You see this large graphic in iTunes Coverflow as you flip through your applications. It's 512×512, hence my suggestion above: start with this one and shrink it down as needed, so you'll always have your canonical One Icon Graphic to Rule Them All™ to serve as the basis for other usage.

The `config.lua` File

The `config.lua` file is where you can specify runtime configuration information that, in a sense, sets up the runtime environment for your application. Along with some other things, it's largely where the virtual screen I mentioned is defined.

The way Corona works is that you design your application to run against a virtual screen, meaning a specified screen size. For example, in Astro Rescue, I've developed it against a virtual screen size of 480×800, a fairly common Android screen size. As you can see, the width and height in this file sets this up:

```
application = {
  content = {
    fps = 30,
    width = 480,
    height = 800,
    scale = "letterbox"
  }
}
```

What happens when you run the game on a screen with different dimensions? Well, Corona does intelligent content scaling for you, meaning it will resize everything to fit the physical screen. So, if the actual dimensions of the physical screen are 960×1600, then Corona simply has to double all the graphics, since your virtual screen size is half the physical screen size, and your application will fill the entire screen. Likewise, if the screen size is actually 240×400 . . . well, first of all, you should probably upgrade your device! Nevertheless, Corona will scale it down to fit in that case as well.

Now, I'm sure the question running through your head is what happens if the screen size is not an even multiple of the virtual screen size? The simple answer is it depends on the scale setting you see there. The letterbox setting that I'm using for Astro Rescue means that Corona will always maintain the same aspect ratio when it scales as the virtual screen, the cost being that you may end up with black bars on the sides of the physical screen, just like when you watch a letterboxed movie on your television.

You could also specify "none" as the scale value, in which case no scaling would be done. This is fine if you only want to support a specific-resolution device, but obviously that limits your potential user base, so it usually isn't what you'll want. The "zoomEven" scale option also maintains aspect ratio but will scale the content to fill the screen, even if that means some content is cut off. Last, "zoomStretch" will fill the screen without cutting off any content, but **will not** maintain aspect ratio. In my experience, most of the time you'll want to use "letterbox" or "zoomEven". You also should design to a screen size that will scale evenly to the greatest number of target physical screen sizes possible. Corona used to recommend using the original iPhone size of 320×480 as your basis, but I personally find that to be a little too small for my tastes. The 480×800 I've used in Astro Rescue will scale nicely on most current devices with fairly little letterboxing, although you do see it on some devices.

Although not shown here, it's important to note that there are two more attributes you can set that impact content scaling in a way: "xAlign" and "yAlign". These tells Corona how you want your scaled content aligned on the physical screen. By default it is centered, which is nearly always what you want. This results in black bars evenly distributed on the sides (or top and bottom) of the screen, just like watching a movie on a television. You can, however, align it to the left or right, top or bottom, if you so choose.

> **Note**   If you're interested (and you probably will be when doing your own games!), there are tricks that
> will allow you to fill that letterbox bleed area with content. It can get a bit tricky to pull off effectively,
> though, so I've left that discussion out here, but a quick look in the Corona forums will turn it up in no time.

The last attribute specified here is `"fps"`, which is the target frame rate of the game. Two values
are valid here: 30 and 60. Note, though, that this is the target rate, so if your code takes more than
33 milliseconds to render a frame then you'll start dropping frames. Also note that this frame rate,
without delving into time-based main loops, affects the speed at which your game runs. For a game
like Astro Rescue, 60 fps would cause it to run too fast.

I'll just quickly mention some of the other attributes that can be present in this file that you may or may
not need to use at some point. As with other things that aren't directly used in Astro Rescue itself, you
should look to the Corona documentation for more details if and when you need these attributes.

The `launchpad` attribute turns Corona LaunchPad analytics on or off. Launchpad is a service offered
to Corona subscribers that helps developers market and monetize their application. Think of things
like ads and social media public relations. It also provides analytic capabilities, which is primarily
what this setting is for. With it, you can see who's running your application, what devices they're
using, all that sort of insightful information.

Last, you can configure options that deal with dynamic image resolution in this file. This is the ability
to swap in higher-resolution versions of your graphical resources for devices like the new iPad with
its Retina display. Sure, you can use dynamic content scaling alone to achieve the same basic
effect, which ensures that your graphics are the right size to fill the screen. However, you do this at
the cost of clarity. Anytime you scale an image, you lose a little clarity. It might only be a little bit, in
which case it's probably going to be fine on most devices. The alternative is to use higher-resolution
images instead, ones that are already sized properly for those high-DPI devices. That way, there's no
clarity loss, no blurriness introduced, and no fuzzy edges and those sorts of artifacts.

To do this, you define an `imageSuffix` attribute under the `content` attribute that defines the naming
convention your graphics will use. For example:

```
{
  ["@2"]=2,
  ["-60p"]=.6
}
```

What this tells Corona is that when your game uses a graphic file named `spaceship.png`, and the
game is running on a device with a screen that is exactly two times the virtual screen size defined
by width and height, it should instead look for a file named `spaceship@2.png` and use that instead.
If `spaceship.png` is a 120×120 image then `spaceship@2.png` should be 240×240. That way, you can
have your art team draw it properly at that size and not simply let Corona resize the smaller version.

The second value, `["-60p"]=.6`, may look a little funky, but all it is saying is that if the physical
screen size is 60% the size of the virtual screen, then use an image named `spaceship-60p.png`
instead. You have complete control over these dynamic sizes.

Caution   It's important to keep in mind that this dynamic substitution happens at runtime, which means that all the different versions of a single graphic must be included in your application bundle. If you aren't careful you can wind up with a file size that is much larger than you expect, even when 90% of the graphics won't even be used on a given device! My advice is to use dynamic content scaling as far as you can, but use dynamic image resolution when it goes too far. If your virtual screen is 320×480 then you're probably fine with dynamic scaling out to 640×960, which just so happens to be the iPhone 4 screen versus the smaller iPhone 3GS. After all, Corona's scaling algorithm is quite good! However, to support the iPad at 1024×768 you may want to consider dynamic substitution for the larger screen to avoid too much blurring.

Summary

In this chapter, you explored the core architecture of the Astro Rescue game. You looked at the configuration files that Corona supports. You explored the Storyboard API and learned how it allows you to break our game into separate scenes.

You also looked at some concepts that tie into all of this, including events and event listeners. You got your first look at some of the system API and display API. Last, you began to understand the overall code structure of the game.

In Chapter 4, you'll start to explore the real core of the Astro Rescue game. You'll see in detail what makes the title scene and main menu scene tick, among other things, and begin to explore things like graphics, transitions, and user interface widgets.

Title, Menu, and Settings Scenes

Okay, so you know Astro Rescue has a title scene, a menu scene, and a settings scene, in addition to the actual game scene itself. In Chapter 3 we saw all these, on top of all of the basic configuration files and the beginnings of the actual code in main.lua.

Now it's time to move into the scenes themselves. Some are quite simple (the title scene), while the others (menu and settings) have a little more meat on their bones, as the saying goes. All three of the scenes we're looking at in this chapter are actually quite small in terms of overall amount of code, but the nice thing about them is they'll force us to look at quite a bit of the Corona API along the way.

I'll kick things off with what is most definitely the simplest of the bunch, the title scene.

Welcome, Ladies and Gents: The Title Scene

The title scene, as shown in Figure 4-1, doesn't have a lot going on, but it introduces a number of Corona API features that you'll use throughout the game. In action, though, it is much more interesting than on the printed page: the background does a cool rotating tunnel-y thingamajig. It's fairly subtle, but gives a nice animated background over which the title graphic can be superimposed.

Figure 4-1. The Astro Rescue title scene

As discussed in Chapter 3, the Storyboard API is used for this scene, which means that it all starts with a scene object:

```
local scene = storyboard.newScene();
```

This call gives you back an object that has all the internal plumbing needed for Corona to work with your scene. That plumbing isn't generally important to you, save for a few bits that leak out into your sphere of responsibility, as we'll see shortly. Going forward, I'll leave this line of code out when discussing other scenes as it's the same for all scenes, but rest assured it's present as the first line of code for each and every scene in the game.

First things first—you have some variables to declare:

```
local bg1;
local bg2;
local rot = 0;
```

Note that all of these variables are declared as local, so they are only visible within this module, meaning to the code in the titleScene.lua file. The variables bg1 and bg2 are references to the background graphic, which you can find in the file titleBackground.png. Why there are two variables, when logically you would expect to only see one (seeing as there's only a single background graphic file), is because of the animation that happens with it (and that's the purpose of the variable rot as well, which just stores a number).

Creating the Scene

That's jumping ahead a bit, though. Before you get to that, you have to see where the scene's work begins, in the `createScene()` method:

```
function scene:createScene(inEvent)

  utils:log("titleScene", "createScene()");
```

Out of habit, I like to have an entry message in each function or method, with the exception of those that are called excessively and would clog up the console window. I also typically have an exit message, but not always. This just makes it easier to glance at the console window when running in the simulator and see the overall flow through my code. That's all this first line of code does, and you'll see similar lines throughout the game so I won't generally mention it again unless there's something unusual about one of the calls.

A Little Jaunt into Audio

The next two lines of code deal with the music that plays behind this scene (in fact, behind all three of the scenes discussed in this chapter):

```
titleMusic = audio.loadStream(utils:getAudioFilename("titleMusic"));
audio.play(titleMusic, { channel = 1, loops = -1, fadein = 500 });
```

The `audio.*` namespace has quite a few functions and properties; `audio.loadStream()` is just one of them. This method is responsible for opening an audio file for streaming, which means chunks of it are read in from storage as it is played, as opposed to `audio.loadSound()`, which you'll see in the game code that loads the audio file into memory completely in one go. Generally, when you want to play music it is better to stream it, since those files tend to be a lot bigger than sound effects used during gameplay. You simply pass this method the name of the audio file to load, including the path. The `getAudioFilename()` in the `utils` class is used here, which handles getting the appropriate type based on operating system and environment, as discussed in Chapter 3.

The `audio.loadStream()` method returns a handle to the audio resource that you can then pass to methods in the `audio.*` namespace, such as `audio.play()`, which starts playing it. You pass that handle to `audio.play()` as well as an options object that defines how you want the audio played. Here, I specify the `channel` to play it on as 1, which you'll recall from Chapter 3 was one of the two channels I reserved for this purpose. I also pass -1 for the `loops` attribute to indicate I want the audio to loop back around at the end and start playing again continuously. You can pass any number for loops. A value of 0 means to play the sound exactly once and stop, 1 means play it once and then loop it once (so it plays twice in total), and so on. Last, the `fadein` value of 500 means that the audio will fade in to full volume over the course of 500 milliseconds, which matches the time it takes the scene to transition onto the screen fully, so the audio plays nicely synchronized with that animation.

> **Note**   Although typically you do not need to reserve channels, I actually have run into some issues that required me to do so. I'm still not sure what the root cause was, but what was happening is that the channel returned by `audio.play()` wouldn't be valid later when I tried to `stop()` the music. This shouldn't have happened and I actually suspect it was a bug in Corona, but the simple solution was just to reserve channels for the two music files that are played in Astro Rescue and use them specifically for each music file. That solved the problem, so my suggestion is don't reserve channels unless you come up against a situation like this where you need to, since it's better to let Corona (and the operating system) manage the channels automatically. I just wanted you to understand why I did it this way.

The other two options you can pass to `audio.play()` are `duration`, which means play the audio for the exact number of milliseconds specified and then stop, regardless of whether the audio was actually finished or not; and `onComplete`, which is a reference to a function that will be called when the audio finished playing. This is referred to as a **callback function** and is a common idiom seen throughout Corona. It allows you to trigger actions when specific events occur, in this case when the audio finishes playing. We'll see such callbacks a number of times as we progress through the Astro Rescue code.

Although I haven't done it here, you might also want to call the `audio.setVolume()` method. This accepts a volume value between 0 and 1, as well as an options object that includes a single `channel` attribute. A value of 0 for `channel` will adjust the volume of all channels, whereas omitting the options object entirely sets the master volume, which is a bit different than adjusting all channels (the volume of a given channel is effectively scaled by the master volume).

> **Tip**   The notion of an options object is very common to many Corona functions so you'll see it all over the place going forward. I personally prefer this API design pattern, since it is more self-documenting. For example, `audio.play(h,{ loop:-1,fadein:500});` is quite a bit clearer than `audio.play(h,-1,500);` since you don't need to go checking documentation for parameter orders and meanings with the options object design. It also means you don't have to worry about breaking your code if you mess up the order, since the order of the attribute in an options object doesn't matter, whereas it does for a plain old function call.

Although not used in Astro Rescue, a few other members of the `audio.*` namespace are worth mentioning now:

- `audio.pause()` and `audio.resume()` allow you to pause and resume a playing audio file, be it a stream or not. You pass to them the channel number to pause or resume.

- `audio.getDuration()` returns the length of a loaded audio resource in milliseconds. You pass to this the handle returned by `audio.loadStream()` or `audio.loadSound()`.

- audio.rewind() and audio.seek() allow you to rewind and start an audio resource playing from the beginning or jump to a specific point in time of the audio resource, respectively. For resources loaded with audio.loadSound() you pass this a channel number, and for those loaded with audio.loadStream() you can actually pass either a channel number or a handle. Resources loaded with audio.loadSound() are allowed to be shared on multiple channels simultaneously, while resources loaded with audio.loadStream() cannot and you must load multiple instances of it if you need to play it on more than one channel at a time. So, the meaning of handle and channel are essentially identical when dealing with resources loaded by audio.loadStream() but not resources loaded with audio.loadSound().

- audio.freeChannels, audio.totalChannels, audio.reservedChannels, and audio.usedChannels are informational properties that tell you, respectively, how many channels are currently free, how many in total are available on the system, how many are reserved, and how many are currently in use.

Our First Foray into Graphics

Now that you have seen how audio works, you can start to look at the other big sense you use when playing a game: the visual. In other words, graphics! Like audio, everything related to graphics is found almost entirely in a single display.* Corona API namespace. Moreover, all of the action takes place using a single entity: the DisplayObject construct. You don't create DisplayObject instances yourself; instead you create graphical elements using methods available in the display.* namespace, such as loading a PNG file:

```
bg1 = display.newImage("titleBackground.png", true);
bg1.x = display.contentWidth / 2;
bg1.y = display.contentHeight / 2;
bg1.xScale = 2;
bg1.yScale = 2;
self.view:insert(bg1);
```

Everything that gets drawn on the screen in Corona is ultimately a DisplayObject. Draw an image using a JPEG file? It's a DisplayObject. Draw a single line? It's a DisplayObject. Draw some text? Yep, DisplayObject again! This is a much more powerful approach than it may at first seem; because the DisplayObject class has a number of properties and methods, it means that anything on the screen has them.

Caution The true at the end tells Corona you want the full-resolution version of the image. By default, Corona will do some internal scaling of larger images to conserve texture space. While that's generally what you want, I've found that many times it will result in images that aren't drawn fully, especially when dealing with full-screen images like the background image. My advice is to always pass true when loading images unless you have a specific reason not to, just to avoid this problem. That being said, watch your texture memory usage and change to true if you see it getting too large.

For example, positioning an image is accomplished easily by setting values for the x and y attributes, as you can see in the previous bit of code. Here, I want to center the background image, so I take the width and height of the screen as available in display.contentWidth and display.contentHeight and divide each by 2.

That takes some explanation, though, because if you've done any work with graphics before you would usually expect that x and y specify the top left-hand corner of the image, but in this case that's not true. By default, DisplayObjects have a reference point that is actually their center, and it is this reference point that you're changing when you update x and y. Now, if you prefer to have the top left-hand corner be the reference point, you're welcome to do so by calling the setReferencePoint() method on your DisplayObject and passing it display.TopLeftReferencePoint. From then on, graphics will position as you expect. You can specify other reference points as well, including all the corners and midpoints on the edges in the same way, but the top left-hand corner and center are the two you'll see the most (and are the only two used in Astro Rescue).

In addition, you can change the size of any DisplayObject by setting xScale and yScale, as done here, to make the background image twice its normal size (the "why" behind that is coming up shortly!)

The final piece of the puzzle is the self.view:insert(bg1); line and it introduces another concept: the DisplayGroup. Every scene has a DisplayGroup associated with it that contains all of the DisplayObjects used in the scene. A DisplayGroup is in fact just a specialized form of DisplayObject that can have child elements. This means that it supports all of the same methods and properties as a DisplayObject does. The benefit to this is that if you have a bunch of DisplayObjects—for example, asteroids on the screen in a game—and you want to do something to all of them, you only need to do it to the DisplayGroup and they're done! Want to make them all twice as big horizontally? Assuming bg is the DisplayGroup they're all in, then you just call bg.xScale=2; and that's that! The self.view reference is the DisplayGroup that Storyboard automatically creates for you and attaches to the scene object created at the top of this source file (self obviously refers to the scene in this context). Calling the insert() method on it, and passing the bg1 DisplayObject reference to it, is all it takes to get the background image into the scene's DisplayGroup. And yes, before you ask, there's a corresponding remove() method to take elements out of a DisplayGroup, but as you'll see in the section on the destroyScene() method, there's a better way than that.

It is important to realize, however, that as you add DisplayObjects to a DisplayGroup you are also effectively defining the z index, or stacking order, of the elements within the DisplayGroup. In other words, an item added after bg1, for example, will appear on top of it. That comes into play because although it isn't shown here, there is another copy of the background image created in the variable bg2. This too gets added to the group, so it would obscure bg1 when drawn (which, since they are the same image, would not visually make any difference).

However, as you know, the background has a little rotation animation thing going on, and the first part to how that works is accomplished with this line of code:

```
bg2.alpha = .5;
```

That sets the alpha, or transparency, of the second copy of the background image to half. This means that bg1 will be visible through it a little bit. I'll jump the gun a bit here and tell you that the rotation effect is accomplished simply by rotating bg1 and bg2 in opposite directions, but that wouldn't accomplish anything if the one on top weren't semitransparent—hence why this line of code is needed.

The last little bit of code in createScene() is this:

```
local gfxTitleHeader = display.newImage("titleHeader.png", true);
gfxTitleHeader.x = display.contentCenterX;
gfxTitleHeader.y = display.contentCenterY;
self.view:insert(gfxTitleHeader);
```

```
end
```

As you know by now, this is creating a DisplayObject, this time the title graphic. Note that this is the last DisplayObject created, and that's no accident: it gets inserted into self.view last, which means it'll be on top of both of the background images.

The Stage

One other important concept to be aware of is the stage. This is a special DisplayGroup representing the screen itself. All DisplayObjects, whether specifically added to a DisplayGroup or not, are automatically a child of the stage. More precisely, if you do not add them to a DisplayGroup explicitly, they are direct children of the stage. If you add them to a DisplayGroup, self.view for example, then they're indirect children of the stage because their parent self.view is a direct child of the stage. If you're working with the Storyboard API, as we are in Astro Rescue, then you generally won't deal with the stage directly at all since you'll be dealing with view-specific DisplayGroups instead.

However, it's important to understand this because what if I didn't add the title graphic to self.view? Well, you should go give that a try! What happens is that when the title scene is transitioned on and off the screen, the title graphic won't be a part of the transition. You see, the transition between scenes is accomplished by animating the self.view DisplayGroup, changing its properties over time really, which, remember, will affect all of its children too. If something isn't in the group then it won't be animated, but it still will be drawn to the screen because it's still a child of the stage, as is the self.view. There are times when you might want that to happen, but usually it'll be a mistake, and an easy one to fix: make sure the offending DisplayObjects are added to self.view and you're good to go.

Starting the Scene

After the createScene() method is executed, the enterScene() method comes next:

```
function scene:enterScene(inEvent)

  utils:log("titleScene", "enterScene()");

  Runtime:addEventListener("touch", scene);

  Runtime:addEventListener("enterFrame", scene);

end
```

The only goal here is to set up listeners for two events: `touch` and `enterFrame`. I'll talk about them in the exact opposite order, just to be different!

You'll recall that in `config.lua` you specified a frame rate of 30 fps. For every one of those frames Corona generates an `enterFrame` event. Now, you could, in theory at least, get away with writing an entire game without ever using that event, but that would be a bit unusual.

Generally, you want to do something for each of those frames. Maybe you want to move the player around the screen, or update the scrolling star field in the background (or rotate some background images—hint hint!). In either case, you want to execute some code when a new frame is about to be drawn so you can do your updates before Corona puts anything on the screen. The `enterFrame` event serves exactly that purpose.

To deal with `enterFrame` you need to listen for the event. When you call the `addEventListener()` on an object that supports it you're saying that object wants to be notified whenever a given event occurs, and when it does, to call the specified function.

You can attach event listeners to many objects, but what if you don't have a specific object to attach it to? That's where the `Runtime` object comes into play. `Runtime` is a global object that Corona maintains for this purpose. With it, you can listen for events that are more global in nature, such as `enterFrame`. The alternative is to have a specific object listen for the event, which you could do, perhaps the title graphic in this case, and do all your work there. That's pretty unusual, though, as you generally want to listen for events at as high a level as makes sense and not force it to a lower level that isn't really necessary.

Take, for example, the other event listener set up here, the one for the `touch` event. Touch events are typically done at a lower level, perhaps the title graphic for example, because frequently the touch interaction is meant for a specific object, so you want to register the touch on that specific object on the screen. What that would mean is that when the title graphic itself is touched, the specified function is called, but not if anything else is touched.

What if you want the user to be able to touch anywhere on the screen, though? That's where `Runtime` comes into play: it handles the touch event on a global level, same as `enterFrame`. It won't matter what object you touch; the event listener you set up will fire.

> **Tip**   In fact, you can have multiple listeners for a given event. So, for example, if you were going to manipulate the title graphic and also the background graphic, you could attach an `enterFrame` listener to both and have the update code in two separate functions. Sometimes that's a good idea as it keeps the code for a given object encapsulated in a sense within the object, but more usually you'll see a single function in the case of `enterFrame` events. The touch event handler is a little different and depends on the use case, but simply put, in this case we want the touch to register anywhere on the screen; hence using Runtime there is the right thing to do.

Now, the astute reader will notice that I didn't pass a reference to a function as the second argument to `addEventListener()` but actually passed a reference to the `scene` object. This too is valid, but it means that you need to ensure you have methods named after the events on the scene object, enterFrame() and touch() in this case. That's a good way to do things because it keeps your code encapsulated within your scene object and avoids any potential naming conflicts. However, the choice is entirely yours. You could pass references to stand-alone functions if you preferred, or even pass functions inline, as I've done in a number of places throughout the Astro Rescue code. Different strokes for different folks! Also, note that if you do this for multiple objects then that single method will need to determine what object was actually touched and act accordingly. This may or may not be work you want to do, but again, circumstances will dictate which approach makes sense.

Exiting the Scene

Just like enterScene(), we have just a very small amount of work to do in exitScene():

```
function scene:exitScene(inEvent)

  utils:log("titleScene", "exitScene()");

  Runtime:removeEventListener("touch", scene);

  Runtime:removeEventListener("enterFrame", scene);

end
```

Any time you add an event handler to Runtime you should remove it, and most usually the place to do so is in exitScene(), with them being set up in enterScene().

> **Note**   Event listeners set up on specific objects don't need to be removed **if** the object is added to self.view because those resources are cleaned up automatically when the scene's DisplayGroup is destroyed by the Storyboard API. However, the caveat is that you can't have any references to the object in your code aside from the DisplayGroup, otherwise that reference will keep the object, and hence the event listener, from being cleaned up. In other words, a memory leak (and maybe worse if that event listener still fires when you don't expect it to!).

The trick here is that you need to pass to removeEventListener() not only the name of the event to stop listening for, but a reference to the function (or object, as is the case here) that handles it. This is tricky because if you use inline functions you won't have such a reference and you'll end up with a memory leak unless the object the listener is attached to gets destroyed automatically as previously described. Basically, be careful with inline event handlers!

Destroying the Scene

When the scene is finally destroyed by the Storyboard API, you get a call to our destroyScene() method:

```
function scene:destroyScene(inEvent)

  utils:log("titleScene", "destroyScene()");

  bg1:removeSelf();
  bg1 = nil;
  bg2:removeSelf();
  bg2 = nil;

end
```

Cleaning up resources in Corona is a two-step process: removing the object and nilling the reference to it. For the two background images we use the removeSelf() method, which is present by virtue of their being DisplayObjects. This one method call takes care of removing the object from its parent group and destroying the resource. However, Lua will maintain a table for this resource, although one with no real value. To get rid of that we have to ensure that any references to the table are nilled out. The variables bg1 and bg2 are the only two such references, so setting them to nil completes the procedure.

> **Caution**   A DisplayObject can only ever, directly at least, be a child of a single DisplayGroup. The DisplayGroup that is its parent could be itself a child of another, but that's fine because the DisplayObject itself is still only the direct child of one DisplayGroup. If you insert a DisplayObject into a DisplayGroup after it was already inserted into another, it is removed from the first and moved to the second. Watch out for this as it's a nasty, subtle bug that's a pain to track down!

Some Unused Scene Event Handlers

If you browse through the Astro Rescue code, you'll notice that the willEnterScene() and didExitScene() methods are present but are empty, save for some logging. These aren't needed for your purposes here, but out of habit I prefer to have all the Storyboard lifecycle methods present so it takes less time later if I need to add something in them. There's certainly no harm in them being present but empty.

Handling Touch

The next method in our scene object is that touch() method I mentioned earlier:

```
function scene:touch(inEvent)

  utils:log("titleScene", "touch()");

  if inEvent.phase == "ended" then
    utils:log("titleScene", "Going to menuScene");
    storyboard.gotoScene("menuScene", "crossFade", 500);
  end

  return true;

end
```

Its purpose is very simple: when the user touches anywhere on the screen, you want to transition to the menu scene. However, touch events are more complex than they might at first seem.

Think about touching something (let's keep it family friendly and go with your phone!). A touch is really a combination of events: the start of the touch when contact is made, perhaps some movements as you glide your finger around the surface, and then the end of the touch when contact is broken. Corona's touch events provide you with this level of granularity in the object passed in to the event handler, inEvent in this case.

This object has a phase attribute that tells you what part of the touch event occurred. I only want to start transitioning to the new scene when the user lifts their finger off the screen, so we look for the ended phase. When it occurs it's a simple matter of calling storyboard.gotoScene(), as we saw in main.lua, and telling it to go to the menuScene. I also want a crossfade animation, meaning the title scene is fading out as the menu scene is fading in, so that's the transition effect I specify. I want this to happen over half a second, so 500 milliseconds is the third argument passed.

In addition to the phase the inEvent object contains other information, such as

- **name**: The name of the event, such as "began" or "ended".
- **target**: A reference to the object that was touched.
- **x and y**: The location on the screen of the touch event.

> **Note** Every type of event, of which touch is just one, has its own sets of attributes. While you'll see a few others, I leave it as an exercise for the reader to take a look at the Corona documentation for the others that aren't used in Astro Rescue.

Continuous Action

Earlier, you saw the event listener added for the `enterFrame` event. As I explained there, since the `scene` object itself was passed as the listener to `addEventListener()`, there needs to be an `enterFrame()` method on the object, and that's the next bit of code:

```
function scene:enterFrame(inEvent)

  bg1.rotation = rot;
  bg2.rotation = -rot;
  rot = rot + 1;
  if rot == 359 then
    rot = 0;
  end

end
```

As you can see, there's not much to it. That `rot` variable that we saw at the start is first used to set the value of the `rotation` attribute of both background images, `rotation` being another of the attributes all `DisplayObjects` have. The rotation occurs around the reference point of the images, which you'll recall is by default the center for a `DisplayObject`. That makes perfect sense here, and is another reason you may want to think twice about changing the reference point: rotations become a little tougher to deal with because you get an off-center rotation, which usually isn't what you want.

> **Note**   This also explains the scaling you saw when bg1 and bg2 were loaded; without that, as the images rotate, you would see corners come into view and the illusion would be broken. Go ahead and comment out the xScale and yScale values to see what I mean.

In any case, the value of `rot` is negated for the bg2 image, which means it'll wind up rotating counter to bg1. Recall that bg2 has an opacity set to half, so bg1 is partially visible through it. With them rotating in opposite directions you get the subtle little animation you see when you run the game. Since 360 and zero are essentially equivalent, the rotation simply loops around to zero when it hits 359 degrees, which gives us a continuous rotation. The `rot` value updates 30 times a second, which as it happens is a nice speed for the effect.

Wrapping up the Title Scene

There's just a small bit of code remaining in `titleScene.lua`, and it's code that executes as soon as the module is loaded, since it's not within any function:

```
utils:log("titleScene", "Beginning execution");

scene:addEventListener("createScene", scene);
scene:addEventListener("willEnterScene", scene);
scene:addEventListener("enterScene", scene);
```

```
scene:addEventListener("exitScene", scene);
scene:addEventListener("didExitScene", scene);
scene:addEventListener("destroyScene", scene);

return scene;
```

You know what this is all about from Chapter 3: all the lifecycle event handlers for the scene have to be registered or none of the code you just looked at will ever execute! Last, the scene object is returned, as required to make this a proper Lua module, and as the Storyboard API dictates we do.

What'll You Have? The Menu Scene

After users leaves the title scene they are transported, as if through some form of magic (!), to the main menu scene. Well, **main** menu scene implies there's another menu scene somewhere, and there's not, so just plain menu scene will suffice. This scene is, err, seen in Figure 4-2 and is actually the most action-packed of all three of the scenes discussed in this chapter, both in terms of what's happening on the screen and what's happening in the code.

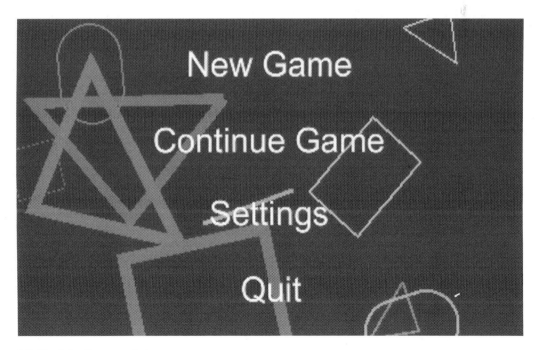

Figure 4-2. The Astro Rescue main menu scene

Creating the Scene

The scene creation begins, as usual, in the `createScene()` method with a little bit of logging and a new method call:

```
function scene:createScene(inEvent)

  utils:log("menuScene", "createScene()");

  self.buildShapes();
```

I'll show you the `buildShapes()` method shortly, but for now I'm sure you can guess by the name that it is responsible for building those shapes you see in the background of the scene. Before that, though, you have some audio code:

```
if audio.isChannelPlaying(1) == false then
  audio.rewind(titleMusic);
  audio.play(titleMusic, { channel = 1, loops = -1 });
end
```

Here we get to see a little more of the Audio.* API in action. Since in `main.lua` you told the Storyboard API to purge scenes any time it switches between them, you have a little bit of a potential problem with the music. You'll recall that the music begins playing in `titleScene`. However, there is another path to the menu scene: after the player stops playing the game. In this situation, the title music would not be playing. To deal with this, the `audio.isChannelPlaying()` method is called to see if channel 1 is playing (remember channel 1 was reserved for this particular music resource). If it is then there's nothing to do, because the user must have come from the title scene (more precisely, the user hasn't started playing the game yet, which is what triggers the music to stop playing). If it's not playing, though, then you have to make sure you start at the beginning by calling `audio.rewind()` on the `titleMusic` stream resource and then start playing it again. This ensures that the music is played in all cases when the menu scene is shown.

Next, you need to create the menu items for the user to click, beginning with the Start Game text:

```
local txtStartGame =
  display.newText("New Game", 0, 0, native.systemFont, 52);
txtStartGame.x = display.contentCenterX;
txtStartGame.y = display.contentCenterY - 170;
txtStartGame:addEventListener("touch",
  function(inEvent)
    if inEvent.phase == "ended" then
      clearGameData();
      audio.stop(1);
      utils:log("menuScene", "Start Game tapped");
      storyboard.gotoScene("gameScene", "zoomOutIn", 500);
    end
  end
);
self.view:insert(txtStartGame);
```

The `display.newText()` creates a text object, which is a `DisplayObject` at the end of the day, so you can manipulate it like any other graphic resource. You pass to this method the text to create, the x and y coordinates of the top left-hand corner of the text, the font to use (either `native.systemFont` or `native.systemFontBold`), and the size of the text. Once the text is created, you position it by manipulating x and y attributes because, again, this is just a specialized `DisplayObject` and that's the simplest way to move one around (yes, there are other ways, as you'll see later).

You also need to add an event listener to it to handle touch events. Recall on the title scene where you used `Runtime` to add the event listener? Well, in this case, you want to register touches on this object only, so the touch event listener is attached to that. I again use an inline event handler here, just because I tend to like that approach since it keeps all the code related to this object contained in the same area of the source, but that's entirely a style choice.

In any case, when the touch event occurs you check to see what `phase` is in progress and in this case, only the event that ended has relevance. So, the user can hold her finger on this text object as long as she wants, but the action won't be triggered until she lifts her finger.

Once that happens, there are a couple of tasks to perform. First, game data needs to be cleared, as discussed in Chapter 3, so that the player is starting fresh. The title music then needs to be stopped, which is a simple matter of calling `audio.stop(1);` where 1 is the channel the resource is playing on (you typically would use a variable here, the one that recorded what channel the resource was played on, but since you reserved this channel specifically for this music, the number is hard-coded instead). Last, a transition to the `gameScene` is started, which you'll start exploring in Chapter 5 when you start getting into the game code itself.

> **Tip** The positions of the menu items are simply eyeballed. The horizontal position is simple: `display.contentCenterX` conveniently provides the x coordinate of the center of the screen, and since a `DisplayObject` by default has a center reference point, this centers all the text. The vertical value, however, is a little trickier and is where the eyeballing comes into play. Once you have the center of the screen with `display.contentCenterY`, you just adjust it up or down as appropriate to get the spacing you want. Sure, I could have calculated this value dynamically based on number of menu items, size of each, and so on, but for a simple menu like this, that's just added complexity. Certainly, if you were doing this game for real to sell, I would suggest going through that extra effort just so that when you move, add, or subtract items later, their positions are maintained automatically.

Next, you have the Continue Game menu option. However, I haven't shown that code here because aside from the text obviously being different, there's only one other difference: the `clearGameData();` call is replaced by a `loadGameData();` call. If you remember from Chapter 3 what these methods do, it should be obvious why this is so: in this case, you need to retrieve the saved game state so the player can pick up where she left off.

The next text object is the Settings option, and again I haven't shown this code (in the interest of sparing the life of a tree or two!) because the only substantive change is in the event handler, where the only thing that needs to happen is to transition to the settings scene.

Finally, you have the Quit menu option, which does have some important differences:

```
local txtQuit = display.newText("Quit", 0, 0, native.systemFont, 52);
txtQuit.x = display.contentCenterX;
txtQuit.y = display.contentCenterY + 170;
txtQuit:addEventListener("touch",
  function(inEvent)
    if inEvent.phase == "ended" then
      utils:log("menuScene", "Quit tapped");
      audio.fadeOut({ channel = 1, time = 500 });
      transition.to(scene.view, { alpha = 0, time = 500,
        onComplete = function()
          os.exit();
        end
      });
    end
  end
);
self.view:insert(txtQuit);

end
```

There's not a **whole** lot more going on here, or so it seems at first, but in fact the callback function here introduces a new concept that is incredibly powerful in Corona: the transition.* API.

With a grand total of only four methods, the transition.* namespace is one of the smallest in Corona land, but despite that it's really one of the most powerful. Take this particular event handler, for example. The goal you're trying to accomplish is to gently fade the screen to black over the course of half a second. Now, you know at this point that you can mess with the alpha attribute of the scene.view DisplayGroup to pull that off. You could set up a variable that has a starting value of 1, since that's the maximum alpha value. Then every time the enterFrame event occurs you could decrease the value by .06 (the maximum alpha value of 1 divided by one-half of our frame rate of 30 fps, so 1 / 15, or .06, rounded down) and update the alpha attribute of scene.view, and you would get what you want.

However, that sounds to me like too much work! Instead, a single line of code can accomplish the same thing! The transition.to() method allows us to animate the attribute(s) of an object over a period of time. The word **animate** here simply means "to change over time." Therefore, first you pass to it what object we want to animate, scene.view in this case, plus an options object. The options object contains two attributes: alpha and time. The time attribute is obvious: how many milliseconds should this transition, or animation if you will, take to complete? 500 milliseconds is half a second, of course, so that is the answer here.

The alpha attribute's value defines the **target** value of the attribute. You're fading to black, which means we want the DisplayGroup to become completely transparent, so a value of 0 is the right answer.

It's optional to have an event handler to a transition like this, but in the case of exiting you actually want to be made aware of when the transition complete so you can shut the application down. So, set up a function and pass it as the value of onComplete, and when it fires you have only to call os.exit().

> **Caution**   One thing to be very aware of is that Apple will not accept applications for publication in their store that have an explicit "exit" or "quit" function like Astro Rescue does, and so using this particular API call in any way in your app will keep it from getting past Apple's scrutiny. As a learning exercise like this, it's fine, but keep this in mind when working on your own games.

In addition to `os.exit()`, which simply shuts the application down, the `os.*` namespace provides a number of other OS-related functions:

- Getting the current system date and/or time: `os.date()` and `os.time()`

- Getting the approximate number of seconds of CPU time the application has used: `os.clock()`

- Getting the amount of time between two time values: `os.difftime()`

- Deleting or renaming a file or directory: `os.remove()` and `os.rename()` (these two are actually a little out of place if you ask me, but so be it!)

Getting back to the notion of transitions though, you also have the `transition.from()` method to use. This works the exact opposite of `transition.to()`: you specify the starting value in the call and the current value of the attribute to be manipulated becomes the ending value.

Whether you use `transition.to()` or `transition.from()`, they share a common set of options. In addition to `time` and `onComplete` they are as follows:

- `transition`: This allows you to specify an easing function, which is used to change the value over time. The default easing function, linear, just changes the value consistently over the specified period (or over the default period of 500 milliseconds). However, if for example you want to speed up the animation the closer it gets to the end, you could specify the `easing.inExpo` function instead. Easing functions are, frankly, a little hard to describe and are better seen, so I won't attempt to document all of them here; the Corona documentation should be your go-to source for that (or, better still, trying each one). Also, note that you can write your own easing function. It's just a regular Lua function with a specific method signature that returns a value each time it's called.

- `delay`: This allows you to specify some number of milliseconds to wait before the animation begins (defaults to none).

- `delta`: This is a Boolean. When false, which is the default, the values you specify for the attributes to be changed are specific values, so if you say `alpha 1` it means animate alpha to a value of 1, assuming a call to `transition.to()`. If you specify `delta` as true, though, then that same value of 1 means change the value of the alpha attribute by one. If the current value were 0, then you would get the same effect. If it were already 1, though, then you'd be changing it to a value of 2 over the lifetime of the transition, which for alpha probably won't do what you want. It seems that Corona clamps the value to 1, so in this case it wouldn't do any harm, but imagine changing colors instead and you can see how you wouldn't get the result you want. Oftentimes, using `true` for delta is convenient if you're moving an object, which of course you can do my manipulating the x and y attributes. If you want to move a spaceship 50 pixels to the right from its current position, for example, setting `delta` to `true` and x to 50 would accomplish that. Setting `delta` to `false` would result in the ship moving to absolute position 50,y where y is its current y coordinate (assuming that wasn't being animated at the same time—yes, you can animate as many attributes at the same time as you wish!).

When you're specifying options for a transition, any attributes of the options object that aren't one of these known attributes are assumed to be the names of attributes of the object you are animating. So, `alpha`, x, y and `strokeWidth` would all qualify for example.

The last important thing about transitions to know is that when you call `transition.to()` or `transition.from()`, what's returned to you is a reference to a tween, which is the term used to describe an animation over time. Often, you won't care about this, but sometimes there will be cases, as is true in Astro Rescue as you'll see in later chapters, where you may want or even need to stop a transition before it completes. When this situation arises you can pass that tween reference to `transition.cancel()` and thy will is done!

The last method in the namespace, `transition.dissolve()`, is a shortcut for a common transition where you transition between two overlapping images, with one fading to transparent while the other fades to opaque. You can accomplish the exact same thing with two simultaneous to and from animations, but this method provides a shortcut since it's so common.

> **Caution**   When using `transition.dissolve()` you do not have access to the onComplete and onBegin callbacks, nor can you cancel it. This is something to think carefully about if you want this sort of transition. While it's more work to deal with two transition calls and potentially two cancel calls, if that's a need in your project you don't really have much choice.

Some Unused Scene Event Handlers

As with the title scene, a few methods are not used in this scene: `willEnterScene()`, `enterScene()`, `exitScene()`, `didExitScene()`, and `destroyScene()`. They aren't needed for your purposes here so they're just empty methods (empty save for the logging, which I personally still like to see in the console so I know things are happening as expected).

Oh, Those Beautiful Shapes!

Now you'll go back to the future and look at that `buildShapes()` method that was called early in the `enterScene()` method. It's a fairly good-sized chunk of code, but it's also relatively simple and straightforward.

```
function scene:buildShapes()

  for i = 1, 10 do

    local shape = scene.createShape();
    shape.xScale = math.random(1, 3);
    shape.yScale = shape.xScale;
    shape:setReferencePoint(display.CenterReferencePoint);
    shape.x = math.random(display.contentWidth);
    shape.y = math.random(display.contentHeight);
    shape.rotation = math.random(1, 360);
    if math.random(1, 2) == 1 then
      shape.rotateClockwise = true;
    else
      shape.rotateClockwise = false;
    end

    shape.rotateTransition = function(inShape)
      if inShape.rotateClockwise then
        transition.to(inShape, {
          time = 3000, delta = true, rotation = 360,
          onComplete = inShape.rotateTransition
        });
      else
        transition.to(inShape, {
          time = 3000, delta = true, rotation = -360,
          onComplete = inShape.rotateTransition
        });
      end
    end;

    shape.rotateTransition(shape);

    scene.view:insert(shape);

  end

end
```

The point of this method is to create 10 random shapes for the background of the menu scene; hence the loop. The first thing done is to call scene.createShape(), which returns a DisplayObject that is some shape (it's random, so you won't know which). Since this is a DisplayObject, you know that all the usual methods and properties are available, so the xScale and yScale properties are set. The value they are set to is determined by a call to math.random(), which simply takes the lower and upper bounds and returns a number within the range (inclusive of the bounds values), so a number between and including 1 and 3 in this case. Note that to maintain a proper aspect ratio, the values need to be set the same, so yScale is set to xScale after its value is randomly set.

Do you remember earlier when I said that DisplayObjects always have their reference point set to center by default? Well, it turns out that isn't **always** true. Specifically, when you draw a graphic from scratch, as the createShape() method does, it isn't true. However, in order to get a proper rotation, you want to use the center point, as previously discussed, so that is done next.

Next, the shape is positioned randomly on screen using the screen's width and height values as the bounds. When calling math.random() with only a single number, the range is automatically taken to be 1 to X, where X is the number you pass in.

> **Note**   You could also pass no arguments, which gets you a number between 0 and 1.

Following that, the amount the shape starts rotated is randomly set, as is the direction it's rotating. Note here that rotateClockwise is what is sometimes referred to as an **expando** attribute, meaning an attribute you add at runtime (expanding on the object, so to speak; hence the name). Lua is a dynamic language and you can do this sort of thing any time you want. This is highly convenient because it means you can avoid having global variables and instead store values that apply to a given object directly on the object.

The next bit is where things get a bit interesting. Again, you add an expando attribute to the shape object, but this time it's a method named rotateTransition(). This is perfectly fine in Lua land, just like expando attribute are. This method kicks off a transition, one for clockwise rotation and one for counterclockwise rotation, depending on the current value of shape.rotateClockwise. In contrast to the transitions described earlier, this one uses that delta attribute to rotate the shape a full 360 degrees (or –360 degrees for counterclockwise rotation) starting from whatever its current value is (remember, it's random, so not doing this via delta would have required more work, something most people like to avoid whenever possible!). When the transition completes, the same rotateTransition() method on the shape is called. The onComplete callback handler receives a reference to the object it belongs to, so you can easily make this call, as you can see.

Last, to kick off the action, make a direct call to shape.rotateTransition(), which you can do like you would for any other method of an object, since that's exactly what it is at this point! This gets the shape rotating. Of course, the shape is inserted into the scene's view as well. Do this 10 times and you have a nice, random background of rotating shapes.

While I'm not sure I'd put a game on the market with this particular background, it certainly serves the purpose of learning here and now quite well.

Creating Graphics from Scratch

The buildShapes() method calls the createShape() method 10 times to create a random shape, which is up next for your review:

```
function scene:createShape()

  local whatShape = math.random(1, 6);
  local shape;
```

First, decide what shape we're going to draw. There's six of them, and each one is drawn slightly differently. Start with the first shape, a simple, plain, boring, straight line:

```
if whatShape == 1 then
  shape = display.newLine(0,0, 75,0);
  shape.width = math.random(1, 6);
  shape:setColor(
    math.random(25, 200), math.random(25, 200), math.random(25, 200)
  );
```

Yep, that's it! The `display.newLine()` method accepts four arguments, X1, Y1, X2, and Y2 where X1, Y1 are one endpoint of the line and X2, Y2 is the other endpoint, and returns a `LineObject` (which is an enhanced `DisplayObject`). Remember, though, that `buildShapes()` is going to randomly move this line around, so what coordinates are used here are kind of irrelevant and really just serve to define the length of the line, which will always be 75 pixels.

I also wanted to introduce some variety into all these shapes by randomly determining their width and color. The `width` is done first, which is just an attribute of `DisplayObject`. The `setColor()` method is then used to randomly determine the color. This accepts three values: red, green, and blue (it can also accept a fourth `alpha` value, but that is optional). I chose the range for all three values as 25 to 200 so that the shapes don't get either too dark or too light behind the menu text.

The next shape is the most complex and is a five-pointed star:

```
elseif whatShape == 2 then
  shape = display.newLine(0,-110, 27,-35);
  shape:append(
    105,-35, 43,16, 65,90, 0,45, -65,90, -43,15, -105,-35, -27,-35, 0,-110
  );
  shape.width = math.random(1, 6);
  shape:setColor(
    math.random(25, 200), math.random(25, 200), math.random(25, 200)
  );
```

First, a simple line is drawn as in the previous section. Then, to that line is appended a series of lines by calling the `append()` method on it. This may look complicated, but all `append()` really does is accept any number of X, Y pairs representing a new endpoint, and the line is extended from its last endpoint to each new endpoint. You can build any vector-type object you like this way. For example, you could build a square manually:

```
local l = display.newLine(100,100, 200,100);
l:append(200,200, 100,200, 100,100);
```

Look at Figure 4-3 to visualize this.

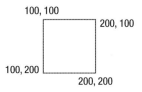

Figure 4-3. The Astro Rescue main menu scene

The line with endpoints 100, 100 and 200, 100 is first drawn, then a line from 200, 100 (the last endpoint of the line) to 200, 200 is drawn to produce the right edge, then from 200, 200 to 100, 200 to make the bottom edge, and last 100, 200 to 100, 100 to complete the square.

> **Tip**   Lua is of course agnostic about how you space things, but I find that writing code where I have to specify multiple X/Y coordinate pairs as X1,Y1, X2,Y2, X3,Y3 with the space between pairs but none between X and Y components makes it clearer.

The third random shape is a rectangle:

```
elseif whatShape == 3 then
  shape = display.newRect(0,0, 150,100);
  shape.strokeWidth = math.random(1, 6);
  shape:setStrokeColor(
    math.random(25, 200), math.random(25, 200), math.random(25, 200)
  );
  shape:setFillColor(0, 0, 0, 0);
```

Corona provides the display.newRect() method for this. All you need to feed it is the upper left-hand and bottom right-hand corners of the rectangle and that's all it needs to draw you a rectangle. As opposed to the two previous shapes, this time you need to use the strokeWidth attribute to set the width of the lines and the setFillColor() method to set the color. Why is that? Well, because display.newRect() returns not a LineObject but a VectorObject, which, like LineObject, is a type of DisplayObject.

The main difference between a VectorObject and a plain DisplayObject is the ability to fill the shape. Since we don't actually want a filled square though, just the outline, filling the square with black (RGB 0, 0, 0) to match the background color works well.

> **Caution**   It also means that if you're working with filled shapes you have to take care with your stacking order, because a filled rectangle will occlude content behind it, unless you also change its opacity. The menu items are drawn after the shapes so we have none of that concern here.

The fourth shape is actually just a specialized form of rectangle, and if you remember grade school, you'll recognize it as a little something known as a square!

```
elseif whatShape == 4 then
  shape = display.newRect(0,0, 75,75);
  shape.strokeWidth = math.random(1, 6);
  shape:setStrokeColor(
    math.random(25, 200), math.random(25, 200), math.random(25, 200)
  );
  shape:setFillColor(0, 0, 0, 0);
```

That shouldn't need any further explanation beyond what was given for the rectangle, so let's instead move on to the next shape:

```
elseif whatShape == 5 then
  shape = display.newRoundedRect(0,0, 150,100, 50);
  shape.strokeWidth = math.random(1, 6);
  shape:setStrokeColor(
    math.random(25, 200), math.random(25, 200), math.random(25, 200)
  );
  shape:setFillColor(0, 0, 0, 0);
```

This is, again, a rectangle. However, it's a specialized kind that has rounded corners, and Corona provides a method for this common need. The only real difference with this as opposed to a plain rectangle is the additional fifth argument passed to display.newRoundedRect(), which is the radius of the corners. I've chosen a radius of 50, which is quite a bit, so that really what you wind up with is an oval. That is done simply so that it's visually different than a rectangle.

The final shape is a triangle:

```
elseif whatShape == 6 then
  shape = display.newLine(100,100, 200,100);
  shape:append(150,40, 100,100);
  shape.width = math.random(2, 6);
  shape:setColor(
    math.random(25, 200), math.random(25, 200), math.random(25, 200)
  );
end
```

With the previous discussion of the star, you have all the tools you need to understand this code as well. I should also point out that for the use case here, the coordinates used to construct this triangle (and the star) don't really matter. As with the line, buildShapes() is going to position this shape anyway, so the coordinates are only relevant in that they are relative to each other and therefore meaningful within the context of drawing the shape initially. If you were instead using these shapes to dynamically construct the background for a level in your game, then the coordinate used would likely have some meaning to the world you are constructing at large.

Only one step remains to complete this method:

```
return shape;
```

```
end
```

Send that shape on back to `buildShapes()` and your work here is done!

> **Note** The only method for shape-drawing that isn't used here is `display.drawCircle()`, which accepts values for X and Y of the center of the circle and its radius. You get back from it a plain `DisplayObject`; there is no specialized subclass like for rectangles and lines. That wasn't used, of course, because a rotating circle wouldn't actually look like it was doing anything!

Wrapping up the Menu Scene

As usual, finish up the settings scene as you finished the previous two, namely by hooking up the event listeners and returning the `scene` object:

```
utils:log("menuScene", "Beginning execution");

scene:addEventListener("createScene", scene);
scene:addEventListener("willEnterScene", scene);
scene:addEventListener("enterScene", scene);
scene:addEventListener("exitScene", scene);
scene:addEventListener("didExitScene", scene);
scene:addEventListener("destroyScene", scene);

return scene;
```

> **Note** The consistent form of a scene's code is one of the main benefits to using the Storyboard API in the first place. Once you have the basic template in place it becomes cookie-cutter and requires no thought or effort on your part, leaving your valuable brainpower free to make your games that much better!

The Choice Is Yours: The Settings Scene

The final scene to explore is the settings scene, as shown in Figure 4-4. It's a very simple scene with just a single option, but it's interesting in that it introduces a whole new facility that Corona has to offer: widgets.

Figure 4-4. The Astro Rescue settings scene

Following the usual instantiation of the scene object comes the first bit of code that touches on the widget.* namespace:

```
local widget = require("widget");
widget.setTheme("theme_ios");
```

To use widgets, you need to include the Corona module for them. This implicitly means that the widget code and resources aren't loaded and available by default, which is an efficiency gain on the part of Corona. Once you have the widget module loaded and you "catch" the returned object resulting from loading the Lua source file for the module, the first thing to do is to decide what theme you want to use.

When you set the theme, which you should do before creating any actual widgets, you reference a Lua file that defines the theme, theme_ios.lua in this case, which is one that is included with Corona. You can create your own theme by defining the attributes such as image resources to use to draw each widget, or modify an existing theme to your tastes. Creating a theme file is a specialized task, though, and is something outside the scope of this book. For the purposes of Astro Rescue, the iOS theme will be fine. This means the settings scene will have an Apple-inspired look to it in terms of the widgets on Android, but that's fine (and some would even consider it a good thing, those that are fans of Apple's aesthetic choices anyway).

Creating the Scene

After that you encounter the createScene() method, as you should be coming to expect when looking at the code for a Storyboard scene:

```
function scene:createScene(inEvent)

  utils:log("settingsScene", "createScene()");

  local txtTitle = display.newText("Settings", 0, 0, native.systemFont, 72);
  txtTitle.x = display.contentCenterX;
  txtTitle.y = 50;
  self.view:insert(txtTitle);
```

This is the title text at the top, created as you saw in the menu scene code.

Following that is the label to the left of the option switch. This again is typical text creation code as you've seen before, with a few differences:

```
local txtAccelerometerControl = display.newText(
  "Accelerometer Control", 0, 0, native.systemFont, 48
);
txtAccelerometerControl:setReferencePoint(display.TopLeftReferencePoint);
txtAccelerometerControl.x = 30;
txtAccelerometerControl.y = display.contentCenterY - 20;
self.view:insert(txtAccelerometerControl);
```

You will note here that the text DisplayObject isn't using its default reference point and is instead switched to the top left-hand corner. This is done simply to make positioning it a little easier: if the reference point was the center then the math to calculate the X coordinate would be just a little more involved. Granted, it still wouldn't exactly be rocket science, but it's not as simple as one hardcoded value (yes, so-called magic numbers in code are generally a Very Bad Thing™, but in a simple case like this there's no real problem doing so).

With the label in place, we can now draw the switch widget itself:

```
local wgtAccelerometerControl = widget.newSwitch{
  left = display.contentWidth - 140, top = display.contentCenterY - 10,
  initialSwitchState = usingAccelerometer,
  onPress = function(inEvent)
    usingAccelerometer = inEvent.target.isOn;
  end
};
wgtAccelerometerControl:scale(2, 2);
wgtAccelerometerControl:setReferencePoint(display.TopLeftReferencePoint);
self.view:insert(wgtAccelerometerControl);
```

A switch widget is your basic, run-of-the-mill Boolean type of widget. It's either on or off, yes or no. By default, you get what is known as an on/off switch, but you can also create a radio or checkbox, two of the more commonly seen types of Boolean widgets. You can do this by passing either radio or checkbox as the value of the style attribute that is passed as part of the options object if you so choose.

> **Note**   Take a look at that funky syntax here: there's no opening and closing parentheses around the option object passed to `widget.newSwitch()`. This is just another form a method call can take if it only accepts a single table as an argument. You can add the parentheses if you wish, and in fact my own personal style is to always use them. However, I wanted to demonstrate this for you if for no other reason than a lot of Corona's documentation uses this form, and I don't want it to hit you out of left field the first time you see it!

The `left` and `top` attributes are of course the position of the widget, corresponding to x and y, and `initialSwitchState` is a Boolean value that determines whether the switch is on or off when initially drawn. Here, the value of the `usingAccelerometer` variable tells you that.

Any time the value of switch changes—that is, when the user flips it on or off—you will need to update the value of that `usingAccelerometer` variable, of course, and that's where the `onPress` attribute comes into play. Here, I define an inline function as its value, since it's a very simple function and I felt it would just clutter the code up to have it stand alone (or be a method of the scene object). Recall earlier when discussing events I mentioned that one of the things passed as part of the event object is the `target`—that is, the object that was touched? That's the case here, and the attribute of a switch widget that gives you the current value is `isOn`, hence `inEvent.target.isOn` gives us the new value for `usingAccelerometer`.

Once the widget creation is completed, there are two more tasks to do. The first is to double the size of the switch, since the default size struck me as a little too small for a good touch target. The `scale()` method takes a horizontal and vertical value that defines how much to scale the widget by, two times in this case. Last, like the title text, the reference point is changed to make positioning a little easier. In this case, we get the right edge of the screen via `display.contentWidth` and then back off from that value by 140 pixels, enough for the double-sized widget to fit without flowing off the right side of the screen.

The final element to create is another widget so the user has a way to get back to the menu, this time a basic button widget:

```
self.view:insert(widget.newButton{
  left = display.contentCenterX - 120, top = display.contentHeight - 65,
  label = "Back To Main Menu", fontSize = 24,
  width = 260, height = 60, cornerRadius = 8,
  onEvent = function()
    utils:log("settingsScene", "Back To Main Menu tapped");
    storyboard.gotoScene("menuScene", "crossFade", 500);
  end
});

end
```

Its creation is much the same as the switch widget, with a few extra attributes. The `label` attribute is of course the text on the button; `fontSize` is the size of that label text; `width` and `height` are the horizontal and vertical size of the button, respectively; and `cornerRadius` is how much of a curve you want the edges to have. You can also do things like change the color of the text (`labelColor`), offset the text by some amount (xOffset and yOffset), change the font to use for the text (font), give the text an embossed effect (emboss), and change the color and size of the border around the button (strokeColor and strokeWidth).

Again, an inline event handler is used. In this case, the onEvent attribute defines that handler, and in fact, this is a bit of a shortcut. You see, a button widget supports onPress, onRelease, and onDrag events that correspond to the various phases a touch on it can go through (onPress and onRelease would always occur but onDrag may not). You can hook one or all of them as you wish, or optionally, you can hook just onEvent, and then check the phase attribute of an event object passed in to differentiate the different phases. Here, though, the phases doesn't actually matter, so there's no check for it, and in fact I don't even bother to receive the event object that's passed in; it'll just be dropped on the floor, so to speak.

Before I move on, although these are the only two widgets used in the game, I want to give you at least a brief overview of some of the others that are available in the widget.* namespace:

- The PickerWheel, shown in Figure 4-5, allows you to select values for one or more data elements each from a range of predefined possible values, all with a skeumorphic interface.

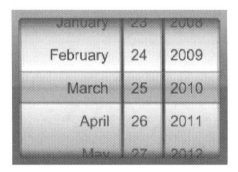

Figure 4-5. PickerWheel widget

- The ScrollView presents an area of the screen that the user can scroll by dragging their finger around. I haven't included an image of this since it's not really much to look at on the printed page, but just imagine how you scroll around pages in a web browser on your phone, and you are picturing a ScrollView.

- The SegmentedControl widget, shown in Figure 4-6, is a multivalue toggle switch where you can select one of a number of predefined, mutually exclusive options. This mimics the types of push-button controls typically seen on old stereo systems where, when you press one button, any others that were previously pressed down will pop back up and only the new selection will be selected down.

Figure 4-6. SegmentedControl widget

▩ The Slider, an example of which you can see in Figure 4-7, allows the user to select a value from a defined range of values by dragging the slider nub across the slider bar.

Figure 4-7. Slider widget

▩ There is also a Spinner widget, which is a rotating circular indicator that lets the user know there is activity going on. This widget needs to be seen in action rather than printed in a book, so I'll just move on.

▩ The Stepper widget in Figure 4-8 allows the user to choose a value from a range of values using single-step increments, up or down.

Figure 4-8. Stepper widget

▩ To help you divide a screen into multiple sections there's the TabBar widget, shown in Figure 4-9. This appears along the bottom of the screen most of the time, and as the user clicks a given tab, the screen changes to reveal different content.

Figure 4-9. TabBar widget

▩ Last, the TableView widget, shown in Figure 4-10, is the more or less canonical way to display a large list of information for the user to browse through in mobile designs. The user can scroll the list up and down by dragging, expand items for more details (if that is one of your design goals), and select items if you apply the proper code.

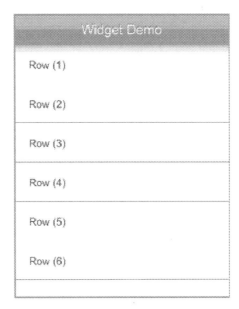

Figure 4-10. TableView widget

As you can see, Corona offers most of the widgets you would need to build most basic user interfaces, and this is an area that Corona Labs is currently putting a lot of effort into building, so it's quite possible there will be an even wider variety of widgets to choose from by the time you read this. As I hope you can see, you can build not just games with Corona but regular, productive applications, too, while still get all the cross-platform goodness you do for games. If you don't mind me saying so, this is very exciting indeed!

Some Unused Scene Event Handlers

As with the other scenes, a number of lifecycle event handlers are present but empty. These are willEnterScene(), enterScene(), exitScene(), didExitScene() and destroyScene(). I think by now you've read enough about this, so enough said!

Wrapping up the Settings Scene

Just like the last two scenes, the lifecycle event handlers are set up and the scene object is returned. I'll save a little ink by not showing it here, but rest assured, it's just like the other two!

Summary

In this chapter, you explored three of the four scenes that comprise Astro Rescue: the title scene, menu scene, and settings scene. Along the way, I introduced a big chunk of the Corona API, including graphics that are both preexisting in the image file as well as those drawn from scratch, audio, UI widgets, and some general-purpose functionality including math functions. I also showed you the transition library for the first time, and you put all of this together to form the functionality behind these scenes.

In Chapter 5, you will begin to tear into the actual game-related code of Astro Rescue itself, and that's where you'll be spending the bulk of the remainder of this book. In the process, you'll gain experience with a lot more of the Corona API, although much of what you were exposed to in this chapter will come back into play many times, although often in different ways.

Chapter 5

The Game, Part 1: Core Game Code

So far, I have covered quite a bit of ground: from the basics of graphics and audio to file operations, from the Storyboard API to the Transition API. You are rapidly building up your repertoire for working with Corona and in the process Astro Rescue is coming together. You've looked at the title scene, menu scene, and settings scene, all very important elements to the complete project.

However, it's not the game itself, and that's the meat and potatoes you're here to see, I know! Well, it's time to go there now—time to start looking at the core of Astro Rescue and see what makes it tick. There is a lot of ground to cover in this chapter, but by the time you're finished you will have gained a significant portion of the knowledge you'll need to write virtually any game you want with Corona.

The Game Scene Kicks It All Off

When the user selects New Game or Continue Game from the menu, the gameScene is launched. As you know, the contract with the Storyboard API says this should be—most of the time, anyway—in a file named gameScene.lua, and in this case it is. That file begins with:

```
gc = require("gameCore");
```

As you'll see, the gameScene is really a pretty sparse object and serves the purpose of an interface between the real game code and the Storyboard API. It's kind of a shim between the two, so to speak. I prefer this decoupling because if I ever want to move away from the Storyboard API for some reason ,then there is no (or, at least, little) impact on my actual game code. Frankly, the gameCore object is what most of this chapter is about, so I'll get to that.

It is, however, important to note that the variable gc is a reference to the gameCore object and is used throughout the code. Remember that, as it'll make the rest of the code make a heck of a lot more sense!

Thinking further along the line of decoupling things as much as possible results in the next three imports:

```
require("gameCoreInputEvents");
require("gameCoreCollisionEvents");
require("gameCoreMainLoop");
```

Each of these Lua source files contains code that is added to the gameCore object—mixed in, if you will. That implies that the import of gameCore must be first, and that is true. Generally, it's good to avoid such dependence on import ordering, but because of the architecture I've chosen it comes into play.

The gameCoreInputEvents.lua file is responsible for adding methods to gameCore for handling all user input events. The gameCoreCollisionEvents.lua file adds code for dealing with collisions between game objects, which, because of what Astro Rescue is, turns out to be where a lot of the action really is in terms of the code. The final import, gameCoreMainLoop.lua, adds in the main loop of the game, which is responsible for handling movement of objects and determining if it's time for the game to end (in conjunction with the code in gameCoreCollisionEvents.lua).

All of those files will be explored in detail in later chapters, but for now you have one final piece of business:

```
local scene = storyboard.newScene();
```

With a scene object in place the Storyboard API can deal with this scene properly. All that's left is adding the life-cycle handlers for it, and that's coming up shortly, but first you have one little detour to make: physics.

The World of the Real: Physics

Okay, nice, something new to talk about! The next two lines of code in gameScene.lua, before the scene life-cycle event handlers get added, are:

```
physics = require("physics");
shapeDefs = require("shapeDefs").physicsData(1.0);
```

In the old days of writing games, the motion of objects was usually pretty linear and nearly always deterministic, in the sense that you specifically wrote the code defining its motion. If you had an airplane flying across the screen, you generally wrote the code to keep decrementing its horizontal position over time, or something along those lines.

That motion isn't particularly natural, though. Although you certainly **hope** a plane always flies in a straight line, especially if you're a passenger, the fact is that it is constantly falling towards the Earth due to gravity! It's only because the forces of lift and thrust combine to keep it in the air that we don't wind up with a lot more visits to mysterious islands with smoke monsters and polar bears on them!

> **Note**   This is of course a reference to the television show **Lost.** I would bet most readers don't need to
> be told this, but it's entirely possible you never saw the show, so just to be safe, I'm telling you!

To simulate the real world, however, what if you wanted that plane to be affected by gravity? On your own, you likely would do something like reduce its vertical position over time, balanced against its level of thrust and lift, taking into account air viscosity and other factors. But what if you then wanted that plane to fly across the surface of Mars? That's different gravity, so you'd need to change your calculations.

Sounds to me like a whole lot of work and complicated math!

Most games didn't bother with this level of complexity years ago because it was too computationally expensive, even if the developer was up to the task. Really, there's a great many games you can write that don't require simulating physics in the first place, and that's still very much true today.

But, what if you want to write the next Angry Birds clone? Well, physics is actually the key to such a game! The way the birds fly off the launcher, arc toward the pigs and their defenses—that's all governed by physics. Not just gravity, but the weight of the bird (which varies by type), the strength the player uses to fling them, and of course the materials they ultimately crash into. Further, how that material reacts is governed by physics, too: whether the objects are made of glass, metal, or wood; how elastic they are (how they bounce, in other words), and other factors.

Having to write the math for all of that would be an exercise in futility for me, I can tell you that much! Fortunately, I don't have to brush off my paltry calculus skills to do so because Corona provides the Physics API for exactly this purpose, and that's of course what that `require()` is for. It brings in the code necessary to work all of that physics magic and presents us with a `physics` reference through which you can access it.

What about that `shapeDefs` object? That's related to physics, too and brings us to the core concept of the Physics API: physics bodies.

You've Got a Great Body There

The great thing about the Physics API is you can bolt it on after the fact. Any graphical element, any `DisplayObject` basically, can be turned into a physics body, which means it will react to gravity and other physical interaction parameters. To be more precise, the physics body is really an extension of a `DisplayObject`, with some extra information it carries related to physics.

Let's say for the sake of argument you have a cannonball graphic:

```
local cannonball = display.newImage("cannonball.png");
```

If you put that on the screen after importing physics, well, nothing will actually happen, because the physics simulation hasn't been activated yet. To do so you only have to call:

```
physics.start();
```

Now, if you put the cannonball on the screen . . . well, **still** nothing will happen! That's because even though you've turned physics on, and Corona is in fact simulating gravity and everything else involved in a physics simulation, it doesn't yet know that this object should be affected by gravity and so won't simulate its motion as part of its physics simulation.

To do that you need to create a physics body and add it to your cannonball, like so:

```
physics.addBody(cannonball, { density = 2.5, friction = .2, bounce = .1 });
```

Now, if you put the cannonball on the screen, you will see that it immediately begins to fall down toward the bottom of the screen. It will gradually gain speed as it does so, exactly as an object falling from the sky does. That's gravity of course, and that's the physics engine at work!

Tip   Although it's not typically something you have to be all that concerned with, Corona uses the popular Box2D physics engine for its physics simulator. In fact, the only time this information tends to come up is if you can't get your physics to act like you want. In that case, knowing that you should research Box2D is helpful, since you'll be able to find plenty of help online, and most of it will apply to Corona just like it does to using Box2D directly. You'll probably need to adjust things a little bit, but generally what applies to Box2D will apply to Corona's Physics API just as well.

The parameters inside the configuration object passed to physics.addBody() defines the physical characteristics of the body. The density attribute is used to determine the object's mass, which determines how much of an effect gravity has on it. In simplest terms: The larger the number, the heavier the object, and the more it'll be affected by gravity (it'll accelerate and fall faster). The friction attribute is how much resistance to the forces exerted on the object there is. This is a value from 0 on up, 0 being no friction. The bounce attribute determines "restitution," which means how much velocity is returned after the object impacts another physics body. This is a value from 0 to 1, where 0 is no bounce and 1 will make the object bounce forever. You rarely want a value greater than .3 unless you are modeling something like rubber because values above .3 result in objects that bounce a lot.

The Curves of Your Body

A cannonball tends to be circular; I'd say that's a reasonable statement! However, by default, a physics body is rectangular. Therefore, the physics body incorporates the circular cannonball, as shown in Figure 5-1.

Figure 5-1. The cannonball and its containing physics body

The white area around the cannonball inside the square would be transparent. This has an undesired effect: collisions between bodies will not always be precise. For example, Figure 5-2 shows a potential collision between two cannonballs.

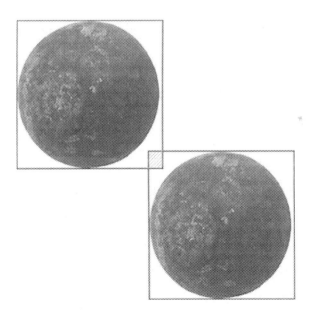

Figure 5-2. The striped square in the middle is where they collide

Now, if these cannonballs were defined as being very bouncy, they would bounce away from each other at this point, and unless they were moving very fast the user would see it as them bouncing away from each other without actually touching! For rectangular objects, this works fine. Imagine a crate, for example: the default body would match the physical object perfectly and there would never be such a problem. For a circle, or other irregular shapes though, it's a potential problem.

If the action is moving fast enough, then you can often get away with this sort of imperfect collision because the player won't be able to see where it doesn't quite match up anyway. This in fact is the case in Astro Rescue except in one specific instance, and that's where shapeDefs comes into play.

While physics bodies are rectangular by default, you can do something more complex by manually defining the body. For starters, you can pass a radius attribute as part of the configuration object passed to physics.addBody() to define a circular body, perfect for our cannonball.

The other option is to define a polygon body. To do so, pass an array of x/y coordinates to physics.addBody():

```
local triangle = display.newImage("triangle.png");
local polyBody = { 0,-19, 19,19, -19,19 };
physics.addBody(triangle,
  { density = 2, friction = 4, bounce = 1, shape = polyBody }
);
```

Assume the triangle.png is a 39×39 pixel image with a triangle drawn in it edge-to-edge and centered. To define a physics body for it that matches its sides, you need to define them clockwise around the shape, as that's what the Physics API requires, and it also must wind up being be a convex shape with no more than eight sides. Therefore, you start with the top vertex of the triangle (which vertex you start at is up to you, as long as you always move clockwise relative to the last coordinate pair provided). The Physics AP requires that the center point of the body is considered point 0,0, so you define the coordinates as you would relative to the origin on an inverted Cartesian graph, meaning positive numbers are movements right and down from the origin and negative movements are left and up. Therefore, to get the coordinates of that top vertex point you'd have to move up 19 pixels on the y axis, or –19 from the center point, with no change on the X axis, so the coordinate is 0,–19. The next point moving clockwise is the bottom right vertex, and that's 19 pixels to the right of the origin and 19 pixels down so that's where 19,19 comes from. The final vertex, the one to the bottom left of the center point, is 19 pixels left on the x axis and 19 pixels down, so –19,19.

For a triangle, defining that body isn't so tough. However, for a larger shape, like, say, the mothership at the top of the screen, with its little landing struts jutting out, it would be quite a burden. Such a definition is precisely what you'll find in that shapeDefs.lua file. In fact, if you have a look in there you'll see that it's a fair bit more complex than that, and includes a number of other body-related configurations, but at its core, that's what it's doing.

Why am I not showing that code and going over it in detail here? The answer is that I didn't write it! I used a tool called PhysicsEditor (http://physicseditor.de) to generate it. This is an extremely handy tool that lets you import a graphic file, the mothership in this case, and then automatically trace the edges of the graphic to come up with the physics body coordinates! It also allows you to edit the other characteristics of a physics body such as density, friction, and bounce. It can then export the code for Corona, among other SDKs, as was done for this file. If you're going to be working with complex bodies like this, I can't recommend using this tool (or another like it) enough!

> **Note**   I worked on a project last year where I had a number of very complex bodies and I was defining
> them by hand. Yes, it works, but man, is it a pain! I wouldn't do that again for all the tea in China. Well,
> okay, maybe for that, because I could turn around and sell it for a lot of money. (Maybe—does China
> even have a lot of tea?! It's research time!)

So, since I didn't write that code, going over it seems a bit superfluous to me. Think of it as you
do Corona: it is code you didn't have to write to accomplish a goal, so unless there's something
wrong in it you probably don't care much about it. Really, though, the important point is that it's
what defines the complex body for the mothership. Later on in the section "Stuff Is Still Better
When It Moves: Sprites Part 2", you'll see where it's actually used to do just that, and you'll see
more of the Physics API as well over the next three chapters, but you've got the basic ideas behind
it at this point.

The Scene Lifecycle Handlers

Honestly, there's not a heck of a lot more in gameScene.lua, but I'll walk you through it nonetheless,
beginning with createScene():

```
function scene:createScene(inEvent)

  utils:log("gameScene", "createScene()");

  gc:init(self.view);

end
```

As stated earlier, the game code itself is decoupled from the scene object, but there is a similar set
of events that need to occur for that game code, beginning with basic one-time initialization tasks.
The gc:init() method of the gameCore object, referenced by the variable gc, does just that. The
DisplayGroup for the scene, self.view, is what all the graphics must be drawn in if you want the
scene transitions to affect them, so it is passed along to gc:init().

The enterScene() method has a similar call into gameCore:

```
function scene:enterScene(inEvent)

  utils:log("gameScene", "enterScene()");

  gc:start();

end
```

The gc:start() method takes care of tasks that need to be done in the game code that should
happen each time the scene is shown. Don't worry, I will of course get into those details soon.

Correspondingly, when you leave the scene you need to stop the game, and there is a gc:stop() method just for that:

```
function scene:exitScene(inEvent)

  utils:log("gameScene", "exitScene()");

  gc:stop();

end;
```

Last, you have the same need when the scene is destroyed as with any scene: to clean up resources that were created when the scene was created. This time, I thought gc:destroy() would a perfectly appropriate name, rather than changing enterScene to start and exitScene to stop:

```
function scene:destroyScene(inEvent)

  utils:log("gameScene", "destroyScene()");

  gc:destroy();

end
```

There's also the willEnterScene() and didExitScene() methods, but they have no corresponding method in the gameCore object, so they are just empty methods.

As with all scenes, there's the final little bit of boilerplate work to do:

```
utils:log("gameScene", "Beginning execution");

scene:addEventListener("createScene", scene);
scene:addEventListener("willEnterScene", scene);
scene:addEventListener("enterScene", scene);
scene:addEventListener("exitScene", scene);
scene:addEventListener("didExitScene", scene);
scene:addEventListener("destroyScene", scene);

return scene;
```

Now you're ready to look at the gameCore object where the real work is done.

Getting to the Heart of the Matter: The gameCore Object

The gameCore object starts innocently enough:

```
local gameCore = {

  levelData = require("levelData"),
```

The levelData.lua file is where the information describing the levels of the game is found. However, it makes much more sense to explain this in the context of drawing a level, which you'll be getting to soon, so you can move on to:

```
gameDG = nil,
```

This variable, and all the rest to come, are members of the gameCore object, not global scope. The gameDG variable is really an alias for the view's DisplayGroup. This is done because outside of the gameScene object you wouldn't have access to self.view, and while there's other ways to make it accessible (e.g., global variable, accessing it through the gameScene object itself), doing it this way makes the code a bit more self-contained within the gameCore object.

```
levelDG = nil,
```

The levelDG variable is another DisplayGroup that will itself become a child of gameDG. The difference is that every object put into levelDG is something that will need to be created and destroyed for each level (whereas gameDG contains not only that, but elements that you don't want to be destroying and creating all the time).

```
topYAdjust = 34,
```

The topYAdjust variable effectively defines the height of the black bar at the top of the screen where the fuel gauge and other readouts are. Elements drawn on the screen are adjusted downward by this amount to account for that space.

```
PHASE_FLYING = 1,
PHASE_DEAD = 2,
PHASE_IN_BAY = 3,
PHASE_LANDED = 4,
phase = nil,
```

When the game is running it can be in a number of phases. The most common case, when the player is actually playing, is the phase defined by the value of PHASE_FLYING. When the player has crashed and the popup is shown asking if he wants to try again, the phase is PHASE_DEAD. When he's entered the landing bay and the level completion popup is shown, the phase is PHASE_IN_BAY. Last, when he's landed and is, presumably, waiting for a colonist to enter, the phase is PHASE_LANDED. The current phase of the game is stored in the phase variable. You'll see where the current phase comes into play later, but suffice it to say that action needs to be paused, or a different action must take place, depending on the current phase.

Caution   Lua does not have the notion of a constant. However, since it would make sense for the phases here to be constants, I've made them all uppercase, which is the typical convention across most languages for constants. It's a reminder to myself that I intend these not to change. However, it's always important to keep in mind that you can change them. Neither Lua nor Corona will or can do anything to force them to be unchangeable.

```
popup = nil,
```

The popup variable stores a reference to one of the popups, either when the player dies or he enters the landing bay and the level is complete.

```
scoreText = nil,
```

The `scoreText` variable is a reference to the text seen on the top of the screen for the player's current score.

> **Note** Don't get too hung up on these variables just yet. My goal at this point is just to give you the general lay of the land. You'll see how these are used throughout the code, and it's not important that you memorize what each of them is right now; just that you have a clear 10,000-foot view of things.

Stuff Is Better When It Moves: Sprites, Part 1

The next bit of code in `gameCore.lua` takes us into another new Corona topic: sprites.

```
ship = {
  sequenceData = {
    { name = "noThrust", start = 1, count = 4, time = 250 },
    { name = "thrustUp", start = 5, count = 4, time = 250 },
    { name = "thrustRight", start = 9, count = 4, time = 250 },
    { name = "thrustLeft", start = 13, count = 4, time = 250 },
    { name = "thrustUpRight", start = 17, count = 4, time = 250 },
    { name = "thrustUpLeft", start = 21, count = 4, time = 250 }
  },
  sprite = nil,
  thrustVertical = nil,
  thrustLeft = nil,
  thrustRight = nil,
  colonistsOnboard = nil,
  fuel = nil,
  maxFuel = nil
},
```

Now, not everything you see here in the ship object is actually related to sprites, so I'll discuss those first. The `thrustVertical`, `thrustLeft`, and `thrustRight` attributes are simple Boolean flags that tell you in which direction(s), if any, the ship is currently thrusting (which results from the player touching the screen or tilting their device, depending on which control scheme they use). The `colonistsOnboard` attribute tells you how many colonists the ship currently has onboard. The `fuel` variable is, naturally enough, how much fuel the ship currently has. Last, `maxFuel` is how much fuel the ship **can** have onboard. There's a little more to that one than it would seem at first, and it has to do with properly drawing the fuel gauge. While that discussion is on the horizon, it's not quite here yet so let's talk about sprites instead, which is where the `sprite` (of course!) and `sequenceData` attributes come into play.

So, what's this sprite thing anyway? In simplest terms, it's a `DisplayObject` with some extra goodness related to animation added in. In more technical terms, a sprite is conceptually a combination of a couple of things: an image sheet (or sprite sheet; the terms are interchangeable), one or more animation sequences constructed based on the image sheet, and the sprite object itself.

Let's talk about image sheets first. These are nothing but plain old images that happen to contain multiple images in them, such as Figure 5-3, which is the alien from Astro Rescue (who I've affectionately taken to calling Evil Otto, in remembrance of the great ColecoVision game Venture, even though the monsters in that game were actually called Hallmonsters and not Evil Otto, but I always think of Evil Otto from Berzerk when I see them so I just go ahead and save a few memory slots in my brain and call them all Evil Otto- but I digress!).

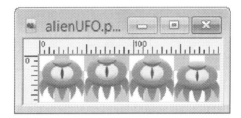

Figure 5-3. *Evil Otto . . . err, Astro Rescue's alien antagonist, in image sheet form*

In this case, it's pretty easy to understand and you can probably guess what's going on here: it's a plain old PNG file that contains four frames of animation to make the alien bob up and down as it moves across the screen. However, the important point is that this single image sheet can be a much more complicated structure. It can contain multiple animation sequences for this game element, and it can even contain sequences for a number of different game elements.

It could, for example, contain the animation sequences for the ship, of which there are a lot more than for the alien, as you can see in Figure 5-4.

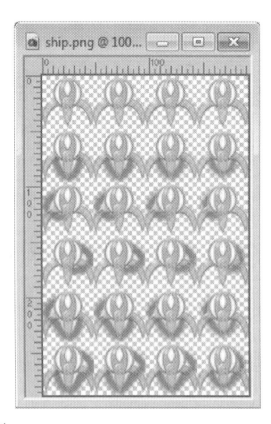

Figure 5-4. Image sheet of the ship

I've tossed around this term **animation sequence** a number of times, but what does that mean? Well, it's nothing more than a collection of individual frames of animation—a sequence of animation frames, in other words.

In this ship image sheet, for example, there are six different animation sequences, arranged in rows, four frames of animation each. The first such row is for when the ship is not thrusting at all (it's either falling due to gravity or has landed). The next sequence, row two, is when it is thrusting vertically only. The third is thrusting left only, while the fourth is thrusting right only. The fifth and sixth are the other two possible thrust cases: thrusting vertically and left or vertically and right, respectively.

The question you have to answer for yourself as you develop your games is how to combine graphics. It's quite possible to have only a single PNG file in your whole project that contains every game element and every animation sequence. There are some benefits to doing this, mainly that the graphic can be highly compressed due to a lot of redundancy in the color palette and pixel patterns. However, in many ways it leads to more complex code and makes maintaining your images a fair bit more difficult (and also makes it easier to run out of texture memory on a real device, since you're loading all your graphics at one time rather than progressively loading things as they're needed). The choice is entirely up to you, though. You could also put each individual animation sequence for each game element in its own file (so, e.g., six different PNGs for the ship).

This may be a bit easier to maintain but will require more code. For my own work, and how I've done Astro Rescue, is to put each discrete game element in its own file that contains all its animation sequences. This is a nice, logical delineation, isn't too difficult to work with, and makes dealing with memory relatively easy.

Okay, so we know what an image sheet is, but how do we turn that into a sprite? It's actually very easy:

```
local mySprite = display.newSprite(
  graphics.newImageSheet("imageSheet.png",
    { width = 50, height = 450, numFrames = 8 }
  ),
  {
    { name = "seq1", start = 1, count = 8, time = 250 }
  }
);
```

The `display.newSprite()` method is the key and gives you back a `SpriteObject`, which is a subclass of `DisplayObject`. This takes two arguments: an `ImageSheet` object and an array of objects where each object defines an animation sequence. The `ImageSheet` object is obtained by a call to `display.newImageSheet()` and you have to give it the graphic file that contains the sheet as well as an object that tells Corona about that sheet. Specifically, you tell it what the dimensions of an individual frame of animation are, as well as how many total frames there are. Notice, though, that you don't need to tell it the overall size of the sheet. This means that Corona will handle sheets of any size and you can organize them horizontally or vertically (e.g., if you wanted 10 frames of 50×50 animation, you could draw them in your sheet straight down so you'd wind up with a sheet that's 50×500).

> **Note**   Corona also has the ability to handle image sheets where individual frames aren't all the same dimensions. This is a more advanced topic, however, and not something that is used in Astro Rescue. It's also not, in my experience, all that common in a lot of Corona projects. Therefore, that capability isn't discussed in this book. The Corona documentation can provide the information you require for this if you have the need. Rest assured, in typical Corona fashion, it's quite easy to do if it's something you need.

The definition of the animation sequences is the other piece of the puzzle. You can define as many sequences as you like; simply add an object to the array passed in. Each sequence needs to define a name (the `name` attribute) for the sequence that you'll refer to later. It also needs to include what frame in the sheet the sequence starts on (the `start` attribute) and how many frames make up the sequence (the `count` attribute). Last, it must tell Corona how fast it should switch between frames (the `time` attribute, which is the time between frame transitions, in other words). The `time` attribute is actually optional and, if not supplied, it will be based on the frame rate of your application. Most times, you'll probably want to define this yourself so your animations will be consistent regardless of frame rate. You can also optionally define how many times you want the sequence to play by specifying the `loopCount` attribute. A value of 0, the default, will cause the sequence to loop until you explicitly stop it. Any other value will run through that many of times and then stop until you explicitly start it again. Last, the `loopDirection` attribute allows you to play the sequence either forward (with a value of "forward", the default) or as a bounce (with a value of "bounce"), which will play it forward, then backward (and it may repeat that or not, based on `loopCount`).

Once you have your sprite, you can activate a given animation sequence easily:

```
mySprite:setSequence("seq1");
mySprite:play();
```

That's it! Your sprite will then cycle through the `seq1` animation sequence (which, in real code, you'll usually want to give a descriptive name; e.g., "walking" if this was a character in the game).

As mentioned earlier, a `SpriteObject` is a subclass of `DisplayObject`, so of course you can do all the usual `DisplayObject` stuff with it. As for what else you can do with sprites specifically, there's not a heck of a lot! In any case, you'll see a few more things as we progress through the code.

Let's not forget about that `sequenceData` attribute in the `ship` object that started this whole sprite discussion. Now you know exactly what it's all about: it's the collection of animation sequences the ship has. The names match up with the sequences described in the ship image sheet. That was pretty simple, wasn't it?

Moving Right Along

A lot of what comes next will be obvious now that you have an understanding of sprites, beginning with the `colonist` object:

```
colonist = {
  sequenceData = {
    { name = "materializing", start = 1, count = 10, time = 1000,
      loopCount = 1
    },
    { name = "standing", start = 11, count = 4, time = 1000 },
    { name = "indicator_onboardShip", start = 21, count = 1 },
    { name = "indicator_pendingRescue", start = 31, count = 1 },
    { name = "walking_left", start = 41, count = 6 },
    { name = "walking_right", start = 51, count = 6 }
  },
  sprite = nil,
  appearCounter = 0,
  FRAMES_BETWEEN_APPEARANCES = 60,
  indicators = { },
  lastAppearancePoint = nil
},
```

Again, we have a collection of animation sequences, as shown in Figure 5-5. This sheet is an interesting case in that some of the sequences have a different number of animation frames than the others, so you wind up with some empty space. This is actually by choice; there would be no problem if these all ran together, either in one straight line (so you'd wind up with an image that's

832×32 pixels: 832 is the width of a frame, 32, times the number of frames, 26). Or it could be arranged in another way, maybe in 4×4 squares of frames. Any arrangement you like will work; as long as the frames are all the same size, Corona will be able to work with it. However, to help visualize the different sequences as a learning exercise, I prefer this layout. That being said, it's important to realize that this **does** uses more texture memory, and usually that's something you want to avoid. For a relatively small image like this, in a relatively small game like Astro Rescue, you can get away with it, but in a larger game, you would be better served by condensing it and having no wasted space.

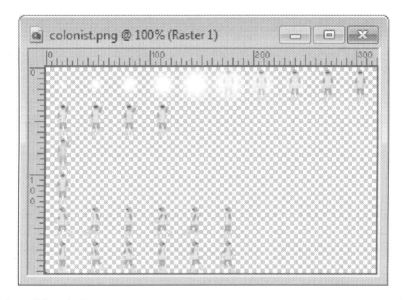

Figure 5-5. Image sheet of the colonist

The "materializing" sequence is for when the colonist first appears on the screen. The "standing" sequence is of course when he's just standing there waiting for you. The "walking_right" and "walking_left" sequences are just that: for when he is walking toward the ship, and which one is used depends on which way he's walking. The "indicator_onboardShip" and "indicator_pendingRescue" are two special cases in that they aren't animations per se. Instead, they are versions of the colonist graphic used to show the indicators in the upper-right corner. This is a good example of how you can use sprites even if you don't need animation; if you simply need to have a couple different versions of a basic static image, you can do it with sprites and only have to maintain one physical graphic file. Whatever suits your needs, Corona will provide it for you!

> **Note** The other attributes of the colonist object start with the `sprite` attribute. This attribute
> is of course is a reference to a `SpriteObject`. The way the game works, there's only ever one
> colonist on the screen at any given time, so a single sprite is all that will ever be needed.
> The `appearCount` attribute is used to determine when it's time for a new colonist to appear.
> The `FRAMES_BETWEEN_APPEARANCES`, a pseudo-constant, is used to ensure at least 2 seconds
> pass between colonist appearances. Remember, the game runs at 30 fps, so 2 seconds is 60 fps. If we
> check every frame to see if it's time for a colonist appear, we can compare to this constant to tell.
> The `indicators` attribute is an array where each element corresponds to one of the colonist indicators
> in the corner. This array gets filled in as the player rescues colonists. Last, the `lastAppearancePoint`
> attribute is used to remember where a colonist last appeared on the screen so that we can avoid a
> colonist appearing at the same place twice in a row and making it too easy on the player!
>
> You may be wondering why I'm creating an object for each of these game entities rather than using
> expando attributes on some plain old `DisplayObjects`. That's certainly a valid way to go. However,
> just from a clarity-of-code perspective I like having everything encapsulated in an object for the ship,
> colonist, and everything else. That also ensures I don't accidentally break anything by creating an
> expando that happens to overwrite or conflict with something Corona expects. As usual, it's up to you
> whether you like this style or not; it'll work either way.

```
explosion = {
  sequenceData = {
    name = "exploding", start = 1, count = 5, time = 500, loopCount = 1
  },
  sprite = nil,
  callback = nil
},
```

The `explosion` object is much like the `ship` and `colonist` objects: it has a `sequenceData` attribute and
`sprite` attribute to deal with the animation, and in addition has a `callback` attribute that, as you'll
see in a chapter 8, is used to execute some code when an explosion finishes doing its **boom** thing.

Next, we have the on-screen controls:

```
controls = {
  left = nil,
  right = nil,
  vertical = nil
},
```

Each of its attributes is simply a reference to a `DisplayObject`, which all get created a little later on
in the code.

```
fuelPod = {
  sprite = nil,
  rotate = function()
    transition.to(gc.fuelPod.sprite, {
```

```
      time = 1000, delta = true, rotation = 360,
      onComplete = function()
        gc.fuelPod.rotate();
      end
    });
  end,
  appearanceRangeFrames = { min = 150, max = 600 },
  framesSinceLastAppearance = nil
},
```

The `fuelPod` object is for when fuel appears for the player to pick up. Here we have a `sprite`
attribute, but notice there's no `sequenceData`. In point of fact, the `sprite` attribute doesn't reference
a `SpriteObject` but instead references a plain old `DisplayObject`. I just kept the attribute name to make
it consistent across all these objects. Sprite animation isn't used for the fuel pod; rather, plain old
Transition API functions are called and that's what the `rotate` attribute references. The function that is its
value performs a transition on the sprite's `rotation` attribute. Again, to me, encapsulating this function
inside the `fuelPod` object makes for a much cleaner style of coding. The `appearanceRangeFrames`
attribute contains two values, which are used to determine when a fuel pod should appear. There will
always be at least 5 seconds between appearances but no more than 10 (these values are numbers
of frames). Last, the `framesSinceLastAppearance` attribute is what is changed with each frame and is
compared to `appearanceRangeFrames` to know when it's time to show a fuel pod.

Like the `controls` object, the `fuelGauge` object is simple:

```
fuelGauge = {
  shell = nil,
  fill = nil
},
```

The `shell` and `fill` attributes reference the components of the fuel gauge, namely the outline of it
(its "shell") and the portion that fills in (and empties) as fuel is used.

The `warningSign` object is next:

```
warningSign = {
  sprite = nil,
  tween = nil,
  fadingIn = true,
  flash = function()
    local aVar = 0;
    if gc.warningSign.fadingIn == true then
      aVar = 1;
    end
    gc.warningSign.tween = transition.to(gc.warningSign.sprite, {
      time = 250, alpha = aVar,
      onComplete = function()
        gc.warningSign.fadingIn = not gc.warningSign.fadingIn;
        gc.warningSign.flash();
      end
    });
  end,
},
```

Once again, we have a `sprite` attribute, but not an actual `SpriteObject` and no `sequenceData` attribute. Like the `fuelPod`, the `warningSign` won't be using sprite animation. It again uses a transition, and when the transition is applied we store a reference to it in `tween` so that it can be stopped later (in contrast to `fuelPod`, whose animation simply runs all the time).

> **Tip**   In general, you should always stop transitions and sprite animations when the object isn't actually on the screen. This will help keep your frame rate up and also reduce battery usage. However, as this is a learning experience I wanted to be sure to show both situations.

The `fadingIn` attribute tells us whether the warning sign is fading into or out of view, which is used within the logic of the `flash()` function. This function is used just like `rotate()` in `fuelPod`. The value of `aVar` is 1 when fading in, or 0 when not fading in, and the `alpha` attribute of the `DisplayObject` is animated toward that value. At the end of the transition, the value of `fadingIn` is inverted and the process is begun again. The result is a pulsating warning sign that fades in and out of view quickly and serves to get the player's attention.

Next up we have our alien:

> **Note**   Originally, the enemy in the game was to have been a spaceship, a UFO if you will. However, when my talented artist buddy Anthony Volpe did his thing with my temporary graphics, he decided that an alien squid-type thing was better, and I agree

```
alienUFO = {
    sequenceData = {
        { name = "default", start = 1, count = 4, time = 200 }
    },
    sprite = nil,
    appearanceRangeFrames = { min = 300, max = 750 },
    frameSinceLastAppearance = 0,
    exitPoint = nil,
    tween = nil,
},
```

Figure 5-6 shows the image sheet. Most of the code is well-known to you by now, so I'll just talk about the new attribute, `exitPoint` (which goes hand-in-hand with tween). When an alien is shown, it starts from some point on the screen (just off the edge of the screen actually). At that time, the game code calculates where it will leave the screen. The motion of the alien is accomplished via a transition of its x/y coordinates from its starting point toward its ending point, which is stored in `exitPoint`. The animation itself is referenced by `tween`.

Figure 5-6. *Image sheet of the alien*

The `plasmaBall` object, whose image sheet is shown in Figure 5-7, is very similar to the `alienUFO` object:

```
plasmaBall = {
  sequenceData = {
    { name = "default", start = 1, count = 4, time = 200 }
  },
  sprite = nil,
  tween = nil
},
```

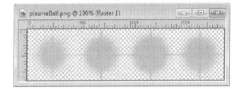

Figure 5-7. *Image sheet of the plasma ball*

Since a plasma ball is only seen when an alien appears, we don't need most of the attributes the objects have had. We just need the `sequenceData`, since this time it's an actual `SpriteObject`, referenced by the `sprite` attribute, and we'll be using the Transition API again to move the plasma ball from the alien to the player's ship, so a reference to the tween is stored in the `tween` attribute once more.

```
sfx = {
  scream = nil,
  screamChannel = nil,
  fuelPodPickup = nil,
  fuelPodPickupChannel = nil,
  sos = nil,
  sosChannel = nil,
  explosion = nil,
  explosionChannel = nil,
  thrusters = nil,
  thrustersChannel = nil
}

};
```

The final attribute of the gameCore object encountered when walking through the code is sfx, which is a collection of references to audio resources. Once again, this organizational structure is a choice. I like having a single object storing all my audio resources so it's easy to remember where they are. It also helps avoid naming conflicts later as I build the code up.

Where It All Starts: Initializing the Game

The first method found in the gameCore object was the one you saw earlier called from createScene() in the gameScene object, init():

```
function gameCore:init(inDisplayGroup)

  utils:log("gameCore", "init()");

  gc.gameDG = inDisplayGroup;

  physics.start(true);
  physics.setDrawMode("normal");
  physics.setGravity(0, 1);
```

As you can see, this is where that gameDG attribute gets populated and is a reference to the DisplayGroup passed in. Referring back to gameScene, you see that's self.view, the DisplayGroup the Storyboard API automatically creates for the gameScene.

Following that, we have some physics setup to perform. Just loading the Physics API doesn't actually do anything on its own, we have to tell the API to start simulating physics first, hence the call to physics.start(). The Boolean passed in tells the physics engine whether physics bodies can "sleep," which means when they come to rest and are not involved in collisions, their motion will no longer be simulated. The value true tells Box2D that bodies **cannot** sleep, while the default value false means bodies **can** sleep (that's a little backwards to most people's thinking, but it is what it is). This is generally a good thing as it reduces the overhead the engine requires; however, there are instances where the simulation will be imperfect and collisions will not work as expected as a result. This was the case in Astro Rescue, as sometimes objects would not register collisions correctly, hence passing true, which tells the engine that bodies should never sleep.

The call to physics.setDrawMode() is actually not necessary as written because "normal" is the default, but since during development it is handy to be able to switch to "debug" or "hybrid" mode, I left that line in. The "debug" mode shows collision engine outlines only (collision detection is something we'll see a lot of in Chapter 8). The "hybrid" mode shows the objects normally with the collision engine outlines superimposed on them. The "normal" mode is of course just the object itself being shown.

> **Tip**   You can also turn sleeping on or off for individual bodies, and I would suggest that be your first course of action if you encounter issues. You should only turn sleeping off if you do encounter problems, though, so that the simulation can be as efficient as possible. If you decide you need to do this, you have only to set the value of the isSleepingAllowed attribute of the body in question as appropriate.

Last, the `physics.setGravity()` call is responsible for describing the gravity used to simulate physics. The arguments are horizontal and vertical gravity components, respectively, measured in meters per second squared. For standard Earth gravity the values 0,9.8 would be used, but since Astro Rescue takes place on another planet with less gravity than Earth, I used 0,1. If the value were 2,1, for example, then gravity would not only pull the player's ship down but also to the right. You can set up whatever sort of wacky world makes sense using these values.

> **Caution**   It's important to realize that collision detection in Corona requires usage of physics. This is something that trips a lot of people up at first. However, it's also important to realize that this does not imply your objects need to be affected by gravity, as you'll see later on. If you really don't want to use the Physics API you can always do "bounding box" calculations on your own to determine when two objects intersect. However, since at the present time Corona does not allow pixel-level manipulations, these calculations will always be approximate at best. Using the Physics API for collision detection allows you to be more precise.

```
gc.loadGraphics();
```

The `loadGraphics()` method is responsible for loading all the graphical resources used during gameplay, but that method is covered in the next section in detail, so for now I'll move on to the audio resources:

```
gc.sfx.scream = audio.loadSound("scream.wav");
gc.sfx.fuelPodPickup = audio.loadSound("fuelPodPickup.wav");
gc.sfx.sos = audio.loadSound("sos.wav");
gc.sfx.explosion = audio.loadSound("explosion.wav");
gc.sfx.thrusters = audio.loadSound("thrusters.wav");
```

You have of course seen sounds loaded before, so this is nothing new.

```
gc.drawCurrentLevel();
```

Like `loadGraphics()`, `drawCurrentLevel()` is a method you'll be exploring in detail in short order, but as I'm sure you can guess it's what is responsible for drawing the screen, namely the ground, for whatever level the game is currently on.

```
gc.resetLevel();
```

The `resetLevel()` method is responsible for resetting state at the start of a level so the game begins properly and consistently. Say it with me: you'll be looking at that soon!

Loading Graphic Resources

Now you're going to start looking at the loadGraphics() method. Much of this will be old hat to you, but there's also some new stuff to explore.

```
function gameCore:loadGraphics()

  local starfield = display.newImage("starfield1.png", true);
  starfield.x = display.contentCenterX;
  starfield.y = display.contentCenterY + gc.topYAdjust;
  gc.gameDG:insert(starfield);
```

First, we need to load the star field background, as shown in Figure 5-8. This has to be done first since you want everything else to be drawn on top of it. Note that its vertical position is determined using that topYAdjust variable you saw earlier. It is pushed down just far enough to leave the empty space you need for the status bar up top.

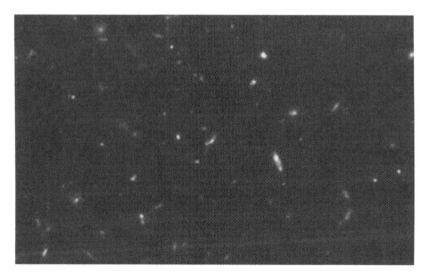

Figure 5-8. *The background star field image (starfield1.png)—thank you, Hubble!*

> **Note**   The star field is actually a section of the famous Hubble Deep Field image. Yes, that's a real picture of space, and nearly everything you see that isn't empty space is a galaxy!

Next up, draw the text that shows the player's current score:

```
gc.scoreText = display.newText("Score: ", 0, 2, native.systemFont, 28);
gc.gameDG:insert(gc.scoreText);
```

Once again, this is nothing you haven't seen before. Notice there is no value after the text, though; that will be drawn later by updating the value of this text object.

Another component of the status bar, in addition to the current score, is the fuel gauge, which is actually a combination of two elements:

```
gc.fuelGauge.shell = display.newImage("fuelGauge.png", true);
gc.fuelGauge.shell.x = display.contentCenterX;
gc.fuelGauge.shell.y = gc.fuelGauge.shell.height / 2;
gc.gameDG:insert(gc.fuelGauge.shell);
gc.fuelGauge.fill = display.newRect(
  (gc.fuelGauge.shell.x - (gc.fuelGauge.shell.width / 2)) + 3,
  (gc.fuelGauge.shell.y - (gc.fuelGauge.shell.height / 2)) + 3,
  gc.fuelGauge.shell.width - 5,
  gc.fuelGauge.shell.height - 5
);
gc.fuelGauge.fill:setFillColor(255, 0, 0);
gc.gameDG:insert(gc.fuelGauge.fill);
gc.ship.maxFuel = gc.fuelGauge.fill.width;
```

The first part is the shell. This is a simple graphic file that is centered horizontally on the screen and positioned vertically based on its own height. You want it to be right at the top of the screen, but remember that its reference point is its midpoint by default. So, if we set y to 0, then it would be half cut off on the top. It needs to move down from that point by half its height, so that's what the code does.

The next part of the fuel gauge is the fill portion inside of it. To do this, we draw a plain old rectangle. The x and y positioning is done effectively relative to the shell and taking into account the thickness of the shell itself. The width and height are similarly based on the size of the shell, minus enough to account for its thickness. The gauge is to be red, so setFillColor() is called with the RGB value for red (255,0,0).

The other task that needs to be accomplished here is to set the maxFuel attribute of the ship object. This is based on the size of the fill portion of the gauge. I did it this way so that I could adjust the size of the gauge as I developed the game, and the rest of the game code would continue to function as expected in all cases. Any time you can avoid hard-coded values in your code it's generally a Very Good Thing™.

Stuff Is Still Better When It Moves: Sprites, Part 2

The next object that gets created is the mothership, shown in Figure 5-9.

Figure 5-9. The mothership (mothership.png)

The mothership is drawn at the top of the screen, and the code that creates it introduces a number of new concepts in the process of doing its thing:

```
local mothershipSprite = display.newSprite(
  graphics.newImageSheet("mothership.png",
    { width = 800, height = 60, numFrames = 1 }
  ),
  { name = "default", start = 1, count = 1, time = 500 }
);
mothershipSprite.objName = "crash";
mothershipSprite.x = display.contentCenterX;
mothershipSprite.y = (mothershipSprite.height / 2) + gc.topYAdjust;
physics.addBody(mothershipSprite, "static", shapeDefs:get("mothership1"));
mothershipSprite.isFixedRotation = true;
mothershipSprite:setSequence("default");
mothershipSprite:play();
gc.gameDG:insert(mothershipSprite);
local mothershipMiddle = display.newImage("mothershipMiddle.png", true);
mothershipMiddle.x = display.contentCenterX;
mothershipMiddle.y = mothershipSprite.height + 32;
mothershipMiddle.objName = "bay";
physics.addBody(
  mothershipMiddle, "static", { density = 1, friction = 2, bounce = 0 }
);
gc.gameDG:insert(mothershipMiddle);
```

At first, it's just like any other sprite in that you need to pass it an image sheet, which is created inline in this case, as well as the animation sequences, of which there's just one this time around.

The first new bit is the setting of objName, which is an expando attribute. This is used later to identify what objects have collided when a collision event occurs.

The x and y locations are set so the mothership is at the top of the screen just below the status bar area.

Next, a physics body is added, as described earlier. Two interesting bits there that are new are the "static" argument and the call to shapeDefs:get(). The latter is a function provided by the code generated by PhysicsEditor that returns the description of the points that make up the outline of the body. That's really all there is to it. As previously discussed in this chapter, that is generated code so it won't be reviewed here (although you probably should take a moment and check it out on your own, just to have a general idea what's going on, but understanding it in detail isn't crucial to what you're doing here).

The "static" argument requires some explanation, though. There are three different types of physics bodies: static, dynamic, and kinematic, and these happen to be the values you can pass to addBody() as well. Static bodies are ones that don't move. The Corona documentation says they "don't interact with each other" as well. While it is true that two static bodies won't interact with each other, in that it won't trigger a collision event, other types of bodies can interact with a static body and produce a collision event. This is demonstrated in Astro Rescue itself: the mothership is static, as is the ground (as you will see later), but the player's ship, which in contrast to the ground and mothership is a dynamic body, can collide with the mothership as well as the ground. The third type of body, kinematic, covers objects that move, participate in collision events, and can be affected by forces (you'll see forces, which are different from gravity, in action later) but are not **affected** by gravity. Things like bullets might be kinematics, and objects that the user can drag around are typically set as kinematic bodies.

Next, the isFixedRotation attribute is set to true. This keeps the ship pointing upright at all times. The default value is false, which results in the mothership tipping left and right if the player's ship crashes into it. Usually, you want the physics simulation to be as accurate as possible, which means if contact is made with another body and the force is off center, then the bodies should tilt as expected. Imagine a teeter-totter on a playground. You remember those, right? The things with the two seats attached by a board balanced on a support in the middle? Well, whichever direction the most force is applied downward to, the side with the heavier kid generally, results in the other side moving in the opposite direction (all other forces being equal). That's the realistic way things work and is normally how you want your physics-based games to react as well. However, if this is not done for the mothership, you will wind up with an unfortunate situation where the mothership slowly seems to fall off the screen! Go ahead and try it—set isFixedRotation to false, run the game, and crash your ship into the mothership on one side. You'll see it slowly start to fall down the opposite way! Fun to watch, but not exactly how you'd expect it to react, and setting isFixedRotation to true deals with that problem.

Last, the default animation sequence, the only one the sprite supports, is enabled and the animation started. In point of fact, there is no actual animation on the mothership, but this leaves open the possibility of adding moving lights or something like that by adding frames later. It would just require altering the value of numFrames and count in the sequence definition.

In addition to the mothership itself, the landing bay (Figure 5-10) is created as well. The landing bay graphic is positioned such that it visually completes the mothership on the screen, hanging below the body of the ship a bit. A physics body is added to it as well so that it can register the collision when the ship enters, and the objName is set to "bay" so we can differentiate that collision event from others later on, as you'll see.

Figure 5-10. The mothership landing bay (mothership.png)

Having the landing bay be a separate element from the mothership itself makes the coding far easier, because you can watch for a collision on each separately and act accordingly in each case. The alternative, where the mothership was one graphic, would have required looking at screen coordinates and such to know when the player's ship hit the bay as opposed to the ship itself, or some other mental gymnastics. Better to take the easier route with two separate images.

Moving Right Along, Redux

When the player is moving too fast and their collision with another object will result in death, a flash warning sign appears. This is a pretty ordinary sprite:

```
gc.warningSign.sprite = display.newImage("warningSign.png", true);
gc.warningSign.sprite.x =
  gc.warningSign.sprite.width - (gc.warningSign.sprite.width / 2) + 2;
gc.warningSign.sprite.y =
  gc.warningSign.sprite.height + mothershipSprite.height + 10;
gc.warningSign.sprite.alpha = 0;
gc.gameDG:insert(gc.warningSign.sprite);
```

It's alpha attribute is set to 0 so that it isn't initially visible, since it's only shown when needed. Its position is set up based on its width, so that it winds up close to the left edge of the screen, and on the height of the mothership, so that it's below that.

Next, the on-screen controls must be set up, but only if the player has chosen to control the game this way via the Settings screen (and this is the default control mode as well):

```
if usingAccelerometer == false then
  gc.controls.vertical = display.newImage("controlVertical.png", true);
  gc.controls.vertical.x =
    (display.contentWidth - (gc.controls.vertical.width / 2)) - 20;
  gc.controls.vertical.y =
    display.contentCenterY + gc.controls.vertical.height + 40;
  gc.controls.vertical.alpha = .2;
  gc.controls.vertical.controlName = "vertical";
  gc.controls.vertical:addEventListener("touch", gc);
  gc.gameDG:insert(gc.controls.vertical);
end
```

That sets up the vertical control on the right and, like the warning size, uses its own dimensions as well as the dimensions of the screen to position it, so that if the graphics are resized later it should still be positioned properly. At least, it should be close; there are some "magic numbers" used here, so they might have to be tweaked, but you probably wouldn't want to make this graphic much different size-wise anyway.

Also, note the controlName expando. This is similar conceptually to the objName set on the game elements in that when a touch event occurs, controlName will help us determine which control was touched and act accordingly. To make use of that value we need an event handler, and unlike some previous scenes, this one is set up on the control element itself. That means that touching the screen will only result in us handling the touch event if it was this control that was touched. Just touching an empty area of the screen won't do so, in contrast to those other scenes that registered touches anywhere. Since a reference to the gameCore object, by way of the gc variable, is what's passed to addEventHandler(), we know there is a touch() method to explore somewhere in our future!

The horizontal controls require a little bit more work to set up:

```
if usingAccelerometer == false then
  gc.controls.left = display.newImage("controlHorizontal.png", true);
  gc.controls.left.x = (gc.controls.left.width / 2) + 20;
```

```
gc.controls.left.y = display.contentCenterY + gc.controls.left.height + 40;
gc.controls.left.alpha = .2;
gc.controls.left.controlName = "left";
gc.controls.left:addEventListener("touch", gc);
gc.gameDG:insert(gc.controls.left);
gc.controls.right = display.newImage("controlHorizontal.png", true);
gc.controls.right.x =
  (gc.controls.right.width / 2) + 40 + gc.controls.right.width;
gc.controls.right.y =
  display.contentCenterY + gc.controls.right.height + 40;
gc.controls.right.alpha = .2;
gc.controls.right.controlName = "right";
gc.controls.right:addEventListener("touch", gc);
gc.controls.right:scale(-1, 1);
gc.gameDG:insert(gc.controls.right);
end
```

It doesn't look much different than the vertical control, until you get to the line with the call to
scale(). What's going on there? Well, to save memory it makes sense to use the same graphic
for the left and right controls, since it's the same thing, just flipped (or mirrored, as it's sometimes
described, because you're talking about a mirror image of the original graphic). However, Corona
doesn't have a native mirroring function (I wouldn't be surprised to see one added before too long
though as it's a very common thing, along with a vertical flip). However, the same thing is easy to
accomplish with the scale() method that all DisplayObjects have. Usually, you pass a horizontal
and vertical scaling factor to this, respectively, so passing 2,2 would double the size of the object in
both directions for example (a value of 1 is 100%). But, Corona provides the special case of negative
numbers, which not only scales but flips on the axis to which you pass the negative value. So, if you
want to horizontally flip the object, you pass -1,0 (0 ensures you don't flip it or scale it vertically).
You could also do both. Say you want to scale it to 300% vertically as well as flip it, and also scale is
200% horizontally; then you'd pass 2,-3. Makes sense, right?

> **Tip**   With Lua and Corona being so flexible, it's trivial to simply add expando methods, just like
> the expand attribute we've seen, so you could always add mirror() and flip() methods for
> horizontal and vertical flipping to all DisplayObjects you create. Even better, create your own
> createNewImage() method that calls display.newImage() first and then adds those
> methods, so you always have it. You can augment the Corona API like this all you like thanks to
> Lua's dynamic nature.

Next, we need to create the sprite for the player's ship:

```
gc.ship.sprite = display.newSprite(
    graphics.newImageSheet("ship.png",
      { width = 48, height = 48, numFrames = 24 }
    ),
    gc.ship.sequenceData
);
```

```
physics.addBody(
    gc.ship.sprite, "dynamic", { density = 1, friction = 1, bounce = 0 }
);
gc.ship.sprite.isFixedRotation = true;
gc.ship.sprite.objName = "ship";
gc.gameDG:insert(gc.ship.sprite);
```

This time it's a dynamic body because we of course want it to react to gravity and any other forces acting upon it, and just like the mothership you don't want it to rotate when it impacts things, or when things impact upon it. The control scheme in the game isn't sophisticated enough for the user to be able to correct the ship when it lists the way it would if isFixedRotation were false, so that possibility is removed entirely by setting it to true so it never lists.

The next game element to set up is the colonist that appears to be rescued:

```
gc.colonist.sprite = display.newSprite(
    graphics.newImageSheet("colonist.png",
        { width = 32, height = 32, numFrames = 60 }
    ),
    gc.colonist.sequenceData
);
gc.colonist.sprite.objName = "colonist";
physics.addBody(
    gc.colonist.sprite, "static", { isSensor = true }
);
gc.colonist.sprite:addEventListener("sprite",
    function(inEvent)
        if inEvent.target.sequence == "materializing" and
            inEvent.phase == "ended"
        then
            gc.colonist.sprite:setSequence("standing");
            gc.colonist.sprite:play();
        end
    end
);
gc.gameDG:insert(gc.colonist.sprite);
```

Recall that the colonist has quite a few different animation sequences as defined in gc.colonist.sequenceData; that's why there's so many frames in the image sheet in comparison to most of the other game elements.

Here you encounter something new in physics: the isSensor attribute. A sensor is an object that registers when collisions occur but does not produce reactive force. In other words, if the player's ship collides with the colonist standing there, that's bad news for the colonist and you want to know about it in the code. However, you **do not** want the ship to react physically to the collision; our code will effectively handle that. Setting isSensor to true does this: you'll get your collision events, as will be discussed in Chapter 7, but they'll have no effect on the ship.

The other part of the equation here is the event listener attached. When the colonist is appearing, which is termed "materializing" within the context of the game, you want to know when that animation sequence completes so that it can switch to the sequence that shows the colonist standing there waving their arms. This event handler deals with that. The "sprite" event type receives notice of a number of different event phases, including "began" for when a sequence begins, "bounce" for when a sequence bounces from forward to backwards while playing, "loop" for when the sequence loops around to play again, and "next" for when a new frame in a sequence is played that doesn't otherwise result in one of the other phases. The other phase, "ended", is for when a sequence ends, and that's what you need to know about about here. Remember though, this event phase will be triggered when any sequence ends, so we also need to check what sequence is playing and ensure the handler only does its thing when it's the "materializing" sequence.

After the colonist sprite comes the explosion sprite (Figure 5-11), seen when the player's ship meets its untimely demise:

```
gc.explosion.sprite = display.newSprite(
  graphics.newImageSheet("explosion.png",
    { width = 70, height = 70, numFrames = 5 }
  ),
  gc.explosion.sequenceData
);
gc.explosion.sprite.isVisible = false;
gc.gameDG:insert(gc.explosion.sprite);
```

Figure 5-11. The explosion image sheet (explosion.png)

There is nothing new there, although note that the explosion is initially hidden, which is only logical.

> **Tip**   While it's quite possible to create this sprite at the time you need it, and destroy it when its animation sequence concludes, it'll generally be more efficient in terms of performance to create all your graphics ahead of time. For small graphics like the explosion, the memory overhead isn't any big deal. For larger graphics, you have to make a trade-off between performance and memory usage, and there is no simple right-or-wrong answer—it's whatever you determine makes sense at a given point in your code.

The fuel pod that appears periodically to help the player is next:

```
gc.fuelPod.sprite = display.newImage("fuelPod.png", true);
gc.fuelPod.sprite.objName = "fuelPod";
gc.fuelPod.sprite.isVisible = false;
gc.fuelPod.sprite.x = -1000;
gc.fuelPod.sprite.y = -1000;
physics.addBody(gc.fuelPod.sprite, "static", { isSensor = true });
gc.gameDG:insert(gc.fuelPod.sprite);
```

It's a static body type because we don't want it to fall down under the effects of gravity, and like the explosion it gets hidden until it's time to show it.

You're probably wondering why the x and y coordinates are set to values that put the fuel pod off screen, since setting isVisible to false does about the same thing. The answer is physics! If you don't do this, then the player's ship can still collide with the fuel pod. Although it's static and set up as a sensor and so won't physically effect the ship, it'll still register collision events. Yes, even when not visible, bodies can affect each other! If you suspect this might lead to some interesting-to-debug situations, you're right! This problem (which in some cases **isn't** a problem, but in this case, it is) can be dealt with later by checking the value of isVisible and simply skipping the logic that occurs in that case if it's false, but another way to achieve that goal is to move the object off screen entirely so a collision simply can't occur. Which way is better is up to you, but I wanted to show you the alternative approach either way.

You're almost done with our graphics setup now. Only two game elements remain, the first of which is the alien:

```
gc.alienUFO.sprite = display.newSprite(
  graphics.newImageSheet("alienUFO.png",
    { width = 48, height = 48, numFrames = 4 }
  ),
  gc.alienUFO.sequenceData
);
physics.addBody(gc.alienUFO.sprite, "static", { isSensor = true });
gc.alienUFO.sprite.x = -1000;
gc.alienUFO.sprite.y = -1000;
gc.alienUFO.sprite.isVisible = false;
gc.alienUFO.sprite.objName = "crash";
gc.alienUFO.sprite:setSequence("default");
gc.alienUFO.sprite:play();
gc.gameDG:insert(gc.alienUFO.sprite);
```

A situation similar to that of the fuel pod, with respect to collisions when it's not visible, applies to the alien, so it is put off screen initially as well. Note the objName value "crash", which is used generically on all elements that the ship can crash into.

Last, you have the plasma ball that the alien shoots at the player's ship:

```
  gc.plasmaBall.sprite = display.newSprite(
    graphics.newImageSheet("plasmaBall.png",
      { width = 24, height = 24, numFrames = 4 }
    ),
    gc.plasmaBall.sequenceData
  );
  physics.addBody(gc.plasmaBall.sprite, "static", { isSensor = true });
  gc.plasmaBall.sprite.x = -1000;
  gc.plasmaBall.sprite.y = -1000;
  gc.plasmaBall.sprite.isVisible = false;
  gc.plasmaBall.sprite.objName = "crash";
```

```
gc.plasmaBall.sprite:setSequence("default");
gc.plasmaBall.sprite:play();
gc.gameDG:insert(gc.plasmaBall.sprite);
```

end

At this point, that code is well known to you. One thing I will point out, however, is that you'll notice the animation sequences on the plasma ball and the alien are started immediately, even though they are not initially visible. For maximum performance, you wouldn't want to start those until those elements were actually visible. However, being a relatively simple game, Astro Rescue doesn't have much concern about performance anyway; even doing things as inefficiently as possible leads to perfectly acceptable performance. Such is the power of Corona! That's probably the battle cry of some little-known Marvel superhero come to think of it, but I digress.

Got to Begin Again: Resetting for a New Level

Every time a new level begins, or the current level is retried, resetLevel() is called to get the state of the game back in the proper condition. Mostly it's a lot of variable resets and fairly mundane bits, but you still need to take a look at it to have the overall picture complete.

```
function gameCore:resetLevel()

  utils:log("gameCore", "resetLevel()");

  gc.phase = gc.PHASE_FLYING;
  gc.popup = nil;
```

The initial state of the game is always PHASE_FLYING, so the action begins immediately when the level is shown. Setting gc.popup to nil ensures code later properly recognizes that there is no popup currently showing (the meaning of **popup** is discussed in the next two chapters—there is more to it than you might imagine!)

```
gc.ship.thrustVertical = false;
gc.ship.thrustLeft = false;
gc.ship.thrustRight = false;
gc.ship.colonistsOnboard = 0;
gc.ship.fuel = gc.ship.maxFuel;
gc:updateFuelGauge();
gc.ship.sprite:setSequence("noThrust");
gc.ship.sprite:play();
gc.ship.sprite.isVisible = true;
gc.ship.sprite.x = display.contentCenterX;
gc.ship.sprite.y = 70 + (gc.ship.sprite.height / 2) + gc.topYAdjust;
gc.ship.sprite:setLinearVelocity(0, 0);
gc.ship.sprite.isBodyActive = true;
```

Resetting the ship is the next chore. This includes ensuring the flags describing the direction of thrust are all false so the ship doesn't start flying around on its own, resetting the count of colonists onboard so the ship starts empty, resetting the fuel gauge to its initial full condition (and redrawing it via a call to the gc:updateFuelGauge() method), resetting the ship sprite's animation sequence so there's no thrust flames coming out, and putting the ship at its starting location.

There's a little bit of new physics here too, namely the setLinearVelocity() call and the setting of isBodyActive. The linear velocity of a physics body is how fast, if at all, it's moving either horizontally or vertically. This value changes over time based on the effects of gravity, collisions, and forces you can apply to the body yourself. To begin with, you don't want the ship to be moving, hence you reset both values to 0. Gravity will begin having an effect immediately, however, and the ship will almost instantly begin moving downward. Setting isBodyActive to true ensures that the ship is simulated as part of the Box2D physics simulation (as I'm sure you can guess, it'll be set to false later on in the code, otherwise this would be pretty pointless!)

```
gc.colonist.appearCounter = 0;
gc.colonist.lastAppearancePoint = nil;
gc.colonist.sprite.isVisible = false;
```

The colonist has to be reset too, including resetting appearCounter so the code begins starting to count toward a colonist appearing. We also clear out the record of the last place on the screen they appeared so all points are available the first time they appear. Of course, the colonist has to be hidden initially too, so that is done.

```
gc.explosion.callback = nil;
```

As you'll see later, when an explosion occurs and its animation sequence completes, a function is called. This is referred to as a **callback function** and a reference to it is stored in gc.explosion.callback. Initially though, there is none, so that must be nilled out.

```
gc.fuelPod.framesSinceLastAppearance = 0;
gc.fuelPod.sprite.isVisible = false;
gc.fuelPod.sprite.x = -1000;
gc.fuelPod.sprite.y = -1000;
```

The fuel pod, as with the colonist, needs to be hidden and the counter reset to start counting toward an appearance. As previously discussed, it is also moved far off screen so as to not interact with the player's ship.

```
if gc.warningSign.tween ~= nil then
  transition.cancel(gc.warningSign.tween);
end
gc.warningSign.tween = nil;
gc.warningSign.sprite.alpha = 0;
gc.warningSign.fadingIn = true;
gc.warningSign.sprite.isVisible = false;
gc.warningSign.flash();
```

The warning sign similarly must be hidden, and this is accomplished by setting its alpha attribute to zero. The trick here, though, is that if the ship had just crashed then the flashing animation would still be occurring, and you need to stop that as well. That's easily accomplished by calling transition.cancel() on the reference to the transition stored in gc.warningSign.tween. The variables associated with the warning sign fading into view are also reset, and the flash() method is called to begin its (at this point, invisible) animation again.

The alien is reset next:

```
if gc.alienUFO.tween ~= nil then
  transition.cancel(gc.alienUFO.tween);
end
gc.alienUFO.framesSinceLastAppearance = 0;
gc.alienUFO.sprite.isVisible = false;
gc.alienUFO.sprite.x = -1000;
gc.alienUFO.sprite.y = -1000;
gc.alienUFO.tween = nil;
```

Since the alien moves across the screen via a transition, you need to stop that movement if it is occurring, just as with the warning sign. The rest of the resetting is, I think, self-explanatory.

```
if gc.plasmaBall.tween ~= nil then
  transition.cancel(gc.plasmaBall.tween);
end
gc.plasmaBall.sprite.isVisible = false;
gc.plasmaBall.sprite.x = -1000;
gc.plasmaBall.sprite.y = -1000;
gc.plasmaBall.tween = nil;
```

The plasma ball is handled very much like the warning sign and alien as well.

Next up are the colonist indicators in the upper-right corner, and these are reset a bit differently. The first step is to get rid of any that are there now:

```
for i = 1, #gc.colonist.indicators, 1 do
  gc.colonist.indicators[i]:removeSelf();
  gc.colonist.indicators[i] = nil;
end
```

Unlike most of the other graphics in the game, these actually are created on the fly, so you have to destroy them at some point so as to not leak memory. Iterating over the gc.colonist.indicators() array allows you to call removeSelf() on them to destroy the graphics resources and then set the reference to nil to avoid the leak.

Once any existing indicators are cleaned up, you then need to create new indicators for the current level:

```
local indNum = 1;
gc.colonist.indicators = { };
for i = gc.levelData[gameData.level][16].colonistsToRescue, 1, -1 do
  gc.colonist.indicators[indNum] = display.newSprite(
    graphics.newImageSheet("colonist.png",
      { width = 32, height = 32, numFrames = 60 }
    ),
    gc.colonist.sequenceData
  );
  gc.colonist.indicators[indNum]:setSequence("indicator_pendingRescue");
  gc.colonist.indicators[indNum]:play();
  gc.colonist.indicators[indNum].x = display.contentWidth - (
```

```
    ((i - 1) * gc.colonist.indicators[indNum].width) +
      gc.colonist.indicators[indNum].width / 2
  );
  gc.colonist.indicators[indNum].y =
  gc.colonist.indicators[indNum].height / 2;
  gc.gameDG:insert(gc.colonist.indicators[indNum]);
  indNum = indNum + 1;
end
```

First, the number of indicators is determined by looking at gc.levelData, which is a data structure that you'll be looking at in just a bit. The data it contains describe a level including its visual structure (the ground and landing pads and such) as well as meta-information, like how many colonists there are to rescue and the coordinates at which an alien or a fuel pod can appear. The colonistsToRescue attribute is what is of interest here.

Now, to build up the gc.colonist.indicators array you have to play a little game: because of the math involved in drawing the indicators, you want the colonist all the way to the right to be the first to appear and then fill them in going left. However, the first element in the array should correspond to that rightmost indicator. In other words, its position on the screen is the exact opposite of its position in the array. This will make working with it later a lot easier, but it means you have to loop backwards here to get the right x/y coordinate calculations for each indicator.

The actual creation of each sprite is straightforward and no different from what you have been seeing all along. The calculation of the x coordinate looks a bit hairy, but it really just boils down to what I was talking about: the first element winds up furthest to the right on the screen. The indNum variable is incremented as that is used to insert the sprites into the array in the usual forward order, counter to the array, and the end result is things are set up as we want them to be on the screen as well as in the array.

Next, we have to deal with some z index issues:

```
if usingAccelerometer == false then
  gc.controls.left:toFront();
  gc.controls.right:toFront();
  gc.controls.vertical:toFront();
end
gc.ship.sprite:toFront();
gc.colonist.sprite:toFront();
gc.warningSign.sprite:toFront();
gc.fuelPod.sprite:toFront();
gc.alienUFO.sprite:toFront();
gc.plasmaBall.sprite:toFront();
```

Calling toFront(), a method of DisplayObject, on all our graphics objects ensures they are in front of the level that will have been drawn right before resetLevel() was called. If this wasn't done, then these graphics would be at least partially obscured by the ground.

Last, the score text has to be reset:

```
gc.scoreText:setReferencePoint(display.CenterReferencePoint);
gc.scoreText.text = "Score: " .. gameData.score;
gc.scoreText:setReferencePoint(display.TopLeftReferencePoint);
gc.scoreText.x = 0;
gc.scoreText.y = 2;
```

As mentioned earlier, the actual score is now appended to the static label and the value of gc.scoreText.text is updated. There is a bit of a trick in order to get the text to be properly left-aligned. Basically, you need to change the default top-left reference point to center, change the text, change the reference point back, and then reset the x/y location. If you don't do all this in exactly this order, then what happens is the text winds up hanging off the left side of the screen a bit. It moves from where it's initially placed in the init() method after the text is changed. This "hack" gets around that that problem.

> **Note**   If you need to use scaling then you should set the x and y scaling both to 1 before changing the text, then set it to display.contentScaleX and display.contentScaleY afterward. Doing so will allow you to have left-aligning at the same time as using scaling.

Kick It Off: Starting the Game

When the enterScene event occurs on the gameScene object, it calls the start() method of gameCore. It is a fairly straightforward method:

```
function gameCore:start()

  utils:log("gameCore", "start()");

  if usingAccelerometer == false then
    system.activate("multitouch")
  end
```

The system.activate() method is used to turn on system-level functions. At present, the only supported option is "multitouch". This means that more than one touch event can be handled simultaneously. Astro Rescue requires this to be true, otherwise the on-screen controls won't work right. For example, without activating this feature, the game won't properly handle presses on the vertical and horizontal thrust buttons and the player won't be able to control the ship properly. You'll learn how touch events are handled in Chapter 7, but this call makes it all work as expected.

Next, we need to set up event handlers for enterFrame so that the core game logic, a.k.a. the main game loop, can run:

```
Runtime:addEventListener("enterFrame", gc);
Runtime:addEventListener("collision", gc);
```

Chapter 6 is where we'll dive into that main loop. In addition, the game wouldn't do much if it didn't have collision events occurring, so an event handler is set up for that. Both of these reference the gameCore object itself by way of the variable gc, so you know from this that there will be an `enterFrame()` and `collision()` method floating around somewhere.

```
if usingAccelerometer == true then
  Runtime:addEventListener("touch", gc);
  Runtime:addEventListener("accelerometer", gc);
end

end
```

Last, if the player has decided to use accelerometer controls, then not only do you need to register to listen for accelerometer events, but you also need to set up a touch listener on the entire screen (as opposed to just the thrust control graphics, as was done earlier when setting up those graphics and when not using accelerometer control). That way, he can use the entire screen as their vertical thrust and control the left and right thrust by tilting their device.

Okay, That'll Do: Stopping the Game

Like two sides of a coin, starting the game has a corresponding stop event as implemented in the aptly named `stop()` method:

```
function gameCore:stop()

  utils:log("gameCore", "stop()");

  if usingAccelerometer == false then
    system.deactivate("multitouch")
  end
```

First, multitouch events are disabled using the `system.deactivate()` method, the opposite of the previously seen `system.activate()` method. This has to be done because multitouch events on something like the menu screen could cause issues: what happens if the user presses two options at once, holds his finger down, and releases at the same time? Since the menu items are triggered during the "ended" phase of the touch event, you'd wind up with two of them firing at roughly the same time. That would lead to all manner of Very Bad Things™ happening.

Next, the physics simulation needs to be stopped:

```
physics.stop();
```

This needs to be done if for no other reason than efficiency: when leaving the game there's no physics involved, so it would be silly and wasteful of CPU power (and therefore the battery!) to keep it running.

Next, the two event handlers attached to the Runtime object that were set up in start() need to be removed:

```
Runtime:removeEventListener("enterFrame", gc);
Runtime:removeEventListener("collision", gc);
```

Especially for event handlers attached to Runtime, you need to be careful to clean these up by removing them when not needed. Imagine if you forgot to do this—it would mean that when you went back to the menu scene, you'd wind up triggering gc.enterFrame() as well as whatever the menu scene might be doing with each frame. That definitely wouldn't wind up being good for anyone!

```
  if usingAccelerometer == true then
    Runtime:removeEventListener("touch", gc);
    Runtime:removeEventListener("accelerometer", gc);
  end

end
```

Similarly, the handlers for the touch and accelerometer events need to be removed, lest you wind up with events occurring on other screens that aren't intended to happen.

Destruction: Cleaning Up After Ourselves

When transitioning from the gameScene back to the menuScene after the game ends, it's important to clean up graphic resources and audio resources, and otherwise remove references to anything that Corona and Lua will clean up automatically. To accomplish this, the destroy() method is called:

```
function gameCore:destroy()

  utils:log("gameCore", "destroy()");

  if gc.sfx.screamChannel ~= nil then
    audio.stop(gc.sfx.screamChannel);
  end
  audio.dispose(gc.sfx.scream);
  gc.sfx.screamChannel = nil;
  gc.sfx.scream = nil;
  if gc.sfx.fuelPodPickupChannel ~= nil then
    audio.stop(gc.sfx.fuelPodPickupChannel);
  end
  audio.dispose(gc.sfx.fuelPodPickup);
  gc.sfx.fuelPodPickup = nil;
  gc.sfx.fuelPodPickupChannel = nil;
  if gc.sfx.sosChannel ~= nil then
    audio.stop(gc.sfx.sosChannel);
  end
  audio.dispose(gc.sfx.sos);
  gc.sfx.sos = nil;
  gc.sfx.sosChannel = nil;
```

```
if gc.sfx.explosionChannel ~= nil then
  audio.stop(gc.sfx.explosionChannel);
end
audio.dispose(gc.sfx.explosion);
gc.sfx.explosion = nil;
gc.sfx.explosionChannel = nil;
if gc.sfx.thrustersChannel ~= nil then
  audio.stop(gc.sfx.thrustersChannel);
end
audio.dispose(gc.sfx.thrusters);
gc.sfx.thrusters = nil;
gc.sfx.thrustersChannel = nil;
```

First to be cleaned up are all the audio resources. This comes down to the same sequence of events for all. First, if the sound is still playing, call `stop()` on it. Then, call `audio.dispose()` to let Corona remove the resource. Last, set both the reference to the channel on which the sound was playing, as well as the reference to the audio resource itself, to `nil`.

> **Note** In truth, nilling out the reference to the channel shouldn't be necessary, but it does no harm. It's always good to be overly concerned with cleaning up resources when you're dealing with resource-constrained mobile devices. Of course, **resource-constrained** doesn't have the same meaning it did just a few short years ago, but you still don't want your game to crash because it causes the system to run out of memory.

With the audio resources cleaned up, it's time to handle the graphics:

```
gc.scoreText:removeSelf();
gc.scoreText = nil;
gc.ship.sprite:removeSelf();
gc.ship.sprite = nil;
gc.colonist.sprite:removeSelf();
gc.colonist.sprite = nil;
gc.explosion.sprite:removeSelf();
gc.explosion.sprite = nil;
if usingAccelerometer == false then
  gc.controls.left:removeSelf();
  gc.controls.left = nil;
  gc.controls.right:removeSelf();
  gc.controls.right = nil;
  gc.controls.vertical:removeSelf();
  gc.controls.vertical = nil;
end
gc.fuelPod.sprite:removeSelf();
gc.fuelPod.sprite = nil;
gc.fuelGauge.shell:removeSelf();
gc.fuelGauge.shell = nil;
```

```
gc.fuelGauge.fill:removeSelf();
gc.fuelGauge.fill = nil;
gc.warningSign.sprite:removeSelf();
gc.warningSign.sprite = nil;
gc.alienUFO.sprite:removeSelf();
gc.alienUFO.sprite = nil;
gc.plasmaBall.sprite:removeSelf();
gc.plasmaBall.sprite = nil;
for i = 1, #gc.colonist.indicators, 1 do
  gc.colonist.indicators[i]:removeSelf();
  gc.colonist.indicators[i] = nil;
end
```

For all of them, do a call to `removeSelf()`and then set the reference to `nil`. These are the canonical steps to properly clean up graphics in Corona.

Note, however, that the graphics added to `levelDG`, things like the ground, aren't cleaned up here. They are actually done next:

```
gc.levelDG:removeSelf();
gc.levelDG = nil;
gc.gameDG = nil;
```

```
end
```

What's interesting here is that although `levelDG` at this point would contain a whole bunch of `DisplayObjects` (as a result of the very next method to be explored), there's no need to remove each of them individually. As it happens, calling `removeSelf()` on a `DisplayGroup` automatically calls it on all of its children, so there's no need to do that manually.

Last, note the setting of `gc.gameDG` to `nil`. While it is true that Corona will clean up the scene's `DisplayGroup` automatically, the code in gameCore would wind up stopping that from happening due to this reference, which would cause Corona and Lua to determine it is not eligible for garbage collection. Setting it to `nil` stops that from happening and ensures garbage collection occurs as you want.

We Need a Playfield: Drawing the Current Level

One of the bigger tasks the code in gameCore.lua has to accomplish is to draw the level, meaning the ground. The `drawCurrentLevel()` is the method specifically responsible for doing that:

```
function gameCore:drawCurrentLevel()

  utils:log("gameCore", "drawCurrentLevel()");

  if gc.levelDG ~= nil then
    gc.levelDG:removeSelf();
  end
```

The first thing to do is to see if there is a level in memory already, as would be the case if this wasn't the first level played this session. When that is true, gc.levelDG is a reference to a DisplayGroup, so in that case a call to removeSelf() cleans up all those resources.

Either way, you need a DisplayGroup into which to put all the graphics, so create one now:

```
gc.levelDG = display.newGroup();
```

That's actually the first time (and the only one, as it happens!) you've seen a DisplayGroup being created manually. Before now, you've only ever seen the one created by the Storyboard API automatically. There's no problem creating your own, and you can in fact create as many as you like. You can even nest them because a DisplayGroup has DisplayObjects as its children, and a DisplayGroup happens to extend DisplayObject. Any time you want to group graphics together, usually to manipulate many at one time, you can create a DisplayGroup, add other objects to it, and then manipulate it. It's an extremely handy thing to be able to do, as this method demonstrates: you'll use it to handle all the ground graphics as one, with no need ever to deal with the individual graphics.

Speaking of individual graphics, that is in fact how the ground is drawn—it's just a series of 32×32 tiles that are used to draw over a 15×25 grid of tiles. The width of a tile (32 pixels) multiplied by the number of tiles across the screen (25) yields a total pixel area of 800, which happens to be exactly the width of the virtual screen to which Astro Rescue is designed. Likewise, the height of a tile (32 pixels) multiplied by the number of tiles down the screen (15) yields a total pixel area of 480, the height of the virtual screen.

Figure 5-12 shows the grid arrangement and should help you visualize what was just described. Each of the squares is a single tile element as defined in the level data discussed in the next section.

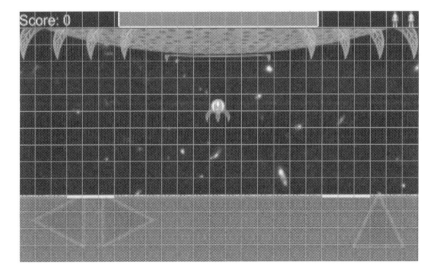

Figure 5-12. The tile grid for drawing a level visualized

That 25×15 grid size is where the loop variables here come from:

```
for y = 1, 15, 1 do
  for x = 1, 25, 1 do
    local pX = 32 * (x - 1);
    local pY = 32 * (y - 1);
    local tileType = gc.levelData[gameData.level][y][x];
```

The x and y location of the next tile to draw is calculated based on the tile's width and height (32) and the row (y) and column (x) being drawn. The type of tile is determined by looking into the gc.levelData structure.

Defining a Level

Let's step out of the flow of examining drawCurrentLevel() a bit and examine this levelData structure. It's an array that looks like this:

```
local levelData = {

  {
    { " "," "," "," "," "," "," "," "," "," "," "," "," "," "," "," "," "," "," "," "," "," "," "," ",
" "," "," " },
    { " "," "," "," "," "," "," "," "," "," "," "," "," "," "," "," "," "," "," "," "," "," "," "," ",
" "," "," " },
    { " "," "," "," "," "," "," "," "," "," "," "," "," "," "," "," "," "," "," "," "," "," "," "," ",
" "," "," " },
    { " "," "," "," "," "," "," "," "," "," "," "," "," "," "," "," "," "," "," "," "," "," "," "," ",
" "," "," " },
    { " "," "," "," "," "," "," "," "," "," "," "," "," "," "," "," "," "," "," "," "," "," "," "," ",
" "," "," " },
    { " "," "," "," "," "," "," "," "," "," "," "," "," "," "," "," "," "," "," "," "," "," "," "," ",
" "," "," " },
    { " "," "," "," "," "," "," "," "," "," "," "," "," "," "," "," "," "," "," "," "," "," "," "," ",
" "," "," " },
    { " "," "," "," "," "," "," "," "," "," "," "," "," "," "," "," "," "," "," "," "," "," "," "," ",
" "," "," " },
    { " "," "," "," "," "," "," "," "," "," "," "," "," "," "," "," "," "," "," "," "," "," "," "," ",
" "," "," " },
    { " "," "," "," "," "," "," "," "," "," "," "," "," "," "," "," "," "," "," "," "," "," "," "," ",
" "," "," " },
    { " "," "," "," "," "," "," "," "," "," "," "," "," "," "," "," "," "," "," "," "," "," "," "," ",
" "," "," " },
    { "2","2","2","3","3","3","2","2","2","2","2","2","2","2","2","2","2","2","3","3","3","2",
"2","2" },
    { "1","1","1","1","1","1","1","1","1","1","1","1","1","1","1","1","1","1","1","1","1","1",
"1","1" },
    { "1","1","1","1","1","1","1","1","1","1","1","1","1","1","1","1","1","1","1","1","1","1",
"1","1" },
    { "1","1","1","1","1","1","1","1","1","1","1","1","1","1","1","1","1","1","1","1","1","1",
"1","1" },
```

```
    { colonistsToRescue = 2 },
    { { x = 2, y = 12 }, { x = 24, y = 12 } },
    { { x = 3, y = 9 }, { x = 11, y = 8 }, { x = 20, y = 7 } },
    { { x = 25, y = 7 }, { x = 1, y = 5 }, { x = 1, y = 6 } }
  },
  ...
};
```

Each row in the topmost array defines a level. Within that, the first 15 rows are the actual data for what tiles make up the ground. Any that are spaces are where no tile is drawn. This means that we could have ground coming up all the way to the top, but in practice that doesn't make a lot of sense from a game-play perspective, so most of the no-space tiles are near the bottom.

The numbers 1, 2, and 3 for tile values correspond to tiles for dirt, the top layer of dirt with the green outline, and dirt with a landing pad, respectively. For the levels with metal ground, the values are 4, 5, and 7 for a filled metal tile, a top-layer metal tile, and a metal tile with a landing pad on it.

Rows 16 through 19 define "meta-data" for the level. Row 16 tells us how many colonists there are to rescue on this level. Row 17 provides a list of objects, each with an x and y coordinate, where each object gives a tile location where a colonist can appear. These coordinates place them right next to the landing pads. The colonists actually get drawn directly above that location, but the coordinates are one of the top-layer tiles next to a landing pad.

Row 18 is like the colonists' points but tells the code where a fuel pod can appear. I chose only two per level, but there's no limitation on how many there can be. They all should be in empty space, however, otherwise the player won't be able to get to them.

Row 19 is similar in that it defines the points from which an alien can come onto the screen. The alien moves in a straight line, so you have to be careful that whatever starting point you choose has a clear flight path all the way across the screen (technically, the alien **could** fly on top of the ground or even the mothership, but it just doesn't look very good).

Finishing Up Level Drawing

Getting back to drawing the level, you left off right at the point where you determined what type of tile is next to be drawn. This information is used to branch accordingly:

```
if tileType ~= " " then
  local material = "Dirt";
  if tileType == "4" or tileType == "5" or tileType == "6" then
    material = "Metal";
  end
```

There's nothing to do when you encounter a tile type of a space character, but for other cases, first assume the material of the tile is dirt, and override with metal for the 4, 5, and 6 tile type codes.

Next, we create the appropriate tile:

```
local tile;
if tileType == "1" or tileType == "4" then
  tile = display.newImage("tile" .. material .. "Fill.png", true);
  tile.objName = "crash";
end
```

```
if tileType == "2" or tileType == "5" then
  tile = display.newImage("tile" .. material .. "Top.png", true);
  tile.objName = "crash";
elseif tileType == "3" or tileType == "6" then
  tile = display.newImage("tile" .. material .. "Pad.png", true);
  tile.objName = "pad";
end
physics.addBody(
  tile, "static", { density = 1, friction = 2, bounce = 0 }
);
```

With the material already determined, you just need to determine whether it's a fill tile, a top tile, or a landing pad tile. For each, there needs to be a physics body attached. Giving the top and fill tiles an objName of "crash" gives you a value to key off of later when we handle collisions to indicate the ship has crashed. Likewise, for the landing pad tile, a value of "pad" is used so the code can differentiate that situation.

```
      tile:setReferencePoint(display.TopLeftReferencePoint);
      tile.x = pX;
      tile.y = pY;
      gc.levelDG:insert(tile);
    end
  end
end
```

For all tile types, set the reference point to the top left corner to make positioning it a little more straightforward. The tile is then inserted into gc.levelDG.

One final step remains:

```
  gc.gameDG:insert(gc.levelDG);

end
```

The entire DisplayGroup that now contains all the tile graphics for this level is inserted into the main DisplayGroup for the scene, and you're off to the races with this level!

Communication Is Key: Showing a Quick Message

As you play the game, you'll see situations when a quick message is flashed on the screen, expands toward you, and gradually fades away. Specifically, this happens when you get a fuel pod or pick up a colonist. The method that accomplishes this is showMessage(), and while the effect is, I think, fairly nice and effective as a transient messaging mechanism, the code behind it is surprisingly sparse.

```
function gameCore:showMessage(inMsg)

  utils:log("gameCore", "showMessage(): inMsg = " .. inMsg);

  local msgText = display.newText(inMsg, 0, 0, nil, 20);
  msgText:setTextColor(255, 255, 0);
```

```
msgText.x = display.contentCenterX;
msgText.y = display.contentCenterY;
msgText.alpha = 1;
msgText.xScale = 1.0;
msgText.yScale = 1.0;
```

A new text DisplayObject is created using the message passed into the method. Its color is set and it is centered on the screen by using the display.contentCenterX and display.contentCenterY values. These are a nice convenience to use rather than having to divide the screen's width and height by 2 yourself.

The alpha attribute is also set so the text is fully opaque, and the scale is set to 1 in both directions. These steps are actually not necessary, but for the sake of coding clarity, I think it's not a bad idea to do them anyway.

Next, a transition is started on this text:

```
transition.to(msgText,
  { time = 1000, alpha = 0, xScale = 30.0, yScale = 30.0,
    onComplete = function(inTarget)
      inTarget:removeSelf();
      inTarget = nil;
    end
  }
);
```

end

The transition takes care of everything in one step: the alpha attribute is reduced over time down to 0 and the text is expanded in both directions. The target values for the scaling are large enough that by the time the alpha value reaches 0, the text has grown way beyond the bounds of the screen.

Last, when the transition completes, the program destroys the text DisplayObject, which conveniently is passed into the onComplete event handler. Setting the reference to nil isn't necessary, but for the sake of consistency with all the other cleanup code, I prefer to have it. Again, being overly concerned with resource management is rarely a bad thing when working with Corona and Lua.

Cut It Out Right Now, You Kids: Stopping Game Activity

The last method in the gameCore.lua file is one used from a couple of places in the game, and its job is to stop any activity currently happening on the screen. This means shutting down transitions, stopping audio, and hiding a few select elements.

```
function gameCore:stopAllActivity()

  if gc.warningSign.tween ~= nil then
    transition.cancel(gc.warningSign.tween);
  end
```

```
if gc.alienUFO.tween ~= nil then
  transition.cancel(gc.alienUFO.tween);
end
if gc.plasmaBall.tween ~= nil then
  transition.cancel(gc.plasmaBall.tween);
end
```

The warning sign, alien, and plasma ball all use transitions to move, as you saw earlier, so if those transitions are occurring they are stopped.

Next, the alien, plasma ball, and the player's ship are hidden from view:

```
gc.alienUFO.sprite.isVisible = false;
gc.plasmaBall.sprite.isVisible = false;
gc.ship.sprite.isVisible = false;
```

Next, you need to deactivate the physics body associated with the player's ship, but there's a little bit of a problem here:

```
timer.performWithDelay(10,
  function()
    gc.ship.sprite.isBodyActive = false;
  end
);
```

The problem is that this method, in at least one situation, will be called from inside an event handler. This is a problem because you are not allowed to manipulate the active state of a physics body from an event handler. So, to be able to accomplish this goal, you need to use the timer.performWithDelay() function. This simply accepts a millisecond value and a reference to a function, which can be inline as it is here if you want. Ten milliseconds is enough for the event handler to complete, so at the end of that interval the isBodyActive attribute will be set to false. The delay is small enough that the user won't notice, and also small enough that, from the standpoint of our code, it happens at virtually the same time as if it were done directly in the destroy() method.

> **Note** There are other attributes that cannot be changed in an event handler, such as bodyType. If you ever encounter a situation where an attribute change in an event handler doesn't seem to be working as expected, check the Corona documentation to see if it's explicitly stated that you can't do that, or simply try the change using timer.performWithDelay().

```
if gc.sfx.thrustersChannel ~= nil then
  audio.stop(gc.sfx.thrustersChannel);
end
```

The thruster sound is actually the only sound resource that needs to be stopped, since all others are temporary sounds anyway, but the thrust sound continues as long as the ship is moving under player control.

Summary

Whew, that was quite a long chapter, wasn't it? Nevertheless, long as it may have been, I think you'll agree it was well worth it!

In this chapter, you covered a lot of ground, including sprites, the beginnings of physics, native UI, and a number of assorted Corona functions. In addition, you got the chance to see more things that have been discussed being used, including the display API, storyboard, transitions, and audio.

All of this was put to good use to start building the core of Astro Rescue, including the basic lifecycle events that are needed, some utility functions, and all the resource management involved.

In Chapter 6, you'll continue exploring the core game code, specifically the main game loop, where most of the real frame-to-frame action takes place. As always, you'll get a chance at some hands-on experience with new elements of Corona, as well as more experience with the things you're becoming familiar with now. Astro Rescue will continue to be built out as a result, and in short order you'll have a full, playable game!

Chapter

The Game, Part 2: Main Loop

Patterns emerge in software engineering in which we realize that one solution to a recurring problem is implemented more often than any other. This is as true in game programming as it is in any other area of programming.

One such pattern is the main game loop pattern. While not every game uses this approach, most—even the vast majority—do. It is so common, in fact, that it usually isn't even talked about as a specific pattern; it's simply the way games are done, 9 times out of 10.

At its core, it is a simple enough concept: you typically have a single function that executes frequently—once per frame being a very common interval—which is responsible for making the core logic of the game happen. This function moves on-screen elements, implements AI, and generally performs any other regularly occurring task needed for the game to run.

Astro Rescue is in no way atypical in this regard, as it does indeed have a main game loop, as implemented in the aptly-named gameCoreMainLoop.lua file, and that is what this chapter is all about.

enterFrame

The specific function to be dealt with here is enterFrame(). In Chapter 5, you saw how a listener was attached to the Runtime object for the "enterFrame" event in the start() method. That results in enterFrame() being called every time Coronal is about to draw a new frame to the screen. You can do whatever you wish in this method, be it simple or complex.

As it happens, the version in Astro Rescue is quite simple. First, we need to deal with three special cases:

```
function gc:enterFrame(inEvent)

  if gc.phase == gc.EXPLODING then
    return;
  end
```

First, you want all game activity to cease when the player's ship is exploding, which you can determine because there is a specific game phase for that. In that case, all you do is terminate the function with a `return`.

```
if gc.phase == gc.PHASE_DEAD then
  gc.showDeadPopup();
   return;
end
```

Similarly, if the player is now dead, which is the state the game ends up in when the explosion animation finishes, then the function needs to terminate early as well. However, in that case, the game needs to show the popup message asking if the player wants to try again or quit, and that is accomplished by showDeadPopup(), as you'll see shortly. Interestingly, you may be thinking that this will continue to occur while the popup is shown because the "enterFrame" event doesn't ever cease from the time the app starts until the time it ends, and you would be correct. It will be the responsibility of showDeadPopup() to **not** show the popup if it's already on the screen.

```
if gc.phase == gc.PHASE_IN_BAY then
  gc.showEnteredBayPopup();
   return;
end
```

As with the case of the player being dead, when she enters the bay there is a popup message that appears as well, so that case gets handled the same as the dead case by calling a method to show the popup and then exiting the enterFrame() function.

With the three special cases dealt with, all that's left to do is the core logic of the game and movement of the on-screen objects:

```
gc.processShip(inEvent);
gc.processColonist(inEvent);
gc.processFuelPod(inEvent);
gc.processAlienUFO(inEvent);
```

You could of course choose to write everything inside the enterFrame() method, and in a simple game like Astro Rescue that might not be so bad, but in anything larger it will quickly become unwieldy. Instead, calling a number of smaller functions for specific tasks is a better pattern to follow.

The first thing that is dealt with is the movement of the player's ship. You'll be looking at that method next, but the executive summary is that there are flags, which you saw earlier, that tell you whether the ship is moving as a result of player interaction, and in what direction. On their own those flags do nothing; it's only the processShip() method interrogating them and actually updating the location of the ship that does anything.

The processColonist() method will take care of showing a colonist to be rescued, if it's time to do so, or moving the current colonist toward the player's ship, if it has landed.

The processFuelPod() method takes care of showing a fuel pod when it's time and, similarly, the processAlienUFO() method takes care of our marauding alien craft.

Although the process isn't complex, sometimes a picture is worth more than all the words of the world combined. So, to ensure it's clear to you what's going on at a high level, Figure 6-1 should solidify it in your mind, I suspect.

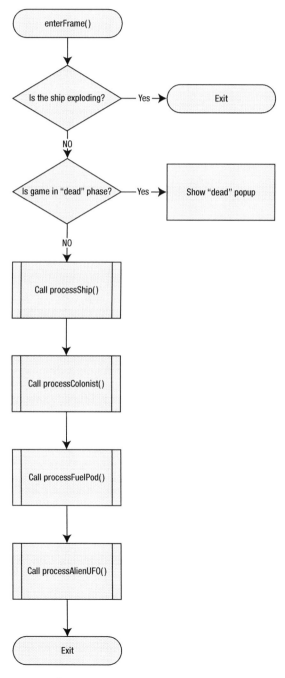

Figure 6-1. *Overall flow of the* enterFrame() *method*

processShip

The next method that is also called from enterFrame() is processShip() and is what's responsible for actually moving the player's ship.

It may seem a little counterintuitive at first glance to move the ship here rather than directly in response to an input event, so let me explain this from a high level before I get into the details of the code.

Let's say you want to move the ship 1 pixel for every screen tap, so you decide to do that in the event handler you set up to handle taps. It isn't hard to imagine that you may get a different number of tap events per frame drawn if the player is tapping madly. What happens if one time they tap the screen three times in between frames, and another time they tap it 10 times in between frames?

The result will be, to the player, a ship that doesn't move at a constant velocity and sometimes "jumps around." Now, that may in fact be what you want on occasion, depending on the type of game you're making, but more often than not you really want a constant rate of movement (ignoring acceleration for the moment).

The way this is accomplished is that the position of the ship is only updated inside the main loop. All that happens in this scenario in the tap event handler is that flags are set to say whether the ship **is** moving or not. Doing this means that you know, based on the frame rate, how many times per second the ship's position will be updated, and it will be constant.

THERE'S MORE THAN ONE WAY TO SKIN, ERR, MOVE A CAT!

The approach to moving the ship described here is referred to as **frame rate-based movement,** but there is another approach, called **time-based movement** or **frame-independent movement.** In that approach, you determine with each frame drawn how many pixels an object should move based on how fast the game is actually running (usually how many frames the last frame took to process). This is useful when your game may have to work on devices that can't produce a constant frame rate, either because some are less powerful or because your game's action sometimes changes in intensity and some frames naturally will wind up taking longer to process than others. Time-based movement avoids the problem of a game running faster on machines that are more powerful and slower on less powerful ones. However, it is a more complex approach requiring more code and can lead to animation that is less smooth because the amount of pixels that an object moves can change suddenly, causing it to appear to jump around.

Frankly, time-based movement is oftentimes simply not needed, but it very much depends on the design of your game. Astro Rescue certainly does not need it, for example—it's simple enough that basing it on frame rate works just fine.

Also, remember that while Corona does provide a way to "lock" the frame rate, if you do too much in your main loop you can cause that frame rate to drop. So, if you go with the frame-rate-based approach you need to be cognizant of this and be careful that in no case will the code executing in your main loop take more time than the frame rate allows (33 ms in the case of Astro Rescue: 1,000 ms / 30 fps = 33 ms/frame). If you do not ensure this, then you will get dropped frames and the game will appear to slow down—not good!

With those preliminaries covered, I'll get into what happens inside `processShip()`:

```
function gc:processShip(inEvent)

  if gc.ship.thrustVertical == true and gc.ship.fuel > 0 then
    gc.ship.sprite:applyLinearImpulse(
      0, -.4, gc.ship.sprite.x, gc.ship.sprite.y
    );
  End
```

Whenever the player has her finger on the vertical thrust button, or on the screen generally when using accelerometer controls, the `gc.ship.thrustVertical` flag will be set. In that case, and if the player has some fuel left, the ship needs to be moved. The trick to this is that you want the ship to accelerate gradually over time. Certainly you could do this ourselves, but why bother? Corona's physics engine makes this possible with far less effort on your part.

The `applyLinearImpulse()` method applies a single, momentary jolt of movement in a given direction to a physics body. This method accepts an x and y component as its first two arguments that tell it how strong the jolt is in each direction. A 0, as in the x component here, means no energy is applied in the horizontal direction. The y value of -.4 means apply energy to push the body upward. The actual value itself is entirely trial and error as you explore what value will result in the movement desired. Since this impulse will be applied with every frame drawn, assuming the flag is set and there is gas left, the value is low. However, it's an additive effect, meaning the overall momentum of the ship builds over time, exactly like we want.

> **Note** There is also an `applyForce()` method that is used to apply a force over time. Similarly, there is an `applyTorque()` method to apply a rotational force to make the body spin over time. An impulse is intended to provide a one-time kick to an object, whereas a force acts on it over time. Either approach would have worked for the ship, but using an impulse as shown provides a somewhat more realistic movement profile for the ship—it simply looks more like what you would expect a hovering spaceship to look like.

```
if gc.ship.thrustLeft == true and gc.ship.fuel > 0 then
  local forceAmount = .2;
  if usingAccelerometer == true then
    forceAmount = .1;
  end
  gc.ship.sprite:applyLinearImpulse(
    forceAmount, 0, gc.ship.sprite.x, gc.ship.sprite.y
  );
end
if gc.ship.thrustRight == true and gc.ship.fuel > 0 then
  local forceAmount = .2;
  if usingAccelerometer == true then
    forceAmount = .1;
  end
  gc.ship.sprite:applyLinearImpulse(
    -forceAmount, 0, gc.ship.sprite.x, gc.ship.sprite.y
  );
end
```

Left and right thrust is handled just like vertical thrust, with one important difference: the amount of force applied differs when using accelerometer control versus touch control. The reason is that the ship winds up moving far too fast using accelerometer control because you can't null it out (i.e., stop the movement) as easily as with touch control, for which you're just lifting your finger off the screen. Therefore, a smaller value is used in that case. Once the amount is determined, an impulse is applied, same as for the vertical thrust case. Negative values move the ship right in this case, since the values are relative to the object's center of mass, so a negative value results in force applied from the left, pushing the body to the right.

```
if gc.ship.sprite.x < 0 or
  gc.ship.sprite.x > display.contentWidth
then
  utils:log("gameCoreMainLoop", "Ship went off screen");
  gc.phase = gc.PHASE_DEAD;
  gc.ship.sprite.isVisible = false;
end
```

If the ship goes off the screen in either direction, then the player is considered dead. The ship is hidden and the phase switched to gc.PHASE_DEAD, which you know from the last section results in the popup message appearing asking if they want to try again or not.

```
if gc.ship.thrustVertical == true or gc.ship.thrustLeft == true or
  gc.ship.thrustRight == true
then
  gc.ship.fuel = gc.ship.fuel - 2;
  if gc.ship.fuel <= 0 then
    gc.ship.sprite:setSequence("noThrust");
    gc.ship.sprite:play();
    gc.ship.thrustVertical = false;
    gc.ship.thrustLeft = false;
    gc.ship.thrustRight = false;
  end
  gc.updateFuelGauge();
end
```

Any time the ship is thrusting in any direction, you need to deduct some fuel. When the player runs out of fuel, the "noThrust" animation sequence is shown, since the ship at this point obviously can have no thrust flames coming out. We also ensure that the three thrust vector flags are set to false. Last, the updateFuelGauge() method is called to redraw the fuel gauge to show the current amount of fuel.

```
local vX, vY = gc.ship.sprite:getLinearVelocity();
if vX > 75 or vY > 75 then
  gc.warningSign.sprite.isVisible = true;
else
  gc.warningSign.sprite.isVisible = false;
end
```

The last step is to see if the ship is moving too fast and to show the warning sign if it is. The getLinearVelocity() method returns to us the rate at which a body is moving in pixels per second. It returns two values, the X and Y components of the body's motion. If either value is greater than the threshold value 75, which again is just a bit of trial and error, then the warning sign is made visible—otherwise it's hidden.

processColonist

Processing the colonist is the next task accomplished in the main game loop. There is a bit more to it than processing the player's ship.

```
function gc:processColonist(inEvent)

  if gc.colonist.sprite.isVisible == true and gc.phase == gc.PHASE_LANDED then
```

If a colonist it currently awaiting rescue, which is the case when isVisible is true, and if the ship has landed, then the colonist should run toward the ship. The first step is to determine how far away the colonist is from the ship:

```
local deltaX = math.abs(gc.colonist.sprite.x - gc.ship.sprite.x);
```

The math.abs() function gives us the absolute value of the difference between the ship and colonist's x coordinate. Use this to move the colonist toward the ship.

First, though, you need to see if the colonist is already at the ship, which could be the case because this method, as you will see, moves the colonist toward the ship with each call.

```
if deltaX <= 1 then

  gc.colonist.sprite.isVisible = false;
  gc.ship.colonistsOnboard = gc.ship.colonistsOnboard + 1;
  if gc.ship.colonistsOnboard <=
    gc.levelData[gameData.level][16].colonistsToRescue
  then
    gc.colonist.indicators[gc.ship.colonistsOnboard]:setSequence(
      "indicator_onboardShip"
    );
    gc.colonist.indicators[gc.ship.colonistsOnboard]:play();
    gc.colonist.appearCounter = 0;
    gc:showMessage("Got 'em!");
  end
```

When there is no longer a delta between the ship and colonist's X location, then the colonist boards the ship. When this occurs, the colonist is again hidden, and the number of colonists on board the ship is incremented. The animation sequence for the appropriate colonist indicator is switched to indicate he has been picked up. The appearCounter for the colonist is reset, making it eligible to show up again, and the "Got 'em!" message is shown.

Now, if the colonist **hasn't** reached the ship yet, then you have to move them toward it:

```
elseif deltaX > 1 and deltaX <= 140 then

  if gc.ship.sprite.x > gc.colonist.sprite.x then
    gc.colonist.sprite.x = gc.colonist.sprite.x + 2;
    if gc.colonist.sprite.sequence ~= "walking_right" then
      gc.colonist.sprite:setSequence("walking_right");
      gc.colonist.sprite:play();
    end
  elseif gc.ship.sprite.x < gc.colonist.sprite.x then
    gc.colonist.sprite.x = gc.colonist.sprite.x - 2;
    if gc.colonist.sprite.sequence ~= "walking_left" then
      gc.colonist.sprite:setSequence("walking_left");
      gc.colonist.sprite:play();
    end
  end

end
```

Remember that we have an absolute value for the delta between the ship and colonist's X location, so if the ship's X value is greater than the colonist's X value is, then the colonist is running to the right, toward the ship. If the animation sequence hasn't already been changed to the "walking_right" sequence, then that is done as well.

Conversely, if the ship is to the left of the colonist then the X location of the colonist is reduced, so they move toward the ship, and the "walking_left" animation sequence is switched as well.

The next task occurs when the colonist is not currently on-screen and/or moving towards the ship. The code needs to decide if it's time for a colonist to appear for rescuing:

```
if gc.colonist.sprite.isVisible == false and
  gc.ship.colonistsOnboard <
    gc.levelData[gameData.level][16].colonistsToRescue and
  gc.colonist.appearCounter >= gc.colonist.FRAMES_BETWEEN_APPEARANCES
then
```

As long as the colonist isn't currently showing and there are still colonists left to be rescued on this level, and if enough time has elapsed since the last colonist appeared, then the colonist can appear.

At this point, one situation that could still be true that you need to deal with is the case where the player just rescued a colonist and is still on the landing pad. In that case, you want to make it so the player has to lift off before the colonist appears; otherwise she might be able to just sit on the pad awaiting colonists all game. Well, not really, since the alien's plasma ball will do them in before that happens, but still, it's better to force her to fly around a bit for the challenge of it.

With this in mind, one quick check is done:

```
if gc.phase == gc.PHASE_LANDED then
  gc.colonist.appearCounter = 0;
  return;
end
```

If the ship is still on a landing pad at this point, just reset the `appearCounter` so that the delay between colonist appearances starts over without the colonist appearing, owing to the return here, which forces the player to have to lift off for a colonist to appear again.

Next is deciding at what tile location the colonist will appear:

```
local whichTile = math.random(1, #gc.levelData[gameData.level][17]);
while whichTile == gc.colonist.lastAppearancePoint do
  whichTile = math.random(1, #gc.levelData[gameData.level][17]);
end
gc.colonist.lastAppearancePoint = whichTile;
```

Recall that the 17th row of data in the level definition provides a list of tile coordinates where a colonist may appear. Therefore, the code randomly chooses a number between 1 and the length of the array that is the 17th row. However, you don't want the colonist to appear at the same place as last time, so compare the chosen tile against `gc.colonist.lastAppearancePoint` and keep randomly choosing a tile until one is picked that's not the same as last time. Once one is chosen, you have to record it in `gc.colonist.lastAppearancePoint`, of course, or this work will be all for nothing next time a colonist appears!

> **Note**   This is actually a rather inefficient way to do this; more important, it could lead to slowdowns. Imagine what would happen if the same tile kept being chosen many times in a row, which could happen since this is random. The main game loop might all of a sudden take longer than its allotted time slice to finish, and you'll get a stutter on the screen. It's not likely to occur in this case so it isn't really a problem, but in general you'd be better off doing something like creating a pseudorandomized list of array indexes at application startup and running through them linearly, looping at the end, and using that to determine the next colonist tile location. It will be less "truly" random than this approach, but will be a constant time hit instead of introducing the unknown time as this code does.

```
local tileCoordinates = gc.levelData[gameData.level][17][whichTile];
local pX = 32 * (tileCoordinates.x - 1);
local pY = (32 * (tileCoordinates.y - 1)) - 16;
gc.colonist.sprite.x = pX;
gc.colonist.sprite.y = pY;
```

Once we know what tile the colonist will appear at, you need to figure out the physical x and y coordinates on the screen at which to place them. The `tileCoordinates.x` and `tileCoordinates.y` values are the x and y coordinates of the tile in the level tile grid, not an actual screen location. To translate to physical coordinate, do a bit of math that is very similar to what you did to draw the screen, and set the sprite's x and y attributes to those calculated values.

Finally, there are just a few small matters to take care of:

```
gc.colonist.sprite:setSequence("materializing");
gc.colonist.sprite:play();
gc.colonist.sprite.isVisible = true;

gc.sfx.sosChannel = audio.play(gc.sfx.sos);
```

end

The colonist's "materializing" animation sequence is played and, of course, the sprite is made visible. Last, the sos audio resource is played so the player doesn't miss the fact that a colonist is now ready to be rescued.

processFuelPod

The processing related to fuel pods is very simple:

```
function gc:processFuelPod(inEvent)

  if gc.fuelPod.sprite.isVisible == false then

    gc.fuelPod.framesSinceLastAppearance =
      gc.fuelPod.framesSinceLastAppearance + 1;
```

If a fuel pod isn't already showing, which can be determined by seeing if the isVisible property of its sprite is false, then the game can continue on. The next step is to increment the counter that lets you know how many frames have elapsed since a fuel pod was seen last.

The next step is to see if that counter exceeds our minimum. This ensures that fuel pods have a minimum amount of time between appearances (150 frames, or 5 s):

```
if gc.fuelPod.framesSinceLastAppearance >=
  gc.fuelPod.appearanceRangeFrames.min
then
  local num = math.random(1, 100);
  if num >= 95 or gc.fuelPod.framesSinceLastAppearance >=
    gc.fuelPod.appearanceRangeFrames.max
  then
    gc.fuelPod.framesSinceLastAppearance = 0;
    gc.showFuelPod();
  end
end
```

If it exceeds the minimum, then a random value between 1 and 100 is chosen. If that value is greater than 95, which means that a fuel pod will appear only 5% of the time it's eligible to, then it will be shown. Alternatively, if you go 600 frames (20 s), which is the maximum time allowed to elapse between appearances, then a fuel pod will be shown for sure.

Once you determine it's time to show the fuel pod, the counter is reset and showFuelPod() is called to actually show it—and that's the next method you'll look at, as luck would have it!

showFuelPod

When processFuelPod() decides that it is time to show a fuel pod, showFuelPod() is called.

```
function gc:showFuelPod()

  utils:log("gameCoreMainLoop", "showFuelPod()");
```

First, do a bit of logging for debugging purposes.

```
local whichTile = math.random(1, #gc.levelData[gameData.level][18]);
local tileCoordinates = gc.levelData[gameData.level][18][whichTile];
```

Next, decide where the fuel pod will appear. The 18th row of data in the level definition provides a list of tile coordinates where a fuel pod may appear. Randomly choose a number between 1 and the length of the array that is the 18th row. Once we know which tile it is, we get a reference to it in tileCoordinates. We now can easily access the x and y values through that variable.

```
gc.fuelPod.sprite.isVisible = true;
gc.fuelPod.sprite.alpha = 1;
gc.fuelPod.sprite.x = 32 * (tileCoordinates.x - 1);
gc.fuelPod.sprite.y = (32 * (tileCoordinates.y - 1)) - 16;
```

Only a single sprite is associated with the fuel pod, so it is made visible and its alpha value reset to full opacity. The physical coordinates of the fuel pod are calculated much like they were in processColonist().

```
gc.fuelPod.rotate();
```

The fuel pod begins to spin by calling its rotate() method, which you'll recall from early chapters uses a transition to accomplish the spin.

```
transition.to(gc.fuelPod.sprite, {
  time = 10000, alpha = 0,
  onComplete = function(inTarget)
    inTarget.isVisible = false;
    inTarget.x = -1000;
    inTarget.y = -1000;
  end
});
```

Last, you need to transition the fuel pod so it gradually fades out of view over the course of 10 seconds. When it is completely faded out, the sprite is hidden and moved off screen to avoid collision events with the ship (since it is still simulated by the physics engine even when invisible).

processAlienUFO

The processAlienUFO() method should already look familiar to you because it is virtually identical to processFuelPod():

```
function gc:processAlienUFO(inEvent)

  if gc.alienUFO.sprite.isVisible == false then
    gc.alienUFO.framesSinceLastAppearance =
      gc.alienUFO.framesSinceLastAppearance + 1;
    if gc.alienUFO.framesSinceLastAppearance >=
      gc.alienUFO.appearanceRangeFrames.min
    then
      local num = math.random(1, 100);
      if num >= 95 or gc.alienUFO.framesSinceLastAppearance >=
        gc.alienUFO.appearanceRangeFrames.max
      then
        gc.alienUFO.framesSinceLastAppearance = 0;
        gc.showAlienUFO();
      end
    end
```

As you can see, the overall structure and flow is the same; the only differences, quite reasonably, are the variables used and the method called when it's time to show a UFO, showAlienUFO().

Because it is essentially what I've already dissected, I'll keep this brief and move on to the next method, which is considerably different than any other: showAlienUFO().

showAlienUFO

The showAlienUFO() method begins very much like showFuelPod() did:

```
function gc:showAlienUFO()

  utils:log("gameCoreMainLoop", "showAlienUFO()");

  local whichTile = math.random(1, #gc.levelData[gameData.level][19]);
  local tileCoordinates = gc.levelData[gameData.level][19][whichTile];
```

After a bit of logging, you then determine which tile represents the alien's starting point. This time, Row 19 contains the list of tiles where the alien can appear, and you'll again randomly choose one of those.

```
gc.alienUFO.sprite.isVisible = true;
gc.alienUFO.sprite.y = 32 * tileCoordinates.y;
```

Next, the alien is made visible and its physical y location set based on the selected tile's y grid location.

But what about the x location? Why isn't that set? The next block of code handles that:

```
if tileCoordinates.x == 1 then
  gc.alienUFO.sprite.x = 0 - gc.alienUFO.sprite.width;
  gc.alienUFO.exitPoint = display.contentWidth + gc.alienUFO.sprite.width;
else
  gc.alienUFO.sprite.x = display.contentWidth + gc.alienUFO.sprite.width;
  gc.alienUFO.exitPoint = 0 - gc.alienUFO.sprite.width;
end
```

The x location of the selected tile will be one of two values: 1 or 25, those being the bounds of the tile locations. However, you want the alien to start a little bit off screen so that it appears to fly in from one side or the other and not just immediately appear on the edge of the screen, as would happen if you used the 1 or 25 values.

Therefore, if the value is 1, the alien will appear from the left side. To get the physical value you just need to subtract the width of the alien's sprite from 0, which puts the alien off screen to begin with. The exit point—that is, the physical location the alien will be moving toward—is then simply the width of the screen plus the width of the alien's sprite.

When the tile x value is 25 we do the same sort of thing in reverse: this time, the alien's starting point is off the right side of the screen and its exit point is off the left, so the calculations are the reverse of what they are for tile x value 1.

```
local firePoint = math.random(1, display.contentWidth);
```

The other thing to decide is where along the alien's line of travel from one side of the screen to the other it will fire a plasma ball at the player's ship. This is a simple random choice using the entire range of the alien's movement as the bounds of the number chosen.

The next step is to make the alien move from its starting point to that chosen firing point:

```
gc.alienUFO.tween = transition.to(gc.alienUFO.sprite, {
  time = 3500, x = firePoint,
  onComplete = function()
    gc.plasmaBall.sprite.isVisible = true;
    gc.plasmaBall.sprite.x = gc.alienUFO.sprite.x;
    gc.plasmaBall.sprite.y = gc.alienUFO.sprite.y;
    gc.plasmaBall.tween = transition.to(
      gc.plasmaBall.sprite, {
        time = 3000, x = gc.ship.sprite.x, y = gc.ship.sprite.y,
        onComplete = function()
          gc.plasmaBall.sprite.isVisible = false;
          gc.plasmaBall.sprite.x = -1000;
          gc.plasmaBall.sprite.y = -1000;
        end
      }
    );
```

This transition occurs over 3.5 seconds. Once the firing point is reached, then the alien has to fire the plasma ball. Its sprite is unhidden and its starting location is the same as the alien's. Next, transition the plasma ball toward the player's ship over the course of 3 seconds. As you will see in Chapter 8, if the plasma ball collides with the ship then the player is dead, but if the plasma ball reaches the location of the ship without a collision then it is simply hidden and moved off screen. Note that the location to which the plasma ball is moving, which is the player's current location, may not be the location of the ship when the plasma ball arrives, as the player can be moving all this time; that's why a collision isn't guaranteed.

The final step is to continue moving the alien toward its exit point:

```
gc.alienUFO.tween = transition.to(gc.alienUFO.sprite, {
   time = 3500, x = gc.alienUFO.exitPoint,
   onComplete = function()
      gc.alienUFO.sprite.isVisible = false;
      gc.alienUFO.sprite.x = -1000;
      gc.alienUFO.sprite.y = -1000;
      gc.alienUFO.frameSinceLastAppearance = 0;
   end
  });
 end
});
```

The interesting thing about this implementation is that the movement of the alien is not a constant linear speed. It will sometimes move fast and sometimes move slowly, and oftentimes will be seen to speed up or slow down after firing its plasma ball. That's because the location from which the plasma ball is fired can be anywhere across the width of the screen, but it will always take the alien 3.5 seconds to move to that point and then off screen from it. If the firing point chosen is 600, for example, and the alien is coming in from the right, that means it will move roughly 200 pixels in 3.5 seconds. It will then fire its plasma ball and move off screen, which means it will move roughly 600 pixels to the left, but it will do that in the **same** 3.5 seconds it took to get to the firing point. Therefore, it will appear to move on screen slowly, fire, and then accelerate off screen.

The way the alien moves is deliberate: it makes the alien a bit more unpredictable and harder to avoid than if it was moving at a constant speed. Since a collision with the alien is bad news for the player, this adds a little bit of challenge, and to me at least, makes the alien a little more visually interesting.

showDeadPopup

When the player dies, showDeadPopup() is responsible for showing the popup message asking if she wants to retry the level or quit the game. The method itself is very simple:

```
function gc:showDeadPopup()

  if gc.popup == nil then

    gc.popup = native.showAlert(
      "Oops", "You died. Tough luck!", { "Try Again", "Quit" },
      function(inEvent)
```

```
        gc.popup = nil;
        if inEvent.action == "cancelled" then
          storyboard.gotoScene("menuScene", "zoomOutIn", 500);
        else
          if inEvent.index == 1 then
            gc.resetLevel();
          else
            storyboard.gotoScene("menuScene", "zoomOutIn", 500);
          end
        end
      end
    );

  end

end
```

First, a check is done to ensure the popup isn't already showing, because this method will be called with every subsequent enterFrame event, and clearly you only want to show the popup the first time through. Assuming it isn't, the Native UI API that Corona provides then will be used to show an alert message. This API is a wrapper around a few platform-specific user interface elements. You can show an alert message, as is done in this method, as well as opening the default mail or SMS application, the application store for the platform, or a number of other UI-related functions (more details on this in the "More on Native UI" section of this chapter).

The alert message used here is a simple popup with a title, some text, and one or more buttons the user can click. The title and text are the first two arguments to native.showAlert(), and the third is an array of one or more buttons (up to five). The first button is considered the default and is colored or otherwise displayed differently to set it apart.

The fifth argument to native.showAlert() is a callback function, inlined in this case. First, it nills the gc.popup variable so that the popup can be shown again when needed. The action attribute will be the value "cancelled" or "clicked". When "cancelled", that indicates that the user closed the alert in some way other than clicking one of the buttons (e.g., clicking the X to close the window in the simulator). That case is handled as clicking Quit is: the game transitions to the menu scene.

If action wasn't "cancelled" then it must have been "clicked", so now the code looks at the index attribute of inEvent to determine which button was clicked. If it was the first one, the Try Again button, then the level is reset and the player can try again. If it was Quit then, again, the menu scene is shown.

showEnteredBayPopup

Similar to showDeadPopup() is showEnteredBayPopup(), seen when the player's ship comes into contact with the landing bay of the mothership. This case requires a bit more work, but not too much more.

```
function gc:showEnteredBayPopup()

  if gc.popup == nil then

    gameData.score = gameData.score + (gc.ship.colonistsOnboard * 100);
```

First, ensure the popup isn't already showing. Assuming it's not, add a value to the player's score based on how many colonists are on the ship.

```
if gc.levelData[gameData.level + 1] == nil then

  storyboard.gotoScene("endingScene", "zoomOutIn", 500);
```

Next, a check is done to see if there is a next level. If there isn't, then the game is over and the endingScene is shown. Otherwise:

```
else

  gameData.level = gameData.level + 1;
  saveGameData();
```

The current level number is incremented and the game data saved so that if the player exits the game, she will continue on the next level, not the one she just completed.

Then, it's time to show an alert:

```
  gc.popup = native.showAlert(
    "Good work",
    gc.ship.colonistsOnboard .. " colonists rescued x 100 points =" ..
    gc.ship.colonistsOnboard * 100,
    { "Next Level", "Quit" },
    function(inEvent)
      gc.popup = nil;
      if inEvent.action == "cancelled" then
        storyboard.gotoScene("menuScene", "zoomOutIn", 500);
      else
        if inEvent.index == 1 then
          gc.drawCurrentLevel();
          gc.resetLevel();
        else
          storyboard.gotoScene("menuScene", "zoomOutIn", 500);
        end
      end
    end
  );

end
```

This works virtually the same as the showDeadPopup() alert code does. The text of the popup is a little more complex, showing the number of colonists rescued and how many points they earned, but otherwise it works the same, so no need to rehash that territory.

Instead, let's talk a little more about what the Native UI API has to offer that wasn't seen in Astro Rescue.

More on Native UI

As mentioned earlier, the Native UI API Corona offers a wrapper around some platform-specific UI elements, as well as some UI-related things. You saw `native.showAlert()`in this chapter, of course, and you've also seen how `native.systemFont` and `native.systemFontBold` are used to get a reference to the native font currently in use by the operating system when you're creating text objects.

Going along, in spirit at least, with `native.systemFont` and `native.systemFontBold` is the `native.getFonts()` method, which returns a list of the fonts available on the system. You can use this if you want to use a specific font but aren't sure if it's available. If it is, you can go ahead and use it, but if it's not available then you can, as one alternative, use `native.systemFont` as a fallback.

Along with the `native.showAlert()` method that you've already seen, there are a couple other methods that show a dialog of some sort to the user.

The `native.showPopup()` method allows you to show a dialog for a specified service. For example, if you want to allow the user to send an e-mail you can call `native.showPopup("email")`. On iOS devices, the popup is displayed within your app, but on Android, the app is suspended and the system's default app for sending e-mail is displayed. You can also pass `"sms"` for sending text messages, `"appStore"` to launch the default app store for the system, or `"rateApp"` to open a "Write Review" dialog (but only for iOS). You can also pass in options as the second argument to `native.showPopup()` to further define what you want to happen (consult the Corona docs for specifics, as the options differ from service to service).

The `native.showWebPopup()` allows you to open a web page (be it a local HTML file or a remote site) into a popup dialog. This accepts at a minimum the URL to open, with a number of options being available such as the size and location of the popup. This is good when, for example, you want to keep the instructions for your application current, so you post them on your web server and open them via `native.showWebPopup()` rather than including them in the application package itself.

In addition, `native.cancelAlert()` and `native.cancelWebPopup()` allow you to programmatically close an alert dialog or web page dialog; for example, if you want it to automatically dismiss itself after 15 seconds of no interaction by the user.

In addition to dialogs, the Native UI API allows you to create a handful of native widgets.

The `native.newMapView()` method allows you to create a `MapView` component to show a map and provides a `DisplayObject` wrapper so you can manipulate it much like any other `DisplayObject`. In contrast to `native.showWebPopup`, which opens a web page in a popup dialog, there is also `native.newWebView()`, which creates a `DisplayObject`, like `native.newMapView()` does, to give you an object you can manipulate that shows a web page in it.

The `native.newTextField()` and `native.newTextBox()` methods are similar in that both create an element for the user to enter text into, again with a `DisplayObject` wrapper so you can manipulate it. The difference is that `native.newTextField()` creates a multi-line, scrollable area for the user to enter text in while `native.newTextBox()` creates a single-line entry area.

> **Note**   One big difference with these native objects is that unlike most other `DisplayObjects`, they always appear on top of other `DisplayObject` and can't be placed into `DisplayGroups`. You can use most of the typical `DisplayObject` methods to manipulate them, but they do not obey the usual `DisplayObject` hierarchy. This is true of all native components.

Last, there are a few miscellaneous functions available to you in this namespace.

The `native.requestExit()` method closes the application on Android gracefully without terminating the underlying application process. In general, it is better to use this rather than `os.exit()`, as is done in Astro Rescue, since it'll make application relaunch faster (and, as per my earlier admonition, will cause your app to be rejected for publication in Apple's App Store for sure). However, if you truly intend to shut the application down, as is the case when you exit Astro Rescue, it is usually better to terminate the process entirely rather than continue to use some amount of memory, in case the user wants to use the app again.

The `native.setActivityIndicator()` method is used to show a platform-specific activity indicator that causes touch events to be ignored while it is visible. Calling this method with `true` shows it; `false` hides it.

Last, the `native.getProperty()` and `native.setProperty()` methods allow you to get and set platform-specific properties, which are called **environment variables** on desktop systems. However, at the time of this writing, only iOS supports this, and only a small set of properties are recognized.

Summary

In this chapter, you looked at the main game loop of Astro Rescue and saw how it triggers most of the core action of the game. You also got a look at a few new physics and math functions. Last, you saw the Native UI functionality Corona provides for interacting with the underlying operating system's native user interface.

In Chapter 7, you'll dive into the aspects of player control and see how the flags used to determine player movement in the main game loop are set when the player touches the screen and/or uses the accelerometer.

The Game, Part 3: Player Control Input

In the now-classic 1983 movie **WarGames,** teenaged hacker-extraordinaire (relatively speaking!) David Lightman hacks into the powerful military computer WOPR and accidentally sets off a chain of events that propels the world toward potential nuclear war. In the climactic final scene, David forces WOPR to play a series of tic-tac-toe games against itself to show that some games inevitably lead to no winner (just like nuclear war, get it?).

While great as a conclusion to a movie, a computer playing itself in tic-tac-toe isn't the most exciting prospect from a purely fun video game perspective. Video games are made for **humans** to play, whether against the computer (to prove the superiority of mankind?) or against other meat bags. Therefore, a key concept in game development is, naturally enough, getting input from the user.

Astro Rescue is of course no exception: the player needs to be able to pilot the ship, rescue colonists, and escape destruction at the hands (err, tentacles?) of the alien foe. Whether it uses touchscreen control or accelerometer control, it wouldn't be much of a game without user input—it would just be another closing scene for another 80s movie! So this chapter, while really not that long, is all about this important topic.

Handling Touch Input

As you'll recall, Astro Rescue allows two modes of user input: touchscreen-only and accelerometer (plus touchscreen) as selected by the player from the settings scene. Touch events and accelerometer events are handled in two separate methods of the gameCore object, and those methods are found in the gameCoreInputEvents.lua file. Let's start with the touch event handler:

```
function gc:touch(inEvent)

  if gc.phase ~= gc.PHASE_FLYING and gc.phase ~= gc.PHASE_LANDED then
    return;
  end
```

The only time touch events should be handled when the gameScene is active is if the game is in the flying or landed (sitting on a landing pad) phase. The flying-around part makes sense; obviously the player needs to control the ship, but why when landed, too? Simple: The player needs to be able to take off again! Vertical thrust events need to occur or they'll be stuck on the ground.

Touch "began" Handling

You'll be handling touch events on the player's initial press on the screen in this branch, which makes sense given that thrust is a continual thing as long as he keeps his finger on the screen, so the next line of code we encounter in this method is:

```
if inEvent.phase == "began" and gc.ship.fuel > 0 then
```

Recall when you looked at the main game loop that there are flags that indicate which way the ship is thrusting, if any. Those flags will be set in this method, but they only need to be set once because the main game loop will continue to apply movement until the flags are unset; there's no need to keep updating anything here. Therefore, you only want to do the work here if we're in the began phase. In addition, the ship can't thrust if there's no fuel, so that is factored in as well.

Vertical Thrust

Next, the game needs to determine which of the on-screen controls were actually touched:

```
if inEvent.target == nil or inEvent.target.controlName == "vertical" then
```

The second clause in that or logic is obvious: a touch on the vertical thruster control should result in vertical thrust. But what about checking for nil? How does that make sense? Remember that when using accelerometer control, the player will touch the screen to initiate vertical thrust. In that situation, no specific target is tapped because the whole screen is registered as the listener for the touch events. The target attribute of the incoming event object is therefore nil, so you need to check for that and handle it the same way as the explicit vertical thrust arrow control.

```
gc.ship.thrustVertical = true;
```

The vertical thrust flag is set to true, so the main game loop will apply that thrust and move the ship accordingly.

```
if gc.phase == gc.PHASE_LANDED then
  gc.phase = gc.PHASE_FLYING;
end
```

The other part of the vertical thrust equation is in the case where the ship is on a landing pad already. There, the logic is simple: get 'em in the air again! The phase is flipped to the flying phase and, as with everything else, the main game loop takes care of the rest.

Left and Right Thrust

Now, what about the left and right thrust controls? Easy enough:

```
elseif inEvent.target.controlName == "left" and gc.phase ~= gc.PHASE_LANDED then
```

As with the vertical thrust, if there's no gas left then the ship is dead in the water. Unlike the vertical thrust, however, we only allow left and right thrust is the ship **is not** on a landing pad. If that clause wasn't part of the logic, then the player could move the ship while on the landing pad and could easily find himself crashing into a wall, so the code won't allow that. After all, a rocket goes up off a launching pad before it starts moving down range toward its orbit, right?

```
gc.ship.thrustLeft = true;
```

The thrustLeft flag gets set and you're good to go.

Right thrust is handled precisely the same way as left thrust:

```
elseif inEvent.target.controlName == "right" and gc.phase ~= gc.PHASE_LANDED then
  gc.ship.thrustRight = true;

end
```

That also closes out the logic for the began touch event.

Touch "ended" Handling

Next up is what happens when a touch event ends:

```
elseif inEvent.phase == "ended" then

  if inEvent.target == nil or inEvent.target.controlName == "vertical" then
    gc.ship.thrustVertical = false;
  elseif inEvent.target.controlName == "left" then
    gc.ship.thrustLeft = false;
  elseif inEvent.target.controlName == "right" then
    gc.ship.thrustRight = false;
  end

end
```

At the end of the day, it's really nothing but doing the exact opposite of what we do for the began event: setting the flags to false when the player lifts his finger off a specific control element.

When All Is Said and Done . . .

The last step is to deal with audio and animations:

```
gc:activateDeactivateSoundsAndAnimations();
```

I'll describe this method later, but for now just keep in mind that it is responsible for playing (or stopping) the thruster sound as well as starting (or stopping) the correct thruster flame animation sequence for the ship.

Handling Accelerometer Input

When the user wants to play with accelerometer controls, the `accelerometer()` event handler method comes into play. It's a surprisingly small bit of code, beginning with this chunk:

```
function gc:accelerometer(inEvent)

  if gc.phase ~= gc.PHASE_FLYING then
    return;
  end
```

As when handling touch input, there's nothing to do when the ship is on a landing pad. The difference here is that since `accelerometer` controls left and right movement only, and that movement is only allowed when flying, there's no need to check specifically if the ship is on a landing pad because even if it is, there's no work to be done here.

```
if gc.ship.fuel > 0 then
```

Once again, the game will only allow movement if the ship has some fuel left, for obvious reasons!

Tilting to the Right

Now, the trick here is to see how far the device is tilted in a given direction. That's easy to do by interrogating the `xInstant` or `yInstant` attributes of the event object, which provide the instantaneous acceleration of the device. In practical terms, that means how far the device is tilted.

There is a trick, though! Have a look at Figure 7-1.

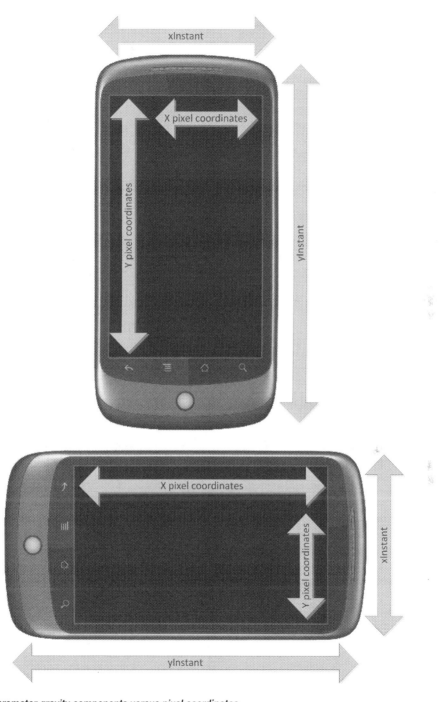

Figure 7-1. Accelerometer gravity components versus pixel coordinates

You have to remember that Astro Rescue is played in landscape orientation only, as seen on the bottom of Figure 7-1. Notice how the X pixel coordinates always run left to right across the screen, regardless of which orientation the device is held in?

That isn't true of the two gravity attributes, however. The xInstant attribute always means the tilt of the device, left to right, **relative to portrait mode** (and yInstant conversely measures tilt up and down, relative to portrait mode). If you rotate the device from portrait to landscape mode, xInstant still measures left and right tilt, and most importantly, **it's still relative to portrait mode**.

All this ultimately means is that when in landscape mode, it's not xInstant we care about, as it would be in portrait mode; it's yInstant. That attribute still measures the tilt of the device up and down, but that's relative to portrait mode, which happens to be left and right now, **relative to the player**.

Once that trick is understood, it's a simple matter of seeing how far the device is tilted:

```
if inEvent.yInstant > .2 then
  gc.ship.thrustLeft = true;
  gc.ship.thrustRight = false;
```

The value of yInstant (and xInstant for that matter) is a value from zero to whatever the maximum the device's hardware provides. What value to use here is completely a trial-and-error thing: .2 feels about right. It ensures that the ship responds to tilts, but not too much. We don't want the slight movements the player's hands subconsciously make to trigger ship thrust, but we don't want him to have to tilt the device so far that he can no longer see the screen, either. When the yInstant value is positive, that means the device is being tilted to the right (again, relative to the point of view of the player), so thrust comes out from the left.

Tilting to the Left

The only difference between checking for left tilt is that the values returned by yInstant are now negative:

```
elseif inEvent.yInstant < -.2 then
  gc.ship.thrustLeft = false;
  gc.ship.thrustRight = true;
```

Otherwise, it is handled the same except that the thrustRight flag is now set to true, of course.

Neutral Tilt

Neutral tilt, or more precisely, the **lack** of tilt, is the last condition you need to account for.

```
    else
      gc.ship.thrustLeft = false;
      gc.ship.thrustRight = false;
    end
  end

end
```

In this case, both flags need to be set to false so the main game loop knows that the ship is not moving anymore; it's effectively in a neutral state.

Again, Out of the Bullpen to Close It out . . .

As with the touch handler, there's one last line in the accelerometer handler:

```
gc:activateDeactivateSoundsAndAnimations();
```

And wouldn't you know, that's the very next thing you need to look at!

Updating Audio and Animations

Once all the flags have been set, whether in the touch handler or the accelerometer handler, the remaining task is to turn the thruster sound on or off and to start the correct animation on the ship. The activateDeactivateSoundsAndAnimations() method is called for precisely that purpose:

```
function gc:activateDeactivateSoundsAndAnimations()

  if gc.ship.thrustVertical == false and gc.ship.thrustLeft == false and
    gc.ship.thrustRight == false
  then
    if gc.sfx.thrustersChannel ~= nil then
      audio.stop(gc.sfx.thrustersChannel);
      gc.sfx.thrustersChannel = nil;
    end
  else
    if gc.sfx.thrustersChannel == nil then
      gc.sfx.thrustersChannel = audio.play(gc.sfx.thrusters, { loops = -1 });
    end
  end
end
```

The first step is to deal with the thruster sound. It's a simple enough block of code: if none of the thrust flags are true, then check to see if the thruster sound is playing, as denoted by gc.sfx. thrustersChannel being nil or not. If it's not, then audio.stop() is called to stop the sound and the reference nilled.

If any of the flags are true, then again you check if the sound is playing already. If it's not (when gc.sfx.thrustersChannel is nil), then start it playing via audio.play(). Piece of cake!

The next step that needs to be done here is to turn on the correct animation sequence for the ship based on which direction(s) thrust is being applied. To do so, you will need to examine the values of the three thrust flags:

```
local tV = gc.ship.thrustVertical;
local tL = gc.ship.thrustLeft;
local tR = gc.ship.thrustRight;
```

There is no technical reason that requires these three variables. In other words, the code would work just fine if instead of tV you used gc.ship.thrustVertical. The only reason I wrote it this way is that it makes the logic checks that follow more concise and easier to read.

> **Tip**   It's also true, however, that there is a small performance gain from doing this. The Lua interpreter won't have to go through a longer scope chain lookup in getting the values while determining the outcome of these if statements, since they are all local and so are as close as possible to their usage in terms of scope. This is a good habit to get into, especially when it makes the code less verbose and, in my opinion at least, easier to follow. That being said, this is what you'd call a micro-optimization, and unless it's in a tight loop, which this isn't, it likely will have virtually no impact on overall performance. But if nothing else, it's a very good thing to know and keep in mind in case you do find a performance issue you need to resolve.

Once we have those three variables, we can begin determining which thrust animation to set:

```
if tV == true and tL == false and tR == false then
  gc.ship.sprite:setSequence("thrustUp");
  gc.ship.sprite:play();
```

If only the `gc.ship.thrustVertical` flag, or `tV` here, is `true`, then the ship is only thrusting upward.

```
elseif tV == false and tL == true and tR == false then
  gc.ship.sprite:setSequence("thrustRight");
  gc.ship.sprite:play();
```

Similarly, `gc.ship.thrustLeft` (`tL`) tells us if it's time to turn on the `thrustRight` animation.

> **Note**   The flags tell us in what direction thrust is extending out from the ship, while the sequence name tells us which direction the ship is actually moving. Remember that they will always be opposite, so when `thrustLeft` is `true`, the flames are coming out from the left side of the ship, pushing it right, so `thrustRight` is the correct animation sequence.

```
elseif tV == false and tL == false and tR == true then
  gc.ship.sprite:setSequence("thrustLeft");
  gc.ship.sprite:play();
```

The same holds true for the `gc.ship.thrustRight` (`tR`) flag, which results in the `thrustLeft` animation being used.

```
elseif tV == true and tL == true and tR == false then
  gc.ship.sprite:setSequence("thrustUpRight");
  gc.ship.sprite:play();
```

The ship can also be moving upward and to the right, which means both `tV` and `tL` would be `true`.

```
elseif tV == true and tL == false and tR == true then
  gc.ship.sprite:setSequence("thrustUpLeft");
  gc.ship.sprite:play();
```

It can also be moving upward and to the left, of course.

```
  else
    gc.ship.sprite:setSequence("noThrust");
    gc.ship.sprite:play();
  end

end
```

Last, if none of the three flags are set, then the ship is not thrusting at all, and is in fact falling toward the ground. In this case there are no flames coming out, which is the noThrust animation sequence.

More on Input Handling with Corona

The user input requirements for Astro Rescue aren't very intensive, but Corona offers quite a bit more than what you've seen in this chapter.

The event object passed into the accelerometer() method, for example, contains a host of other attributes that may be of interest to you:

- deltaTime tells you how long, in seconds, it has been since the last accelerometer event.

- isShake will return true if the device was shaken by the user. However, the meaning of the term **shake** is dependent on the underlying operating system and even the device itself.

- xGravity and yGravity provide the amount of acceleration due to gravity in the x and y directions, similar to xInstant and yInstant, but xGravity and yGravity are measures over a longer period of time than those two. There are also zInstant and zGravity attributes that measure acceleration for the z axis (toward and away from the user).

There are also a number of additional attributes for touch events that were not used in Astro Rescue, including:

- time is the time in milliseconds at which the touch event occurred, as measured since the application started.

- x and y give you the coordinates of the touch event. Related to this is the xStart and yStart attributes, which tell you where the touch began. This is useful in situations where you want to track movement relative to the "began" phase of a touch. For example, say you want to determine if the place where the player lifts his finger is to the right of where he initially put his finger down. You might do something like:

```
if inEvent.phase == "ended" then
  if inEvent.x > inEvent.xStart then
    print("to the right");
  end
end
```

Although in a sense tangential to user input, you can also listen for events that deal with device orientation. Events of type "orientation" receive an event object with a delta and type attribute. The delta attribute gives you the number of degrees of difference between the orientation switched from and the orientation switched to. The type attribute returns one of "portrait", "landscapeLeft", "portraitUpsideDown", "landscapeRight", "faceUp", or "faceDown", indicating the new orientation of the device.

The other type of user input often seen in mobile applications nowadays is gyroscope input, at least on devices containing a gyroscope. Many of the same types of attributes for the previously discussed input events are present on the event object for a gyroscope event, such as deltaTime and of course name (which has a value of, unsurprisingly, "gyroscope"). Also provided are xRotation, yRotation , and zRotation attributes, which measure the rate of rotation around a given axis, measured in radians per second.

Summary

In this relatively brief chapter, I showed you the most important aspect (in some ways) of Astro Rescue: user input. You saw how both touch and accelerometer input events are handled, and how the various flags that are used in the main game loop are set based on that input.

You also explored some parts of the Corona API dealing with user input that aren't actually used in Astro Rescue, to give you a feel for what else you can do with it, including device orientation events and gyroscope input.

In Chapter 8, you'll look at collision handling. While this is another key element of Astro Rescue (and nearly any video game), it also uses a fairly small amount of code—further testament to the power Corona puts in your hands!

The Game, Part 4: Collision Events

In most action-oriented games, the notion of collision detection plays a primary role. Whether it's detecting when Mario lands on a Koopa Troopa, or when Pac-Man gobbles a power pellet, or when Master Chief mêlées with a Covenant grunt, being able to detect when two objects come into contact is part and parcel of many types of games.

Astro Rescue is no exception. The gameCoreCollisionEvents.lua source file contains the event handler function (along with some related "stuff") that is responsible for handling such events. In a very real sense, this code, although rather small in volume, is responsible for making the game work. I know, you could say that about the main game loop (and I think I may have, in fact!), but really, without collisions the game would just be a nifty little demonstration of Corona's drawing and input capabilities. With collisions, though, it becomes a real game.

When Worlds Collide

Collision detection is the ability to detect when two images, or sprites in typical game parlance, touch. For instance, in Astro Rescue you need to know when the player's ship is destroyed by the alien's plasma ball, or when the ship bumps into part of the landscape and therefore unceremoniously blows up.

There are a number of collision-detection algorithms out there to consider using—there's no one-size-fits-all answer. One type is brute force: your code could check each pixel of one image against each pixel of another, looking for any that share the same x/y coordinates. While this yields 100% accurate detection, it is slow, and more important, it isn't currently possible in Corona because you don't have pixel-level access to DisplayObjects (at the time of this writing at least).

Bounding Boxes Collisions

Another method, described visually in Figure 8-1, is called bounding boxes. It is a very simple method: it checks the coordinates of the four corners of the objects and nothing more. If the corner of one object is within the "bounds" of the other, a collision has occurred.

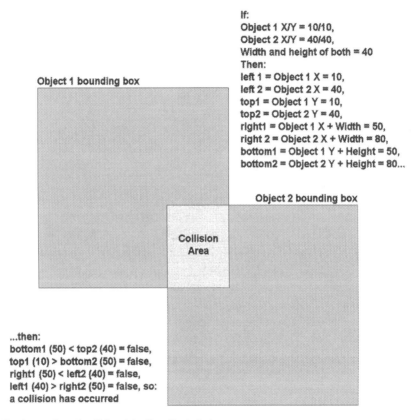

Object 1 bounding box

If:
Object 1 X/Y = 10/10,
Object 2 X/Y = 40/40,
Width and height of both = 40
Then:
left 1 = Object 1 X = 10,
left 2 = Object 2 X = 40,
top1 = Object 1 Y = 10,
top2 = Object 2 Y = 40,
right1 = Object 1 X + Width = 50,
right 2 = Object 2 X + Width = 80,
bottom1 = Object 1 Y + Height = 50,
bottom2 = Object 2 Y + Height = 80...

Object 2 bounding box

Collision Area

...then:
bottom1 (50) < top2 (40) = false,
top1 (10) > bottom2 (50) = false,
right1 (50) < left2 (40) = false,
left1 (40) > right2 (50) = false, so:
a collision has occurred

Figure 8-1. Bounding boxes–based collision detection, illustrated

As illustrated in Figure 8-1, each sprite has a square (or rectangular) area around it, called its bounding box, which defines the boundaries of the area the sprite occupies. Note how the lower-right corner of Object 1's bounding box is within the bounding box of Object 2. This represents a collision. You can detect a collision by running through a series of tests comparing the bounds of each object. If any of the conditions are untrue, then a collision cannot possibly have occurred. For instance, if the bottom of Object 1 is above the top of Object 2, there's no way a collision could have occurred. In fact, since you're dealing with a square or rectangular object, you have only four conditions to check, one for each corner, any one of which being false precludes the possibility of a collision. Simply put, if the corner of one object is within the bounding box of another, a collision has occurred.

This technique is certainly doable in Corona, and is in fact common, in addition to being rather speedy and easy to code. However, this algorithm does not yield perfect results because not all game objects are perfect rectangles. Some are circles, some might not fill a square entirely on one side, and so on.

For example, if this technique were to be used in Astro Rescue, you would have some situations where the plasma ball registers a hit on the ship, but if you watch carefully enough, they never actually physically touch. This can happen anywhere there is empty space around the edges of the ship sprite, because even though the corner of the plasma-ball sprite might cross the boundaries of the ship sprite, it only intrudes into the ship sprite's empty space, not actually the ship itself. In other words, the bounding boxes can collide without the object itself actually touching—it's enough to be considered a hit when, in reality, it's not.

Sometimes this is adequate. In many game situations, you really don't need any more precision than this; the gameplay won't be negatively impacted by this bit of imprecision. However, in Astro Rescue, it might lead to the player finding it unfair to have to be, in a sense, **too** accurate in their control movements, given the relatively small screen sizes of most mobile devices relative to the size of the game objects. It would be a little frustrating because it would require the player to be a little **too** perfect to avoid collisions (e.g., this would also affect flying near the ground). While this could be fixed with pixel-level detection, that's not available in Corona, at least not at the time of this writing.

So, if you want a more accurate collision detection, you need to do something else. Fortunately, in Corona, an answer can be found in the physics library.

Physics-Based Collisions

The one collision detection built into Corona (not counting bounding boxes, which you can always use) is implemented when using physics. Recall from our earlier discussions of the physics engine in Corona that using physics is entirely optional. Well, that's true, unless you need collision detection. In that case, say hello to the Physics API, whether you need to simulate physics or not!

Now, to be clear, you aren't forced to have a physics environment per se, meaning objects don't need to be affected by gravity and that sort of thing. That's what I meant when I said "whether you need to simulate physics or not." You can create physics bodies and simply not have them be affected by gravity, in which case you use them like plain old sprites, except that will activate their ability to receive notification of collision events.

To use collision, there are two steps you must take. First, create physics bodies for the objects that can be involved in collisions. This is absolutely no different than creating any bodies you've already seen. Second, register for notification of the "collision" event, either on specific objects or on the global Runtime instance—again, no differently than you've seen other events handled.

As with touch events, a collision event has a "began" and "ended" phase, which in this case means when contact begins and when contact is broken between the two objects. In addition, there are "preCollision" and "postCollision" events that you can optionally watch for that give you notification right before two objects are about to interact and right after they finish interacting.

Whenever one of these events occurs, the event object passed in contains two attributes, object1 and object2, which provides a reference to the tables of each object involved in the collision—in other words, a reference to the DisplayObjects involved in the collision. You can interrogate them as needed and act appropriately based on their identity. When you listen for these events on an object itself, you'll also get an attribute named other that references the other object the collision was with. This is handy because when handling collision events on Runtime, you will need to examine both object1 and object2 frequently to determine what to do, whereas with a local event handler on an object, you automatically know what one of the objects is (namely, the one to which you attach the listener), so your code can be a little simpler. In Astro Rescue, I use the global listener approach, so you'll see a little bit of this relatively more complex code. Therefore, my suggestion is **generally** to use local event listeners whenever you can, even if Astro Rescue doesn't!

The event passed in to a `postCollision` event handler, regardless of whether the handler is local to an object or global, also contains `force` and `friction` attributes that you can use to determine the force of the collision. Note, however, that both `preCollision` and `postCollision` can be "noisy," meaning you may get many of them for a given collision as the forces of the two objects begin to interact. Therefore, use them with caution.

> **Caution**   One important point to keep in mind is that if you attempt to manipulate the objects involved in a collision inside the collision event handler, you will almost certainly crash the Box2D physics engine underlying Corona. The workaround for this typically seen is to "wait a bit" by either setting a flag that some other code will read later on to do the manipulation, or use something like `timer.performWithDelay()` to defer the changes for some period of time.

Collisions, Visualized

Sometimes, when you're working on collision detection, it helps to be able to visualize the objects as Box2D sees them. This is easily accomplished by passing `"debug"` to the `physics.setDrawMode()` method, as called from `gameCore.lua`. Normally, `"normal"` is passed, so that you see the actual graphics as intended. However, passing `"debug"` results in something like what you see in Figure 8-2.

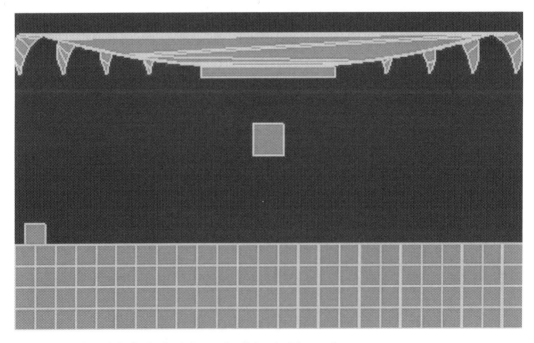

Figure 8-2. Corona's view of physics bodies in terms of collisions in debug mode

Now, you can clearly see how each `DisplayObject` is seen in terms of collision detection: our ship, the square floating in the middle, the ground tiles, and our colonist (the square to the left). All of these are simple bodies so they are just plain old squares. The mothership, by contrast, is a complex body made up of a number of segments, and you can see how each is outlined for collision detection purposes. Even the landing bay, the rectangle below and centered on the mothership, can clearly be seen.

Another option you have, which is shown in Figure 8-3, is to pass "hybrid" instead of "debug". This gives you something of a mixed view: you will see the usual graphics with the collision detection outlines superimposed on them. Either way, this trick, so to speak, can be extremely helpful when debugging why collisions aren't working as you expect in your games. Not only can you see the outlines, but also information about the physics body besides collision detection data, which is presented in beautiful TechniColor-coding these outlines for your pleasure:

- Orange outlines mean dynamic physics bodies

- Dark blue outlines are kinematic bodies

- Green outlines are static bodies

- Gray means a body is sleeping and not actively being simulated

- Light blue means joints in complex bodies

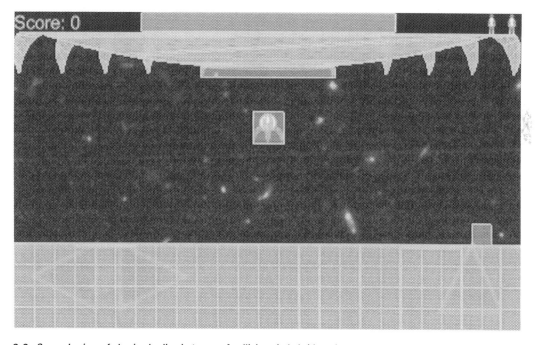

Figure 8-3. Corona's view of physics bodies in terms of collisions in hybrid mode

Forward unto the Code

With the high-level look at Corona collision detection out of the way, you can get into the code for handling them in Astro Rescue:

```
function gc:collision(inEvent)

  local colObj = inEvent.object1.objName;
  if colObj == "ship" then
    colObj = inEvent.object2.objName;
  end
```

The collision event is attached to the global `Runtime` object, as you saw when you looked at the `gameCore.lua` file, and it results in the `collision()` method of the `gc` object being called. The first task is to determine which objects collided. Since you know, by virtue of Astro Rescue's game play, that the ship is always involved in any given collision, the task here is to determine what the **other** object is. This is what I was talking about earlier: if the event handler were instead attached to the ship, then this wouldn't be necessary. However, since that's not the way I wrote the code (bad me!), this code effectively has to do what Corona does automatically when using a local handler. Fortunately, the code is simple enough: get the name (as set by the setup code way back in `gameCore.lua`) of `object1` into the variable `colObj` and see if it's our ship. If it is, then you know that the other object involved in the collision is referenced by `object2`, so get **its** name. Of course, if the name of `object1` **isn't** `"ship"`, then you already have the name of the other object in `colObj` and you're done.

```
if gc.phase ~= gc.PHASE_FLYING and colObj ~= "crash" then
  return;
end
```

Next, since collision events should only be processed when the ship is flying, and since collisions with anything that doesn't have a name `"crash"`, such as a fuel can, won't result in an explosion, you need to abort if these conditions aren't met.

These Are Bad, M'Kay? Crashing into Stuff

Assuming you get past that one quick check, the next step is to determine what the ship collided with and act accordingly. Of course, you only want to handle collisions during the `"began"` phase, so you check for that as well—first, in fact.

```
if inEvent.phase == "began" then

  if colObj == "crash" then

    utils:log("gameCoreCollisionEvents", "Crash");
    gc:showExplosion(gc.ship.sprite.x, gc.ship.sprite.y);
```

Any object with a name "crash", which includes the tiles that make up the ground, the mothership (not counting the landing bay part), the alien, and the plasma ball, results in a fiery death of our colony-rescuing hero. In that case, a call to the showExplosion() method, passing in the location of the ship, takes care of everything. You'll be looking at that method later in this chapter.

Set 'er Down Gently: Landing on a Pad

Of course, the ship may have come into contact with a landing pad instead, and that's what the next branch of the if statement that began in the last section is for. The name "pad" is what you look for in that case.

```
elseif colObj == "pad" then

  utils:log("gameCoreCollisionEvents", "Pad contact");
  local vX, vY = gc.ship.sprite:getLinearVelocity();
  if vX > 75 or vY > 75 then
    utils:log(
      "gameCoreCollisionEvents",
      "Pad crash (Too fast: vX(75)=" .. vX .. ", vY(75)=" .. vY .. ")"
    );
    gc:showExplosion(gc.ship.sprite.x, gc.ship.sprite.y);
  else
    utils:log("gameCoreCollisionEvents", "Safely landed");
    gc.ship.sprite:setSequence("noThrust");
    gc.ship.sprite:play();
    gc.ship.thrustVertical = false;
    gc.ship.thrustLeft = false;
    gc.ship.thrustRight = false;
    gc.phase = gc.PHASE_LANDED;
  end
```

Now, when the ship encounters a landing pad you have some further work to do because it may have been going too fast. After all, you're going through the effort of simulating physics in this game, which means you probably want **some** degree of realism to it. So, if the player attempts to land while going too fast, as indicated by the flashing warning sign in Figure 8-4, that's probably something that's not too good for our poor little ship—I mean, unless it's built out of unobtanium of course, as any good sci-fi fan knows!

Figure 8-4. JANE, STOP THIS CRAZY THING!

To make this determination, you examine the linear velocity of the ship, or how fast it's moving in the x and y directions. The getLinearVelocity() method is added to the ship's sprite DisplayObject when the physics body is added to it and returns two values, which are captured in the vX and vY variables. If either of these values is greater than the (arbitrary) threshold value 75, then that's bad news for the player. The code also logs the values, which is really more for testing purposes than anything else (it's how I was able to determine what a good threshold value was—just trial and error—but I could see what the values were when it "felt" right to me). Once again, showExplosion() is called in this case, too.

Assuming the player doesn't suffer a fiery death from too forceful a landing, though, you end up in the else branch. Here, the animation sequence of the ship is changed to turn off the thruster flames, and the three movement flags are set to false so that our main game loop stops moving the ship. Of course, the phase attribute of our gameCore object is changed to gc.PHASE_LANDED so that the rest of the code base will be aware of the fact that the ship has successfully landed, triggering the colonist to move toward the ship, assuming there's one near.

You're All Clear, Kid, Now Let's Blow This Thing and Go Home! Entering the Landing Bay

The next object that the player's ship can collide with is the landing bay of the mothership:

```
elseif colObj == "bay" then

  utils:log("gameCoreCollisionEvents", "Entered landing bay");
  gc:stopAllActivity();
  gc.phase = gc.PHASE_IN_BAY;
```

In this case, the only tasks necessary are to ensure that all game activity ceases, hence the call to `stopAllActivity()`, which you previously looked at, and to switch to `PHASE_IN_BAY` so the main loop will show the popup on its next iteration.

Err, Sorry, Sir: Hitting a Colonist

While entering the landing bay is a good thing—presuming colonists have been rescued—there is a much worse situation: what if the ship hits a **colonist?** That is decidedly less positive, well, for the colonist at least! I suppose if the player does this on purpose they may in fact be playing a different game that they may find more enjoyable . . . perhaps the game should detect if you've done this too many times and offer links to mental health professionals? Eh, I digress.

```
elseif colObj == "colonist" and gc.colonist.sprite.isVisible == true then

  gc.sfx.screamChannel = audio.play(gc.sfx.scream);

  gameData.score = gameData.score - 50;
  if gameData.score < 0 then
    gameData.score = 0;
  end
  gc.colonist.sprite.isVisible = false;
  gc.colonist.appearCounter = 0;
```

The test is whether the ship has in fact come into contact with the colonist, but also whether the colonist is visible or not. Remember that the game only ever hides the colonist, so there's a chance of a collision when the sprite is hidden, which you don't want. If these conditions are met then the game plays a little scream sound, and deducts some points from the player's score (that seems like the **least** we should do, right?!) The game also hides the colonist and resets the appearCount so the main loop starts counting down to when the colonist should be positioned and shown again.

> **Note**   The scream sound is the famous Wilhelm Scream, voiced by Sheb Wooley in 1951 for the movie **Distant Drums**. It is now a public-domain stock sound that has been used in many movies over the years, including the **Star Wars, Lord of the Rings,** and **Indiana Jones** series, as well as numerous video games.

Getting Gas Isn't Always a Social Faux Pas: Fuel Pods

The last branch in the `collision()` method deals with the situation where the ship comes into contact with a fuel pod.

```
    elseif colObj == "fuelPod" then

      gc.sfx.fuelPodPickupChannel = audio.play(gc.sfx.fuelPodPickup);
      gc:showMessage("Got Some Fuel");

      gc.fuelPod.sprite.isVisible = false;
      gc.fuelPod.sprite.x = -5000;
      gc.fuelPod.sprite.y = -5000;
```

```
      gc.ship.fuel = gc.ship.fuel + 50;
      if gc.ship.fuel > gc.fuelGauge.fill.width then
        gc.ship.fuel = gc.ship.maxFuel;
      end
      gc.updateFuelGauge();

    end

  end

end
```

Pretty simple stuff here: play the fuel pod pickup sound (the sound of a can of soda being opened) and a call to showMessage() to show the "Got Some Fuel" message with the 3-D expanding message effect. The game hides and moves the fuel pod offscreen to avoid any collisions occurring before it's shown again. It also updates the amount of fuel the ship has. This is slightly tricky in that the amount of fuel is also used when drawing the fuel gauge as its width, so you have to cap the amount of fuel to that width. Last, the call to updateFuelGauge(), which you'll get to shortly, is responsible for redrawing the fuel gauge with the correct new width so it fills up and shrinks like a status/progress bar typically does.

> **Note**   Always remember that making an object invisible doesn't necessarily stop collisions involving it from occurring, but moving it off-screen does. Also remember that the coordinates here are relative to the virtual screen size used for the game, so while–1000, –1000 might not be offscreen on a device with a physical screen size of 1280×1024, it will be if the virtual screen size is 800×480, as it is here.

Show Me The Boom!

Although at this point I have fully covered collision detection as used in Astro Rescue, there are two methods in the gameCoreCollisionEvents.lua source file that go along with collision detection, the first of which is showExplosion(), called any time the player's ship meets an early end, as shown in Figure 8-5.

Figure 8-5. That fireball probably looks pretty from inside the ship—if you can get past the AGONIZING BURNING SENSATION!

```
function gc:showExplosion(inX, inY, inCallback)

  utils:log("gameCoreCollisionEvents", "showExplosion()");

  gc.stopAllActivity();

  gc.phase = gc.EXPLODING;

  system.vibrate();
```

After some initial logging, all game activity is stopped via gc.stopAllActivity(); so that things like the alien, or a plasma ball, are done away with. The phase of the game is changed accordingly as well to effectively notify our main loop that the ship is in the process of exploding and its movements should be shut down, among other things.

On devices that support haptic feedback—that is, vibration—the call to system.vibrate() is used to cause a little vibration, perfect for an explosion event.

> **Note**   In the simulator, `system.vibrate()` results in a system beep being heard. On devices that don't support haptic feedback, nothing happens. For Android devices you need to include `android.permission.VIBRATE` in the `androidPermissions` section in your `build.settings` file. If you forget to do this, your app will **probably** be fine and the device just won't vibrate as expected (although you'll almost certainly see an exception in the logs about it). However, because of the Android security architecture, an exception **may** be thrown back to the application, resulting in you game unceremoniously crashing. This is true of any "trusted" function for which you need to specify a permission on Android devices. The bottom line is simply this: don't to forget to add permissions as necessary!

```
gc.explosion.sprite.isVisible = true;
gc.explosion.sprite.x = inX;
gc.explosion.sprite.y = inY;
gc.explosion.sprite:setSequence("exploding");
gc.explosion.sprite:play();
gc.explosion.callback = inCallback;
gc.explosion.sprite:addEventListener("sprite",
  function(inEvent)
    if inEvent.target.sequence == "exploding" and
      inEvent.phase == "ended"
    then
      gc.explosion.sprite.isVisible = false;
      gc.phase = gc.PHASE_DEAD;
    end
  end
);

gc.sfx.explosionChannel = audio.play(gc.sfx.explosion);

end
```

Showing the explosion is a simple matter of showing the sprite (remember there's a single sprite for the explosion; it is just moved around as needed) and positioning it at the x/y coordinates passed in, which happen to correspond to the center of the ship. The "exploding" animation sequence, the only one this sprite supports, is played, and you register a callback for when the animation sequence completes. When it does, the sprite is hidden and the game phase changed, which will result in the "You're dead" popup being shown by the main loop next time through. Oh yes, and what explosion wouldn't be complete without a bit of audio loudness? So, the explosion sound is played as well, and that's how you blow up the hero!

Are We on "E" Yet?

The final method to look at is responsible for updating the fuel gauge any time the amount of fuel on the ship changes, either due to the player activating thrusters or picking up a fuel pod:

```
function gc:updateFuelGauge()

  if gc.fuelGauge.fill ~= nil then
    gc.fuelGauge.fill:removeSelf();
    gc.fuelGauge.fill = nil;
  end
```

The gc.fuelGauge.fill field references the red bar in the middle of the fuel gauge, which is the part that expands and shrinks. While there are a number of ways this could be done, in terms of changing the size of the existing DisplayObject, or perhaps masking it somehow, I decided the easiest way is simply to recreate it with the appropriate new size. So, first, the existing one is destroyed:

```
  if gc.ship.fuel > 0 then
    gc.fuelGauge.fill = display.newRect(
      (gc.fuelGauge.shell.x - (gc.fuelGauge.shell.width / 2)) + 3,
      (gc.fuelGauge.shell.y - (gc.fuelGauge.shell.height / 2)) + 3,
      gc.ship.fuel, gc.fuelGauge.shell.height - 5
    );
    gc.fuelGauge.fill:setFillColor(255, 0, 0);
    gc.gameDG:insert(gc.fuelGauge.fill);
  end

end
```

Next, assuming the ship has some fuel left, a new DisplayObject is created, a new rectangle in this case. The x/y location is calculated based on the width of the outer white box and its center. This is done so that if I wanted to rearrange the status bar area of the game (which I did during development), I only had to move the "shell" portion, the outer white box, and the fill portion of the fuel gauge would automatically be positioned properly as well. The width of the new rectangle is the amount of fuel the ship has. Recall from earlier that the maximum amount of fuel the ship can have is dependent on the width of the fuel gauge itself, so these two values directly correspond to each other. The height is simply the height of the shell, minus a few pixels, so that the fill fits nice and snug inside the shell.

The fill color of the new rectangle is inserted into the gameDG DisplayGroup, and you have yourself a resized fuel gauge corresponding to the amount of fuel on the ship at that point.

Summary

In this chapter, you looked at how collisions are handled in Corona using the Physics API, as well as some alternative methods that could be used instead of that facility. You also saw how explosions are created and how the fuel gauge is updated as fuel is consumed.

In the next chapter, you'll wrap up your exploration of Astro Rescue by looking at endingScene.lua, which is where you find the screen the player sees when they win the game, along with a few new Corona tricks.

Chapter **9**

Wrapping Up

Welcome, my friend, to the final chapter in our exploration of Astro Rescue! You've seen a lot so far, gotten quite familiar with a large chunk of Corona SDK, and built a nice little game in the process. There's only one piece missing now, and that's the ending scene, the player's reward for a job well done!

It's not a particularly lengthy bit of code, but it does introduce a few new concepts, a few new things that Corona has to offer. So, let's not waste much time with preliminaries—let's dive right into things.

A Few Variables to Start

The last few chapters have been an exploration of the core code behind Astro Rescue. Of particular interest is to remember that they represent a chunk of code that in a sense piggybacks on a Storyboard API scene, meaning the core game code is decoupled from the scene code.

The benefit of that abstraction is that if you later decided not to use the Storyboard API at all, perhaps instead opting to write your own similar facility, you shouldn't have to alter the core code much, if at all. The tradeoff of course is a little more complexity (typical of most abstractions in programming).

The benefit of having it all be part of the scene, which is slightly less complexity in terms of less abstraction (vis-à-vis a scene object that then delegates work to functions it calls, possibly in another object), is good for smaller scenes, like the earlier title and menu scenes, and that goes for the ending scene here as well. As such, you're dealing with just a single source file this time, endingScene.lua, which begins innocuously enough:

```
local scene = storyboard.newScene();

local endingMusic;

local capturedImage;
```

You start off with just a few variables defined within the scope of this module. Of course, you have to create a new scene object, something you've seen plenty of times before. This scene will have its own music playing, so you'll define a variable to reference that. Last, you have captureImage, which has to do with making this scene work at all.

> **Tip**   There's nothing that says you can't use the decoupled approach while still only having one source file. Simply combine all the gameCore*.lua files into gameScene.lua without changing anything else and that's what you have. However, I would argue that doing so makes for messy code. Certainly, a source file of that length tends to be a lot more difficult to navigate. As with so many things in Corona, the choice is up to you, but my suggestion is to logically break your code into multiple source files along whatever boundaries make sense, regardless of whether you decouple anything in terms of the architecture of the code.

When I say "making this scene work," what does that actually mean? When you complete the game to reach the scene, you will be greeted with some cheery music, a final score and a little graphical effect all superimposed over a gradient-filled background. The effect I speak of is, roughly, like a spotlight bouncing back and forth across the text. In Figure 9-1, you can see the scene when the spotlight is pretty much centered on the screen.

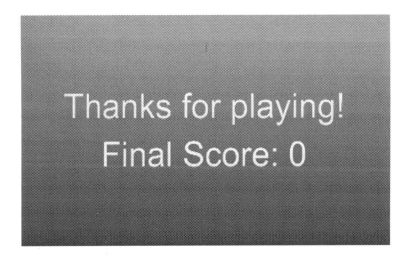

Figure 9-1. Spotlight centered

Over time, the spotlight bounces left and right, highlighting portions of the screen and reducing illumination on the other half. For example, in Figure 9-2, the spotlight is focused on the right side of the screen, leaving part of the left to be dimmed.

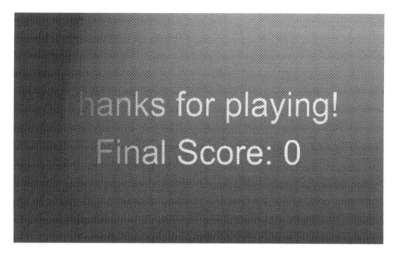

Figure 9-2. Spotlight to the right

Likewise, in Figure 9-3 you can see the spotlight focused on the left side of the screen, leaving the right side in the dark.

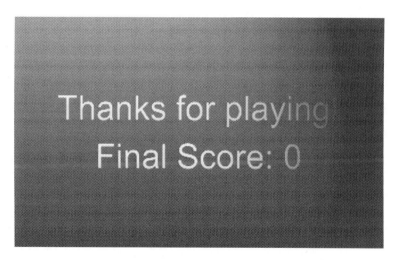

Figure 9-3. Spotlight to the left

Obviously, this is one of those times where the printed page just doesn't suffice, so if you haven't done so yet I'd suggest you take the time to play through the game to see this in action. Fortunately, if you're lazy, like me, then you'll just hit the thrust up button a few times to get through each level without rescuing any colonists to get to it quickly. Hey, we're programmers after all, not emergency rescue technicians—we can take a shortcut if we want!

The bouncing is a nice, gentle bounce, not a linear movement left and right. That movement, the gradient background, and the spotlight effect are all new Corona capabilities for you to check out!

Creating the Scene

You have to fill in the blanks, so to speak, for the scene's lifecycle methods now, beginning with createScene():

```
function scene:createScene(inEvent)

utils:log("endingScene", "createScene()");

endingMusic = audio.loadStream(utils:getAudioFilename("endingMusic"));
audio.play(endingMusic, { channel = 2, loops =- 1, fadein = 500 });
```

A little logging, and then the music immediately starts music playing. The getAudioFilename() method is again used, as it is everywhere you have to load audio resources, to abstract out any platform-specific issues that need to be dealt with. Once it's loaded, the music begins playing, with a slight fade-in that matches the scene transition time. It plays on a loop, using a specific channel for the same reasons as already discussed when you looked at the title and menu scenes.

Next, you have to create that gradient background:

```
local bgGradient = display.newRect(
  self.view, 0, 0, display.contentWidth, display.contentHeight
);
bgGradient:setFillColor(
  graphics.newGradient( { 255, 0, 0 }, { 0, 0, 0 } )
);
```

First, a rectangle is created that is sized to fill the screen. Next, the rectangle is filled, and what is passed to setFillColor() is not RGBA component values, as you saw in the menu scene, but is instead a gradient object created by a call to graphics.newGradient(), in this case a gradient that runs from red to black.

A gradient object can be used to fill many DisplayObjects, including text, but **not** including circles and rounded rectangles. A gradient has a starting color and an ending color, both of which you specify. Corona then creates all the steps between those two colors automatically. You can specify the starting and ending colors in a number of formats:

- { gray }: A shortcut for creating a grayscale color.
- { gray, alpha }: A shortcut for creating a grayscale color that also lets you control opacity.

※   { red, green, blue }: The typical RGB components, as shown in the ending scene code.

※   { red, green, blue, alpha }: RGB components again but now with the additional alpha (opacity) value.

The starting and ending colors are required, and you can then also optionally include a third argument to graphics.newGradient() that specifies the direction of the gradient. The default value, "down", is what is used in the ending scene. You can also specify "up", "left", or "right".

That's actually all there is to creating gradients with Corona! As I said, you can apply gradients to most things, including text, as you can see here:

```
local txt1 = display.newText(
  self.view, "Thanks for playing!", 0, 0, native.systemFontBold, 72
);
txt1:setReferencePoint(display.CenterReferencePoint);
txt1.x = display.contentCenterX;
txt1.y = display.contentCenterY - 50;
txt1:setTextColor(
  graphics.newGradient( { 255, 255, 255 }, { 255, 255, 0 } ) )
);
```

The first line of text is created just as you've seen text created in the past; nothing new or special here. The text is moved off the center of the screen by 50 pixels, and—spoiler alert—the next line of text will be moved down 50 pixels as well, which makes the entire two lines as a whole look to be centered nicely.

Once the text is created, the game creates a gradient to fill it with, this time running from white to yellow. It just makes the text look a little more interesting than the plain white text you saw in the main menu.

The second line of text is created in the same way:

```
local txt2 = display.newText(
  self.view, "Final Score: " .. gameData.score, 0, 0,
  native.systemFontBold, 72
);
txt2:setReferencePoint(display.CenterReferencePoint);
txt2.x = display.contentCenterX;
txt2.y = display.contentCenterY + 50;
txt2:setTextColor(
  graphics.newGradient( { 255, 255, 255 }, { 255, 255, 0 } ) )
);
```

Of course, the final score is shown on this line, but otherwise that and the vertical position are the only differences.

The next step is to ensure that the user will begin a new game next time by clearing all game data:

```
clearGameData();
```

That method was explored way back when you looked at `main.lua`. Just to refresh your memory, it is responsible for resetting the level to 1 and the score to 0, and then saving the game state file so those values are used next time they start a new game (or "continue" the game, which means the same thing at that point).

The next thing you have to add is the code that allows the spotlight effect to work as expected—at least, part of it:

```
capturedImage = display.captureScreen();
self.view:insert(capturedImage);
```

Now, you have to imagine the screen at this point in time: the background gradient was created, then the text, so right now the screen is in its final form, minus the spotlight. I'll jump ahead slightly and tell you that the spotlight effect is subtractive, not additive, meaning that rather than illuminating portions of the screen it's actually dimming areas, or excluding them from view—masking those parts, if you will.

To make the spotlight effect work you need to capture the complete image first, meaning the screen itself, as it appears without the spotlight in play.

That's what `display.captureScreen()` does. It takes a snapshot of the display as it currently exists. Yes, this is how you can take snapshots of your game! It gives you back a `DisplayObject`, with which you can then do whatever you want: anything you can do to a `DisplayObject` generally, including saving it to a file. To do so, pass `true` to `display.captureScreen()`, which actually saves it to your device's photo album as a JPEG file (or as a PNG if running in the simulator).

> **Note**   To be able to save a snapshot like this on Android, you need to add the `android.permission.WRITE_EXTERNAL_STORAGE` permission to your `build.settings` file.

When you call `display.captureScreen()`, you get a `DisplayObject` back as mentioned. This also means that, in the usual fashion with `DisplayObjects` created after others, it is on top of everything else currently on the screen.

Therefore, after this line of code executes, you have one screen-sized `DisplayObject` that has the background gradient and the two lines of text, but those individual objects are **not** children of it! It simply appears that way—they have the individual background rectangle with the gradient, and the two text objects are still there, but now obscured by the full-screen `DisplayObject`.

That leads to the next step in this process:

```
bgGradient:removeSelf();
bgGradient = nil;
txt1:removeSelf();
txt1 = nil;
txt2:removeSelf();
txt2 = nil;
```

This removes the original objects drawn to the screen, since you no longer need them.

Turning the Spotlight On

Now it's time to create that spotlight effect. To do so, you're going to make use of Corona's bit mask functionality. First, the code:

```
capturedImage:setMask(graphics.newMask("circlemask.png"));
capturedImage.maskDir = 1;
capturedImage.maskXNext = (display.contentWidth / 3);
capturedImage.maskXDir = 1;
capturedImage.maskScaleX = 4;
capturedImage.maskScaleY = 4;
```

Looks simple enough, right? I'll break it down, starting with the first line, and more specifically, the call to `graphics.newMask()`.

A bit mask, which is what `graphics.newMask()` creates, is a structure that allows you to "mask off" portions of an image. A bit mask is created from a mask image, such as `circlemask.png` used here, which you can see in Figure 9-4.

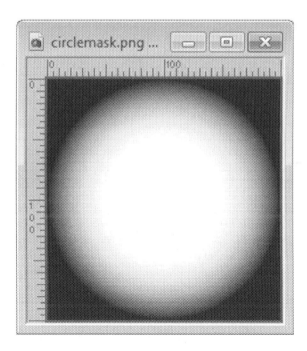

Figure 9-4. circlemask.png

The image is converted to grayscale internally by Corona, or it may already be grayscale, as is the case with `circlemask.png`. Any pixels in the mask image that are white will be transparent, any that are black are opaque, and any that are in between will have a varying degree of opacity. All you do then is apply the mask to a `DisplayObject` via a call to its `setMask()` method, which you can conceptualize as the mask image being superimposed over the target image. Then, the mask does its thing: any pixel in the mask image that is not black will allow the corresponding pixel in the target image to be visible, to varying degrees based on the level of gray of the pixel. Likewise, any pixel that is black in the mask image will cause the corresponding pixel in the target image to be blocked from view.

> **Note**   A bit mask image must follow two rules: its width and height must be even multiples of 4, and it must have a black border around it of 3 or more pixels in width.

By default, the mask image will be centered on the image it is applied to, which just so happens to be exactly what you want here. Just as important for our purposes here is the fact that the maskScaleX and maskScaleY attributes allow you to scale the mask. If you didn't do that, what you'd see is a fairly tiny little circle in the middle of the screen just kind of bouncing left and right. It wouldn't look so hot. By scaling it up, it largely fills the screen and only the edges around the circle, the black portions in the mask image, get obscured as the spotlight moves.

Get That Spotlight Moving!

Speaking of the spotlight moving, that's accomplished with our old friend the Transition API, and the fact that a mask can be moved, and that its x/y location is relative to the DisplayObject to which it is applied.

```
capturedImage.transition = function()
  capturedImage.tween = transition.to(capturedImage, {
    time = 2000, maskX = capturedImage.maskXNext,
    transition = easing.inOutQuad,
    onComplete = function()
      if capturedImage.maskXDir == 1 then
        capturedImage.maskXDir = 2;
        capturedImage.maskXNext = -(display.contentWidth / 3);
        capturedImage.transition();
      else
        capturedImage.maskXDir = 1;
        capturedImage.maskXNext = (display.contentWidth / 3);
        capturedImage.transition();
      end
    end
  });
end;
```

The maskDir, maskXNext, and maskXDir attributes, which are custom attributes added to the mask object that I intentionally didn't mention earlier when you saw the mask being created, are used to make the transition work. The maskDir attribute tells you which direction the mask is currently moving in. When it's a value of 1, the mask is moving right to left. When it's a 2, it's moving left to right.

We create a tween over a 2-second period of time that moves the mask from whatever its current location is (centered on the captured image initially) to the value of maskXNext. The value maskXNext is initially set to, (display.contentWidth / 3), results in the mask moving to the left of center a bit. When the tween completes, the direction is reversed and the mask is set to move to the right, a bit off-center.

The other trick here is the used of easing.inOutQuad as the transition easing function. Easing in general was discussed in Chapter 4, but as a refresher, it allows you to specify that the motion of a tween isn't linear but instead gives the impression of forces like friction and gravity affecting an object as it moves. In the case of the spotlight, it gradually slows down as it reaches its outer position (whether left or right of center), stops, and then begins moving in the other direction, only to repeat the slowdown as it reaches the other extreme. It's a nice, subtle little effect that looks a lot better than just a straight left-to-right motion at a constant velocity.

Of course, none of this would matter if not for:

```
capturedImage.transition();
```

That kicks off the animation and gets the spotlight moving.

As amazing as it seems, that's more or less all the code behind this scene! It doesn't take much to produce some relatively impressive things with Corona, something I hope by this point you've seen for yourself a number of times. However, even if most of what makes this scene what it is has been explored already, there are in fact a few more bits of code to look at.

Other Scene Methods

The remainder of the methods in this scene are all old friends, starting with willEnterScene():

```
function scene:willEnterScene(inEvent)

  utils:log("endingScene", "willEnterScene()");

end
```

Okay, admittedly, not much to see there! In enterScene(), which is next, there's only slightly more:

```
function scene:enterScene(inEvent)

  utils:log("endingScene", "enterScene()");

  Runtime:addEventListener("touch", scene);

end
```

The user can tap anywhere on the screen to exit this scene and return to the main menu, so you naturally need a touch event handler attached to the Runtime object, again calling the touch() method of the scene object.

What about exiting the scene, you ask? The exitScene() method is here for that, too:

```
function scene:exitScene(inEvent)

  utils:log("endingScene", "exitScene()");

  Runtime:removeEventListener("touch", scene);

  audio.stop(2);

  transition.cancel(capturedImage.tween);

end
```

Once the touch event listener is removed, the music is stopped. Once again, since this music was played on a specific channel, you need to stop that specific channel, unlike the sound effects during gameplay.

You also need to stop the animation of the spotlight. Since that's just a basic tween created with the Transition API, the `transition.cancel()` method does the trick, passing the reference to the tween stored on the `capturedImage DisplayObject` as a custom attribute.

There is also a `didExitScene()` handler, in case it's needed later, but for now it's not needed and is therefore just an empty "do-nothing" method.

```
function scene:didExitScene(inEvent)

  utils:log("endingScene", "didExitScene()");

end
```

Last, `destroyScene()` is present to clean up when the scene is destroyed by the Storyboard API and the title scene is shown again:

```
function scene:destroyScene(inEvent)

  utils:log("endingScene", "destroyScene()");

  audio.dispose(endingMusic);
  endingMusic = nil;

  capturedImage:removeSelf();
  capturedImage = nil;

end
```

This only leaves the `endingMusic` and the `capturedImage DisplayObject` to clean up, so once you use the appropriate API methods to remove them and `nil` out their references, you're good to go.

Touch Events

The touch handled method that was set up in `enterScene()` is the next method encountered as you walk through this source file.

```
function scene:touch(inEvent)

  utils:log("endingScene", "touch()");

  if inEvent.phase == "ended" then
    utils:log("endingScene", "Going to menuScene");
    storyboard.gotoScene("menuScene", "zoomOutIn", 500);
  end

  return true;

end
```

It's a standard touch handler, nothing special, that triggers a `storyboard.gotoScene()` call to transition back to the menu scene at the behest of the user.

Kicking It All Off

The only thing left to do, having fully defined the scene object with all its associated lifecycle methods and event handlers, is to add the listeners for those lifecycle events:

```
utils:log("endingScene", "Beginning execution");

scene:addEventListener("createScene", scene);
scene:addEventListener("willEnterScene", scene);
scene:addEventListener("enterScene", scene);
scene:addEventListener("exitScene", scene);
scene:addEventListener("didExitScene", scene);
scene:addEventListener("destroyScene", scene);

return scene;
```

When that's done, the code has only to return the scene object so it can be used by the Storyboard API.

As a famous pig once said: "That's all, folks!"

Summary

In this chapter, you looked at the last bit of code that makes up Astro Rescue, the ending scene. In the process, you explored some new Corona functionality, including gradients and masking. You had a chance to see one last use of the über-useful Transition API as well as some old friends such as event handling and audio.

In the next chapter, you'll look at some miscellaneous bits of Corona functionality that, while not used in Astro Rescue, most certainly could have been, and that you may well want to use in your own game projects. Some of those things include online scorekeeping, embedded database support and in-game ads (typical of "free" games), to name a few.

The Postgame Show

Imagination is more important than knowledge. For knowledge is limited, whereas imagination embraces the entire world.

—Albert Einstein

All of the biggest technological inventions created by man—the airplane, the automobile, the computer—says little about his intelligence but speaks volumes about his laziness.

—Mark Kennedy

A stroke of the brush does not guarantee art from the bristles.

—Kosh Naranek

I'm sorry, Dave. I'm afraid I can't do that.

—Some uppity computer that needs a swift kick in the pants

Odds and Ends

Okay, look, I realize that Astro Rescue isn't likely to challenge Angry Birds for a spot on the top-selling apps list in any app store out there. It's a neat enough game for the learning exercise it was meant to be, but it's not likely to take the gaming world by storm.

So, let's ask ourselves: what sorts of things might you want to add to it if the goal was actually to sell it and make some cash money from it? Certainly there are all sorts of things you might think of: better graphics and sound would likely be near the top of the list; more levels for sure; a wider variety of obstacles to overcome. The list is only limited by your imagination.

But since this is still a book focused on learning Corona, what sorts of things might be discussed that, at the same time, will further your knowledge of what the SDK has to offer? That's what this chapter, in a somewhat isolated fashion from Astro Rescue itself, is all about!

In it, you won't actually be modifying the Astro Rescue code—you're effectively done with that phase of things. However, you'll look at, in no particular order, a few topics, a few odds and ends (hey, that'd make a great chapter title, wouldn't it?!) that would likely make the game better, and ultimately more saleable, if you wanted to go down that path. This will also nicely round out our look at the Corona SDK and, while it can't be said that this chapter will examine every last nook and cranny, it will conclude a fairly robust and rather comprehensive look at what Corona provides you as an application developer.

Files Are So Passé: SQLite Database

In Astro Rescue, the save game state is saved in a plain old text file that happens to contain a JSON-ified version of a Lua table. This generally works very well, especially in a case like this where the data to be saved are small and so can easily be read and written all at once.

The story might be considerably different, however, if you were writing a contacts application, for example, where you want to save phone numbers, addresses, and the like for people you know. In that case, while you could imagine doing something like Listing 10-1—and in Lua that makes a fair bit of sense—the solution falls apart quickly when you have to write the contacts object to disk in its entirety every time, not to mention read it all just to look up one specific contact!

Listing 10-1. Writing Some Contacts out to Disk the "Old-Fashioned Way"

```
json = require("json");

local contact1 = {
   firstName = "Bill",
   lastName = "Cosby",
   phoneNumber = "555-123-4567"
};

local contact2 = {
   firstName = "Robert",
   lastName = "Kennedy",
   phoneNumber = "555-888-9999"
};

local contacts = { contact1, contact2 };

local path = system.pathForFile("contacts.json", system.DocumentsDirectory);
if path ~= nil then
   local fh = io.open(path, "w+");
   fh:write(json.encode(contacts));
   io.close(fh);
end
```

Then, to find contact information for John's younger brother, you'd need to read in the entire contacts object, decode the JSON back into a Lua object, then scan through it to find the correct object. Once this gets larger than just a handful of contacts, it's obviously not going to be a particularly good way to do it.

What's This SQLite You Speak of?

A far better answer is a true and proper database of some sort. Thankfully, Corona provides just such a capability via its sqlite3.* package. This package contains functions that deal with SQLite databases.

If you're not familiar with that, let me explain. SQLite is an open source library that implements a SQL-based database engine. This library is small, cross-platform, self-contained (it doesn't require a server to run), and, perhaps most important for Corona, embeddable. SQLite is used by many products out there, including iOS itself, where it is supplied by default; the popular Firefox browser, where it's used to store user configuration information, among other things; the desktop Skype client; and the well-known Dropbox, which uses it to store data in its client application.

In terms of how you use SQLite, it looks a whole lot like any relational database you've ever used. There are tables, which you query with SQL (Structured Query Language). It has support for things like transactions, indexes, constraints, triggers, and most of what the SQL92 dialect offers.

In Corona land, SQLite is available on all supported platforms and in the simulator. On iOS, as mentioned, SQLite ships with the operating system. On Android, however, a compiled version needs to be added to your generated binary (something you'll see how to do in the very next chapter!), and it adds about 300 KB to the size of that binary.

Let's Create a Database Already!

A database can be in-memory only, which means it will only exist for the duration of the application's current execution, or it can be persisted to disk. The latter case is probably the more common, so let's see how that's done, in Listing 10-2.

Listing 10-2. Fisher Price's My First SQLite Database™

```
require "sqlite3"

print("SQLite Version: " .. sqlite3.version());

db = sqlite3.open(system.pathForFile("app.db", system.DocumentsDirectory));

db:exec([[
  CREATE TABLE IF NOT EXISTS contacts (
    id INTEGER PRIMARY KEY autoincrement,
    firstName TEXT,
    lastName TEXT,
    phoneNumber TEXT
  );
]]);

db:exec([[
  INSERT INTO contacts (firstName, lastName, phoneNumber) VALUES (
    "Bill",
    "Cosby",
    "555-123-4567"
  );
]]);

db:exec([[
  INSERT INTO contacts (firstName, lastName, phoneNumber) VALUES (
    "Robert",
    "Kennedy",
    "555-888-9999"
  );
]]);

for r in db:nrows("SELECT * FROM contacts") do
  print(
    r.id .. " = " .. r.firstName .. " " .. r.lastName .. " : " .. r.phoneNumber
  );
end
```

Of course, it all starts with importing the sqlite3 module. After that, if you want to, you can get the version of the SQLite engine in use. If you run this in the simulator you'll see a version number of 3.7.14.1 (at least as of this writing).

After that, it's time to open a database. You can have as many as you want, and you can store them where you want. However, as is best practice in nearly all cases where you have data related only to your application that you want to save to disk, the system.DocumentsDirectory value should be used to limit visibility to your application and ensure it has full read/write access on all platforms. The database name, contacts.db here, is entirely up to you.

Once the database is open it's time to create a table. The basic syntax for nearly everything you'll do with a SQLite database in Corona takes the general form:

```
file:exec([[ SOME SQL HERE ]]);
```

You can, and for readability probably should, use line breaks in the SQL, as I've done in the example code. Here I am assuming you have some knowledge of SQL generally, but even if you don't I suspect the SQL used to create a table is pretty self-explanatory. The table will only be created if it doesn't exist already, to keep you from overwriting any existing data.

The id field is the primary key of the table and is a number, an INTEGER to be precise. It also uses the AUTOINCREMENT qualifier, which means that every time a row is inserted into the table, this field will be a number generated by incrementing the value of the last inserted row. In this way, the value of the field is always unique and hence works as a primary key.

> **Note**   Case is not generally important in SQL. However, my own convention is to always put SQL keywords in caps, and I also try to make sure the field names, however I choose to capitalize them, match everywhere, meaning in the SQL as well as in any objects I might create from a SQL query.

The other three fields are defined as TEXT type fields and aren't keys or anything, so their definition is straightforward. However, the interesting thing about SQLite is that the column type is really more of a suggestion than anything else! You can, in fact, store a string in the id field, or you can store a number in either of the name fields. The data types you specify are really "affinities," which gets into how the values are stored on disk versus what you get when you retrieve them—most of which you can ignore 9 times out of 10, frankly.

The long and short of it is that you can either

- specify data types (from among TEXT, NUMERIC, INTEGER, or REAL) when creating tables and then ensure you never try and store the wrong type in a field (because SQLite will do it regardless!), or

- not specify a data type at all and go about your business storing anything you like anywhere!

SQLite will happily work either way and you most likely won't ever know the difference. My suggestion, however, is to exercise a little bit of self-discipline: specify the data types and stick to them. To me, that's a lot less likely to come back and bite you somehow later!

Once you have a table created, you can go about inserting data into it with a regular old SQL insert statement. Since the id field auto-increments, you don't need to pass a value for it.

Gettin' at Your Data

You can read back your data in two basic ways. As shown in the sample code, if you want to retrieve multiple rows and iterate over them, then the nrows() method of the opened database object is your best bet. It returns an iterator over a result set, which you can then easily use in a loop. Within the loop, the variable r is a pointer to the next object in the result set, and you can then access the fields in a straightforward way.

Even if your query is more specific, say . . .

```
SELECT * FROM contacts WHERE id=4
```

. . . you can still use this approach, but then of course you know you'll always get only one result (unless you get none, which is perfectly valid). In this case however, there's another way you can do it:

```
rs = db:exec(
  "SELECT * FROM contacts WHERE id=4",
  function(udata, numCols, cVals, cNames)
    print(udata, numCols, json.encode(cNames), json.encode(cVals));
  end
);
```

Here, the function inline in the exec() call passed as the second argument will be executed for each result in the result set of the query. So, while you can in fact handle multiple items this way as well, it is, in my mind at least, a more natural fit for handling one, if for no other reason than it physically **looks** like it's meant for that. Whether you agree with that or not, it's nice to know you can use this sort of callback approach. By the way, the arguments that are passed to the function are the following:

- ▓ udata is user data that you can use to persist information between invocations of the callback
- ▓ numCols is the number of columns in a given row of the result set
- ▓ cVals is the column values
- ▓ cNames is the column names

Last, note that in this approach, if the callback returns a nonzero value then the iteration stops and all subsequent SQL statements are skipped. Returning nothing at all is considered a zero return, so the loop will continue as shown in the previous code snippet.

> **Tip**   The underlying API that Corona uses is provided by the open source luasqlite3 project. Their documentation is actually more expansive than the Corona documentation, so if you're ever unsure about how to do something with SQLite in Corona, take a look here for more extensive information: http://luasqlite.luaforge.net/lsqlite3.html.

Data Amnesia: In-Memory Databases

The database in the example here is stored on disk and persists between application runs. What if you have some transient data that you only need while the application is running? An in-memory database might be a better answer in that case. To create one, you have to make only one slight change. This:

```
db = sqlite3.open(system.pathForFile("contacts.db", system.DocumentsDirectory));
```

becomes this:

```
local db = sqlite3.open_memory()
```

From that point on you use the database exactly the same as any other. When the application shuts down, however, that database is destroyed and you start fresh the next time the application runs (so, you probably wouldn't want to do this for a contacts database as in this example, but you get the idea!).

Talkin' to the Outside World: Network Access

A mobile device is a personal thing. Generally speaking, it belongs to a single user, and most of the time a single user is using it at a time. Therefore, when you write a game for a mobile device, they are, more times than not, geared toward that single-player experience.

It's also usually the case that the assets the game needs are downloaded when you install the game as part of the game package itself (read: embedded within the executable file you install). While that is still the most common model, more and more games are being released that, in large part due to the size of their graphics, audio, and other assets, require you to download from an app store what is really a pretty small executable, which then downloads all the additional resources when you first run it. This allows you to get the application on the user's device as quickly as possible while also working around the size limitations all app stores currently have (although those size restrictions have been relaxed considerably in all stores over the past few years).

It also allows you greater flexibility. Perhaps you only want to download assets as they are actually needed. Imagine a game when you are walking around a virtual world. Why should the user need to spend 20 minutes upon first launch downloading the entire world, when you can instead only force her to download a small portion in, say, 30 seconds? The rest of the world, the tavern on the far side of a level for example, can be downloaded when she actually arrives. Or, perhaps you want the world to grow over time. Users can download the new areas as they become available without having to explicitly install a new version of your game.

All of this requires network access, and Corona is there to help you in this area! The SDK actually provides two pertinent packages: the `network.*` package and the `socket.*` package.

Some Basic Network Functionality

The `network.*` package provides some very basic, high-level networking support. First, it allows you to check network status, shown in Listing 10-3.

Listing 10-3. Hello? Hello?! Anybody out there?!

```
function networkStatusListener(inEvent)
  print("address", inEvent.address);
  print("isReachable", inEvent.isReachable);
  print("isConnectionRequired", inEvent.isConnectionRequired);
  print("isConnectionOnDemand", inEvent.isConnectionOnDemand);
  print("IsInteractionRequired", inEvent.isInteractionRequired);
  print("IsReachableViaCellular", inEvent.isReachableViaCellular);
  print("IsReachableViaWiFi", inEvent.isReachableViaWiFi);
end

if network.canDetectNetworkStatusChanges then
  network.setStatusListener("www.google.com", networkStatusListener);
else
  print("Network reachability checking not supported");
end
```

First, the `network.canDetectNetworkStatusChanges` field tells you whether the platform the app is currently running on is capable of reporting network status. At present, only Mac and iOS are capable of doing that. So, if your app is on an Android device, or the simulator on Windows, the value here will always be `false` and there's no reliable way to tell if network connectivity is available to your application in this situation, other than to simply try a request and handle it if it fails.

If it is available, however, then you can create a listener function and pass it to `network.setStatusListener()`. That function will then be called any time network status changes. However, note that this works on a per-target host basis. In other words, in the example it's checking to see if the host `www.google.com` is reachable. The consequence of this is that it's possible for `www.google.com` to be down and not responding, which will register in the code as network connectivity not being available when it actually is. This actually makes sense if you think about it: generally, it's only a single host you'll want to talk to anyway. You can also pass a comma-separated list of hosts if you truly are interested in more than one, or if you want to have a more generic check of network connectivity (it's less likely that five different hosts would all be down at the same time, so if you can reach even one you know network connectivity is available).

Within the listener function, `networkStatusListener()` in the example, you can determine what host was reached (`inEvent.isReachable` and `inEvent.address`)—that is, if it was actually reachable, because remember that this function will be called if it's **not** reachable, too; it's called any time network status **changes**, not necessarily when connectivity is working. You can also determine over what type of connection it's reachable (`inEvent.isReachableViaWiFi` and `iEvent.isReachableViaCellular`, which are good if you need to download a lot of data and only want to do so over a Wi-Fi connection), if the user will need to interact with the application to reconnect to the host (`inEvent.isInteractionRequired`, e.g., if a password is required), and if the connection will be brought up automatically or not (`inEvent.isConnectionOnDemand`).

Once you know whether you can reach an appropriate host or not, you can proceed to make requests to that host for resources. For example, let's say you want to retrieve a file available via HTTP on a web server. Listing 10-4 shows that this is a simple task indeed.

Listing 10-4. US Defense Spending at Work!

```
function networkListener(inEvent)
  if (inEvent.isError) then
    print("Network error!");
  else
    print(inEvent.response);
  end
end

network.request(
  "http://tycho.usno.navy.mil/cgi-bin/timer.pl", "GET", networkListener
);
```

If you run this in the simulator you'll see that what is output to the console window is an HTML document retrieved from the US Naval Observatory's web server showing the current time in various time zones. It's just a dump of the "naked" HTML document of course, since there's no web browser to parse and render the document, but that's good enough for our purposes here. All you do is pass the URL, HTTP method, and callback function reference to network.request(), and you get back whatever resources are at that location on that server, or an error if something goes wrong.

If you need to send data, you can do that too, as a POST request. All you do is add as a fourth argument to the network.request() call that is an object with an attribute named body that contains the POST data (properly URL-encoded of course, if necessary). Don't forget to change the third argument to "POST" as well and you're good to go passing whatever data to the server you'd like.

You can even mess around with the request headers by adding a headers attribute to the object passed as the fourth parameter in name = value pair form. A complete example of both POST and header manipulation is shown in Listing 10-5. Although the site being called doesn't care about these headers or the POST body, the request works just fine, and if you throw a network sniffer on your PC you'll see the headers and POST body sent across the wire regardless.

Listing 10-5. POST and Header Manipulation in One Go

```
function networkListener(inEvent)
  if (inEvent.isError) then
    print("Network error!");
  else
    print(inEvent.response);
  end
end

hdrs = { };
hdrs["Accept-Language"] = "en-US";
local rData = {
  headers = hdrs,
  body = "Miscellaneous%20Value"
};

network.request(
  "http://tycho.usno.navy.mil/cgi-bin/timer.pl", "POST", networkListener, rData
);
```

> **Caution** The one other attribute you can set on your data object passed as the fourth argument to `network.request()` is `timeout`, which specifies how long the request should wait before failing. The default is 30 seconds; however, this attribute is currently only supported on iOS and Mac, so use it carefully. With great power comes great responsibility, as Uncle Ben so wisely reminds us every chance he gets. Seriously, the guy is annoying—even from beyond the grave!

What if you want to download a file instead? Well, you certainly could just grab the response in the callback function via `inEvent.response` as in the previous example, but then you're responsible for what gets done with it, which means extra work on your part. Perhaps you want to stash it in a SQLite database as you played with in the previous section. That's perfectly fine and maybe even the best choice in some cases, but there's a good chance you'll want to save it to a file, and the `network.*` package has you covered if you do.

Take a look at Listing 10-6. It's a simple example of grabbing an image off a web site and displaying it on the screen.

Listing 10-6. Who Says Buying a House Is Hard??

```
function callback(inEvent)

  if (inEvent.isError) then
    print("Download no happen, sorry!");
  else
    display.newImage("house.png", system.TemporaryDirectory, 48, 48);
  end

end


network.download(
  "http://etherient.com/img/home.png",
  "GET",
  callback,
  "house.png",
  system.TemporaryDirectory
);
```

The `network.download()` method takes care of getting the file at the specified URL, using the specified HTTP method (which would likely always be GET, but you could use others if the server requires it), the callback listener function to execute when it's retrieved (or when an error occurs), the name of the file under which to save the content retrieved from the server and the location where to save it. The `callback()` function then just displays the image from the file system.

Nothing says you have to retrieve images, of course; you could retrieve any arbitrary data file this way, say map data or lists of valid servers to use in a multiplayer situation or whatever else your imagination can conjure up.

> **Note** It's important to understand that both the `network.request()` and `network.download()` methods are asynchronous (as evidenced by the use of a callback function). This of course means that the code following their invocation will execute even before the response comes back, so you need to write your code with that in mind.

There's More to Networking than Getting Content

The other option that Corona offers is the `socket.*` package. This allows you to get a little more low-level than just HTTP requests, although it can do that, too. It also provides support for other protocols including FTP, SMTP, and DNS.

The `socket.*` package is built on the open source LuaSocket library and provides its functionality to your Corona applications. For example, say you want to send an e-mail. That's easy to accomplish, as shown in Listing 10-7.

Listing 10-7. An E-mail . . . a . . . Err . . . Causes the US Post Office to Close Forever?!

```
smtp = require("socket.smtp");

msg = smtp.message({
  headers = {
    to = "fzammetti@etherient.com",
    subject = "Corona rocks!"
  },
  body = "Yeah, so, that was fun."
});

r, e = smtp.send({
    from = "fzammetti@omnytex.com",
    rcpt = "fzammetti@etherient.com",
    source = msg,
    server = "zammetti.com",
    port = "587",
    user = "XXX",
    password = "YYY"
});

if (e) then
  print("Error: ", e)
end
```

Whew, that's almost **too** easy, isn't it? Once you import the `socket.smtp` module, it's a simple matter of creating an `smtp.message` object, setting the appropriate headers and message body on it, and then calling `smtp.send()` to send it, specifying the sender, recipient (`rcpt`), the message object you created, SMTP server and port, and (optionally) a username and password under which to log in.

> **Note**   For either the `network.*` or `socket.*` packages you'll need to add the
> `android.permission.INTERNET` permission to your `build.settings` file to allow network access on
> the Android platform.

As mentioned, the LuaSocket library is used by Corona to provide this functionality. For much more detailed documentation than what you'll find in the Corona SDK documentation, refer to `http://w3.impa.br/~diego/software/luasocket/reference.html`.

I'm Always Losing My Gym Sockets: Socket Networking

The e-mail example is just that: an example. It's meant to be just enough to give you a starting point. If you need to use DNS services (such as getting a host name from an IP address or vice versa), or you want to send and receive files via FTP, or want to URL-encode or escape data, then you'll need to refer to the location mentioned and use the e-mail example as a rough starting point.

However, one other topic I want to demonstrate is building a socket-based client/server. This becomes very useful if you want to do direct player-to-player gameplay. Take a look at the example in Listing 10-8.

Listing 10-8. A Simple TCP Client Example

```
socket = require("socket");

server, err = socket.tcp();
if server == nil then
  print(err);
  os.exit();
end

server:setoption("reuseaddr", true);

res, err = server:bind("*", 0);
if res == nil then
  print(err);
  os.exit();
end

res, err = server:listen(5);
if res == nil then
  print(err);
  os.exit();
end

Runtime:addEventListener("enterFrame",
  function()
    server:settimeout(0);
    local client, _ = server:accept();
    if client ~= nil then
      local receivedContent, _ = client:receive("*l");
      if (receivedContent ~= nil) then
```

```
        print(receivedContent);
        if receivedContent == "ping" then
          client:send("pong");
        end
      end
      client:close();
    end
  end
);

local _, port = server:getsockname();
print("localhost listening on port " .. port);
```

This example shows how to construct a server that listens on a port and echoes what it receives to the console, and if it receives the string "ping" responds to the caller with "pong".

Once you import the socket module, the next step is to create a socket with the socket.tcp() call (and yes, you can do UDP if you like as well). After a quick check to ensure that was successful, set the reuseaddr option on it. This allows for IP addresses to be reused, which is especially important for this to work in the simulator, since it and the host machine will share the same IP address.

Next, bind the socket to a port using the server:bind() method. Passing "*" and 0 as arguments as done here means that any available port will be used.

Next, tell the server to start listening for incoming requests and check if it's running as expected. The number passed to the server:listen() method is the backlog number, which means how many requests can be queued waiting for service from this server.

Next, you need to ensure that our Corona app doesn't end after this code is executed, so set up an enterFrame listener. Skip that for just a moment and instead jump down to the last two lines. The first, the one with the call to server:getsockname(), returns the IP address and port the server is listening on. The port number is then echoed for reference.

> **Tip**   The use of the underscore in a couple of lines here is something you haven't seen before. This is a convention when a function returns multiple values that indicates you don't care about that particular value. Lua will discard it and not bother you about it. No need to create a variable that will just be ignored, after all!

Now, going back to the enterFrame handler, the first line, the call to server:settimeout(0), is very important because it ensures our usage of the server isn't blocking. If you didn't do this, you'd find that the app freezes inside the enterFrame handler, which isn't good to say the least! Setting the timeout like this avoids that.

Next, you get a client object that connects to the socket the server is using. With this client you can then accept connections and check for any received content. Passing *l to client:receive() indicates that you want to read a line of text from the received content, if any. Assuming you did get some content, print() it to the console and reply if the proper trigger phrase is received. Last, the client is closed and the handler function ends, to be triggered again with the next enterFrame iteration.

You can test this by running the example code in the simulator and noting the port the server is listening on. If it's 64613 for example, fire up your favorite telnet client (such as PuTTY or Tunnelier) and connect to `localhost:64613`. Once it connects, enter "ping", and see that you get "pong" back, and that what you type is echoed to the simulator console.

LUAFileSystem

During the course of exploring the Astro Rescue code, you learned how to read and write files. As you'll recall, most of that functionality is housed in the `io.*` package. That's not the only package that Corona offers for dealing with the file system, though. The other, `lfs.*`, provides access to the features of the open source LuaFileSystem (`http://keplerproject.github.com/luafilesystem/index.html`).

This library provides a number of features, including the ability to manipulate directories (add and delete them), the ability to scan the contents of a directory (to list the files and directories it contains) and manipulating attributes of files and directories (among other things). You can see some of this in action by looking at Listing 10-9.

Listing 10-9. Using the LuaFileSystem to Mess with, Well, the File System!

```
local lfs = require("lfs");

-- List files in the documents directory.
for f in lfs.dir(system.pathForFile("", system.DocumentsDirectory)) do
  print(f);
end

print("------------------------------------------------------------");

-- Add a directory to the temporary directory.
tempDir = system.pathForFile("", system.TemporaryDirectory);
if lfs.chdir(tempDir) then
  lfs.mkdir("A_New_Directory");
  for f in lfs.dir(tempDir) do
    print(f);
  end
end

print("------------------------------------------------------------");

-- Update timestamp of access on the new directory.
dirPath = system.pathForFile("A_New_Directory", system.TemporaryDirectory);
lfs.touch(dirPath);
attrs = lfs.attributes(dirPath);
print(attrs.modification);

print("------------------------------------------------------------");

-- Now delete that new directory.
lfs.rmdir("A_New_Directory");
for f in lfs.dir(tempDir) do
  print(f);
end
```

The first block of code lists all the files and directories within the documents directory. To do this, the `lfs.dir()` method is used, which returns an iterator that you can then iterate over, where each object returned by the iteration is a file or directory that is a child of the target directory. The `system.pathForFile()` method, which you've seen before, is used to reference the directory you're interested in scanning.

The second block of code adds a directory named A_New_Directory to the temporary directory. Before doing that, though, you need to change the current working directory so that the directory is created where you intend it to be, and the `lfs.chdir()` method is what allows you to do this. Once the working directory is changed the `lfs.mkdir()` method lets you create the new directory using the specified name. The code then redisplays the contents of the temporary directory so you can see that the new directory was created.

The third block of code uses the `lfs.touch()` method to effectively update the timestamp on the directory. Once that is done, the `lfs.attributes()` method gets a collection of various attributes about the directory, one of which is the modification attribute, or when the directory was last touched. This value (in milliseconds) is displayed.

The last block removes the new directory using `lfs.rmdir()` and redisplays the contents once more to see that the directory was, in fact, removed.

You can see the results of executing this program in Figure 10-1.

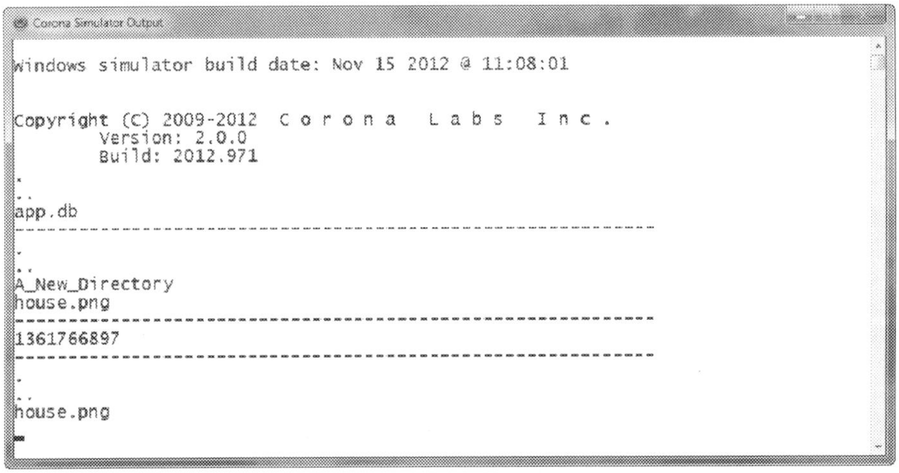

Figure 10-1. Proof, admissible in court (although IANAL), that the LuaFileSystem functionality in Corona works!

If you're familiar with Unix command lines, you'll quickly realize that the LuaFileSystem methods match closely with the typical commands you would use on the command line. Similarly, the attributes available for a file or directory are those that you can typically see in a command line environment.

The `lfs.*` package augments the `io.*` package, and even some of the functionality present in the `system.*` package, to give you greater access to the underlying file system of the device your application is running on. Use it wisely, my young Padawan!

> **Note**   This example does not do any sort of error checking. That's just to make it as simple as possible for you to digest. If you're going to use this package for real, though, you'll want to refer to the Corona and LuaFileSystem documentation to ensure you react to errors properly.

Ads

The monetization model of mobile apps is an interesting discussion to have. There are a number of approaches, from direct charges for a given application to in-app purchases to just making the application entirely free.

Another common approach is the ad-supported model. Here, you generate revenue based on ads displayed within your application. You are paid by a given ad supplier that you work with. While I'm sure you can imagine creating this code yourself, and it wouldn't be all **that** tricky, Corona again is here to make it even easier for you!

I won't be giving you a working example here as I have in other sections because in fact, I can't; to do so would require you have a key provided by one of the two supported ad services, InMobi or Inneractive. That's something you would have to get on your own. However, I can talk in generalities here and give you the basic picture of how it works, which is actually quite simple (something I know I've said time and again about Corona!).

There are actually only three basic steps.

Step 1: import the ads module.

```
local ads = require("ads");
```

Step 2: initialize the ads subsystem.

```
ads.init("inmobi", "xxx");
```

This assumes you're using the InMobi ad network; otherwise pass `inneractive` instead as the first argument (or another value corresponding to another ad provider, as Corona supports them). The second argument is the unique key the ad provider assigns to you when you sign up to work with them.

Step 3: show an ad (who saw that one coming, right?!)

```
Ads.show("banner320x48", { x = 0, y = 10, interval = 30, testMode = false });
```

The first argument is the type of ad to show, which more or less means how big the ad banner is to be. Note though that the dimensions you see in the values are in points, not pixels, so on a Retina display device like the iPhone 4 the values are doubled in pixels. Also note that for the Inneractive provider, you actually have a choice of type of ad rather than simply size as for InMobi.

The value you pass here depends on what the ad provider supports. The possible values, as present, are as follows:

- For InMobi: `banner320x48` or `banner300x250` on all devices, or `banner728x90`, `banner468x60`, or `banner120x600` on the iPad only

- For Inneractive: `banner`, `text`, or `fullscreen`

The second argument is an object that can contain a number of attributes. The x and y attributes are simply where on the screen the ad banner is to appear. The `interval` attribute tells Corona how frequently, in seconds, to change to another ad. The `testMode` attribute, when `true`, tells the ad provider you're using a testing account and they shouldn't process ad views like they normally would in terms of statistics or payments to you.

Last, you can hide the ad currently showing by calling the aptly named `ads.hide()` method. No ads will show up again until `ads.show()` is called once more.

That is essentially all there is to putting ads in your games! It's a simple API for sure, and once you sign up with one of the ad providers you can get going in no time. Pretty sweet, huh?

In-App Purchases

An ad-supported model of application monetization is all well and good, but it's certainly not the only option. Another common approach to making money with your games is the in-app purchase route. Here, the user downloads a game, sometimes for free, sometimes for a small cost. As they play and advance in the game they are presented with the opportunity to purchase additional content to continue. This content can take many forms including buying access to additional levels, power-ups that give their in-game character new abilities, options that allows them to customize things in the game, and anything else that you as the developer dream up that you think is a good candidate for monetization. When the user can do this from within the game itself, this is an in-app purchase.

Corona's `store.*` package contains functionality for dealing with this. It currently supports the Apple iTunes store and the Google Play market for Android. Other storefronts, such as Amazon or Barnes & Noble, may be supported in the future, but currently are not.

As with the discussion of ads, I can't show you complete, working example code that you can play with because this all depends on your having accounts set up on one or both of the app stores. You can, however, get a good feel for how this works, as with ads.

The basic flow of events to perform an in-app purchase looks something like what you see in Listing 10-10.

Listing 10-10. An Example of In-App Purchases

```
local store = require("store");

store.init(
  function (inEvent)

    if inEvent.transaction.state == "purchased" then
      print("Complete");
      print("productIdentifier", inEvent.transaction.productIdentifier);
      print("receipt", inEvent.transaction.receipt);
      print("transactionIdentifier", inEvent.transaction.identifier);
      print("date", inEvent.transaction.date);

    elseif inEvent.transaction.state == "restored" then
      print("Restored (already purchased)");
      print("productIdentifier", inEvent.transaction.productIdentifier);
      print("receipt", inEvent.transaction.receipt);
```

```
      print("transactionIdentifier", inEvent.transaction.identifier);
      print("date", inEvent.transaction.date);
      print("originalReceipt", inEvent.transaction.originalReceipt);
      print("originalinEvent.transactionIdentifier",
        inEvent.transaction.originalIdentifier
      );
      print("originalDate", inEvent.transaction.originalDate);

   elseif inEvent.transaction.state == "cancelled" then
      print("Cancelled by user")

   elseif inEvent.transaction.state == "failed" then
      print("Purchase failed: ", transaction.errorType, transaction.errorString);

   else
      print("D'oh! Something went wrong!");

   end

   store.finishTransaction(inEvent.transaction);

  end
);

if store.canMakePurchases then

  store.loadProducts(
    {
      "com.etherient.myGame.purchaseableItem1",
      "com.etherient.myGame.purchaseableItem2"
    },
    function(inEvent)
      for i = 1, #inEvent.products do
        print(inEvent.products[i].title);
        print(inEvent.products[i].description);
        print(inEvent.products[i].price);
        print(inEvent.products[i].localizedPrice);
        print(inEvent.products[i].productIdentifier);
      end
    end
  );

  store.restore();

  store.purchase( { "com.etherient.purchaseableItem1"} );

else

  print("You are not allowed to make in-app purchases on this device");

end
```

The first step is a call to store.init(). Well, the first step is actually to import the store module, but you know that! What you pass to store.init() is a callback function that will respond to the various events that can occur when you attempt to make a purchase. Let's come back to that in just a moment.

Once you initialize the store, what happens next depends on what you're trying to do. One thing you might do is check if in-app purchases are allowed on this device by checking store.canMakePurchases. In iOS at least, purchases can be disabled, usually for parental control purposes, so it's a good idea to check this first lest your code blow up later (which the example code would do, by the way, since the check is performed and then promptly ignored—this is just an example, not production code!)

Something else you'll probably want to do is call store.restore(), which will restore any purchases this user has already made. This will result in your callback function being called and the restored branch executed for each item restored. What you do at this point is up to you: maybe you need to download the new content, or maybe you check to ensure it's already done and do nothing in that case.

You also might want to list all the items available for purchase. To do this you can use the store.loadProducts() method. You pass to this a list of identifier strings for items that can be purchased for your game. The store responds with information about it including description and price, which are probably the most important attributes. In the example code, the information is simply printed to the console; in a real game you'd want to show them to the user and let them select, of course.

> **Note**   The string identifiers are things you create in the storefront you are working with. All the attributes are stored there as well. I haven't gone into those details because they vary from store to store, but you'll get at least a sense of what's involved in the very next chapter when I discuss distributing your game.

Ultimately, making a purchase is what you're here to do, and the store.purchase() method, not surprisingly, lets you do that. You pass to it a list of string identifiers for what the user wants to purchase; once again, the callback function you registered with store.init() will be called, once for each item; and the outcome of the transaction will determine what branch in that function is taken. You, as the person wanting to make money, are hoping for the purchased or restored branch (they may try to purchase something that's already purchased, which would get you to the restored branch, although if you think about it that's a flaw in your user interface!). You might hit the cancelled branch if the user changes his mind about the purchase, or failed if something goes wrong, such as his credit card being declined. Any unknown errors are handled in the else branch.

> **Tip**   The store API has no method to set the quantity for a purchase at present. For this, you need to cheat: just specify an item multiple times in the call to store.purchase() and Corona will do the equivalent of setting a quantity for you.

Last, when you're done with the transaction, call store.finishTransaction(), passing it the object passed into the callback by way of inEvent.transaction, and everything gets buttoned up nicely. If you fail to do this, the store you're communicating with will assume the transaction was simply interrupted and will attempt to resume it the next time the application is launched. Since this isn't a great user experience, you'll want to ensure you call this function for sure.

Social Gaming

One of the somewhat newer aspects to gaming, whether mobile or not, is the introduction of so-called social aspects. This can mean many things to different people, but one thing that it frequently means is online tracking of scores, leaderboards and such, that compare you to other players. There are a number of popular mechanisms for doing this; just as with ads, as discussed earlier, there are providers that will track this information for you. These third-party libraries include the iOS Game Center, which just so happens to be the only one that Corona supports out of the box!

> **Warning**   Previously, Corona also supported OpenFeint, which was a very popular cross-platform game network but which no longer exists as such, having been acquired by another company. Corona subsequently dropped support for it. This unfortunately means that there is no longer a cross-platform game system that Corona supports out of the box. At this point you would have to explore other possible third-party options that may exist, roll your own service (which is far outside the scope of this book), or simply live with only supporting these sorts of features on iOS devices for the time being. Corona has recently made their Corona Cloud service available too, which provides some of these same services to Corona SDK subscribers.

Something else that people very frequently mean when talking about social gaming is integration with Facebook. Simple things like being able to post their high scores or telling their friends what they're playing at the moment are popular these days.

Let's start with how you can hook into Game Center, and potentially other game networks that Corona may one day support.

Game Network Integration

As with ads and in-app purchases, I'll have to talk in generalities here because without signing up with one of these providers, I can't properly show you working code. Like those topics, however, I can provide you a good overview to help you started if you want to use these mechanisms.

As with ads and in-app purchases, the API Corona provides for game network integration, packaged in the gameNetwork.* namespace, is very simple and boils down to three steps (or two, depending on how you look at it):

- Call gameNetwork.init() after importing the module by including require("gameNetwork") in your code and passing to it as its first argument the name of the game network to work with (currently only gamecenter is a valid value).

- Call gameNetwork.show() to show information from the provider.

- Call gameNetwork.request() to send or request specific information.

A second argument can optionally be passed to the `init()` method. This argument is a callback function that handles certain lifecycle events, determined by a number of different factors, such as:

- When the value in the `type` attribute of the event object passed in is `showSignIn`, that means the Game Center sign-in screen is about to be shown, and your game now has the chance to pause itself or perform any other tasks that are specific to your game and that need to occur before the sign in view is shown.

- When the `data` attribute of the event object passed in is `true`, that means sign-in was successful and you can continue with your game code accordingly. When the value is `false`, sign-in failed and you can branch as appropriate there, too.

- If any errors occur, such as network errors, values will be populated in the `errorCode` and `errorMessage` attributes of the event object.

- When the value init is present in the `type` attribute, that means the sign-in view was dismissed and you can continue your game code to handle the results of the login.

Note   In iOS, if your app is "backgrounded," your app will automatically be logged out of Game Center. In that case, it will automatically attempt to log in again when the app is resumed. Your callback handler function will be invoked again in this case, so you must code it to handle this case appropriately as well.

Once everything is initialized, you can go about showing or getting/setting information. For example, to show a leaderboard of high scores for the past week, you can do:

```
gameNetwork.show(
  "leaderboards",
  { leaderboard = { timeScope = "week" }
});
```

The first argument is what you want to display, the second is a data object that further defines the request. This object is optional in many cases but you will probably use it more times than not. In this case, only the `timeScope` attribute is present, which takes a value of `week`, `today`, or `alltime` to define what range of data you want.

As another example, let's say you want to send a friend request on Game Center. For that, you might do:

```
gameNetwork.show(
  "friendRequest",
  {
    message = "I'm desperate, please like me!",
    playerIDs = { "G:111111111", "G:222222222" },
    emailAddresses = { "none@none.com" },
    listener = myCallback
  }
);
```

Here, the message attribute is obvious, I'd say. The playerIDs is the list of identifiers of Game Center users you want to send the request to. The emailAddresses attribute is a list of e-mail addresses for players you want to send a request to. Last, the listener attribute references a function that will receive callback events. This attribute is actually applicable for nearly all gameNetwork.show() calls, although is optional.

Now, what happens when you want to record a high score? That's easy enough! The code for that looks something like this:

```
gameNetwork.request(
  "setHighScore",
  {
    localPlayerScore = { category="com.etherient.Engineer", value=25 }
  }
);
```

Want to get a list of the achievements your game supports? Here you go:

```
gameNetwork.request(
  "loadAchievementDescriptions",
  { listener = myCallback }
);
```

Assuming myCallback() is a function that appropriately does something with the achievements, like display them most prominently, you're good to go.

Last, what about unlocking an achievement the player just got? Simple enough:

```
gameNetwork.request(
  "unlockAchievement",
  {
    achievement = {
      identifier = "com.etherient.five_levels_finished",
      percentComplete = 100,
      showsCompletionBanner = true,
    },
    listener = myListenerFunction
  }
);
```

As you can see, the API isn't particularly difficult, but this sort of social interaction is exactly the sort of thing players have come to expect from modern games, and thankfully Corona gets you there with a minimum of effort.

Facebook Integration

Now let's talk about working with Facebook. The first step is to register your application with Facebook. This will get you a unique app ID that you'll use with the Corona facebook.* package.

Once you have it, you'll need to enable Single Sign-On (SSO) for iOS apps (for Android you can skip this step). This amounts to modifying your `build.settings` file like so:

```
settings = {
  iphone = {
    plist = {
      CFBundleURLTypes =
      {
        {
          CFBundleURLSchemes =
          {
            "fbXXXXX",
          }
        }
      }
    }
  }
}
```

> **Caution**   The nesting of this configuration must be exactly as shown here or all manner of hellspawn will be brought forth upon the Earth . . . or your app just won't work. Why risk it, I say?

Replace fbXXXXX with the Facebook ID provided when you registered your application.

Once that's done, the next thing your app will have to do is log the user in to Facebook. This is accomplished by a call to `facebook.login()`. To this method you pass:

- Your app ID as the first argument.

- A reference to a callback function as the second argument. This function is passed a fbconnect event object that contains information you'll need, including: phase (with possible values login, loginFailed, loginCancelled, or logout, which allow you to determine how your code should react), type (with possible values session, request, or dialog, which tell you what type of call your code made to trigger the callback) and token (the access token generated by a login request).

Once the user is successfully logged in, you can make `facebook.request()` calls to accomplish various tasks. For example, if you want to get a list of the user's friends, you can do:

```
facebook.request( "me/friends" );
```

This returns a JSON object to your listener function (event type "request") that you can parse and work with.

To post a message to the user's activity feed:

```
facebook.request(
  "me/feed",
  "POST",
  { message = "I'm playing the most awesome game ever!"}
);
```

Last, to upload a photo, perhaps a screenshot of the player completing the game, you could do:

```
facebook.request(
  "me/photos",
  "POST",
  {
    message = "I won! I won! I won!",
    source = {
      baseDir = system.DocumentsDirectory,
      filename = "screenshot.png",
      type = "image"
    }
  }
);
```

Now, all of this requires you to build the UI for posting and displaying information yourself. There's another way though: you can allow Facebook to do it! This is accomplished with the `facebook.showDialog()` method. You pass this a string that tells it what dialog you want to show, and optionally a second argument that defines the data to use when showing the dialog. This data is specific to the call you want to make. For example, to show a dialog allowing the user to post to their timeline, you might do:

```
facebook.showDialog("feed", {
  link = "www.etherient.com",
  caption = "Check out this site!",
  description = "It's a cool site, seriously!"
});
```

See this page for details on what calls are possible and what data to pass for each: `http://developers.facebook.com/docs/reference/dialogs`.

Last, when you're all done with Facebook, you can log the user out like so:

```
facebook.logout();
```

Yep, that's really it! With just a few lines of code you can allow your players to obnoxiously declare to all their friends and family how great they are at your game. It's what Facebook is for, after all! (Oops, I seem to have forgotten the sarcasm tags there . . . they're implicit, though!)

Analytics

The final topic for this chapter is something users of your application will probably never see, but that can be of great importance to you as an application developer: analytics.

Analytics allow you to collect information about your application and how people use it. Want to know how many people install your game? Analytics. Want to know how often people play it? Analytics. The number of in-app purchases of a given type? Analytics. Information about crashes? I'll give you one guess!

The Corona `analytics.*` package makes it easy to do this and more. The API present here is the model of simplicity itself. First, call:

```
analytics.init(xxxx);
```

The value you pass to `analytics.init()` is a key given to you by the analytics service you sign up with. At the time of this writing, Flurry (`www.flurry.com`) is the only service supported. Flurry is a free service that tracks a great deal of data for you, including custom data, and then presents to you a web-based interface for viewing it all. You can slice and dice the data in various ways to visualize that data however you need to in order to get the information you're after.

If all you did was the `analytics.init()` call, Flurry would automatically track a host of information for you, such as number of unique users who launch your app, average session length, and more. However, that's only part of the equation! You can also do this:

```
analytics.logEvent(xxxx, yyyy);
```

In this case, xxxx is a string defining a custom event. In this way, you can track situations specific to your application. For example, if you are writing a Pac-Man clone, maybe you want to track how many ghosts players eat. For this, you might pass a string `ghostsEaten`, and Flurry will then track this for you. The second argument, which is optional, is a table with key-value pairs that provide more information about the event. This way you might track how many Blinkys, Pinkys, Inkys, and Clydes are eaten.

Corona Launchpad

One other option to be aware of with regard to analytics is Corona Launchpad. Once you become a Corona SDK subscriber you'll automatically have access to this service. With it, you will **by default** get a number of basic analytic data points, among other services. The only "special" thing you need to do to turn this on is to build your app with a distribution provisioning profile for iOS or a private key for Android—and don't worry, the next chapter is where I'll talk about those things if they aren't familiar to you!

> **Note**   During testing, you can also record data for iOS apps by using an ad hoc provisioning profile. You'll still need to use a private key for Android builds. This lets you collect information from your beta testers, for example, before your app is fully baked.

In Figure 10-2 you can see an example of what the data display on the Corona web site looks like. As you can see, it's not a lot of information, but it's certainly helpful.

Figure 10-2. Okay, so my game isn't doing too well, but still, it illustrates the idea just fine anyway!

The data collected, it should be noted, is not 100% real-time. There is a delay of up to 24 hours in fact, and there is some buffering logic in place for when devices don't have a persistent network connection, so you won't miss anything in those cases.

Finally, while this is all more or less automatic, you do of course have the option of not participating. You can simply remove the application from your dashboard on the Corona web site, where you find this data. However, that will only effectively hide your app from view—it will still be transmitting data to the Corona cloud. To avoid this, too, you need to add `launchPad=false` to your `config.lua` file.

> **Note**   Usage of `analytics.logEvents()` is not recorded by the Corona Launchpad analytics feature. At least, I am unaware of any way to see it if it is. The statistics captured by this service, while certainly useful, really are pretty basic in nature. If you need something more robust, take a look at Flurry for sure.

One final note: By law, when you are using analytics you are now required to include a privacy policy in your application that a user can easily view at will. Unless you fancy yourself a trial lawyer, or have a bunch of spare cash lying around to hire such a lawyer, I suggest keeping this in mind!

Summary

In this chapter, you covered a wide range of topics, from data storage in a SQLite database to in-game ads and purchases, from location awareness services to more advanced networking capabilities. You also looked at things like analytics and some more advanced file system capabilities.

In the next and final chapter, you'll look at the last logical step in creating a Corona app: packaging it up and getting it into the various app stores for a variety of mobile platforms. This is the final piece of the puzzle that you'll need to bring Astro Rescue to a real conclusion, as well as your knowledge of Corona. After reading it, you should have all the basic information you'll need to start creating your apps, be they games or not, and to get them out into the world at large.

What are you waiting for? Turn the page, let's get to it!

Chapter 11

Testing and Publishing

So you've spent months of your life hacking away at code, generating art resources, mixing audio, and making sure everything works in the Corona simulator. You've polished and you've tweaked and your game is ready for the eyes of someone other than yourself to check out. Or, maybe not—maybe it's just time to see how it runs on a real device. (Of course, you probably would have done that before this point, but work with me on this one!)

In other words: it's time to build and package your application in a form you can deploy to a real device and, perhaps, to others' devices as well.

More than that, it might be time to **publish** your game to an app store and start seeing that sweet, sweet money come a-rollin' in!

Both of these topics are what this chapter is all about. Here, I'll show you how to create the appropriate packages that can be run on a real Android or iOS device, I'll show you some ways to get those files onto the device, and I'll talk about what it takes to get your app published.

In addition, I'll talk about some techniques for debugging an application on a real device (some of which was touched upon in Chapter 10 under "Analytics").

Let's start with the simplest case first, though: getting your app onto a real Android device.

Feed the Robot: Building for Android

Building your app for Android is perhaps the easiest possibility, so let's begin there.

Before you can do that, though, you need to ensure that your system has what it needs to build Android applications. At this point I assume you have installed Corona itself (if you haven't, what have you been doing all this time?!). This allows you to build apps targeted for the simulator, as you well know by now. To be able to then build for Android depends on what your operating system is. If you're running Mac then you already have everything you need, assuming at least you're not on an ancient Mac!

> **Note**   For Windows, however, you have an additional step: you need to install the Java Development Kit, or JDK, if you don't have it already installed. This is provided by Oracle. At the time of this writing, the full link is `http://www.oracle.com/technetwork/java/javase/downloads/index.html` but you can find it easily enough on `www.oracle.com` if that link fails.

> **Caution**   You should not install JDK 7 as there are issues with this and Corona (more precisely, Android only supports the 32-bit version of JDK 6 and you'll get keystore password errors if you try and use JDK 7). This goes for Mac as well as Windows platforms. While in theory you can install both 6 and 7 side by side and get Corona to work by ensuring there is not a path environment variable that points to JDK 7, I frankly could never get this setup to work, and so I go with the "better safe than sorry" approach of just sticking with JDK 6 until Android allows JDK 7 to be used. There are threads in the Corona forums dealing with this, though, if you want to try to get it to work.

It's a perfectly typical installation so I'll skip going over it in detail. Once you have it installed, you're ready to go.

> **Caution**   You'll need the 32-bit version, not the 64-bit version. Unfortunately, if you currently have the 64-bit version installed, you'll need to uninstall it and install the 32-bit version instead. Alternatively, you can configure your system to ensure that the 32-bit version, which you can install side by side with the 64-bit version, is the default and is what Corona will use. I can tell you from experience, however, that this can be tricky sometimes to get working, so if you have any choice at all I recommend only installing the 32-bit version.

The procedure for building an Android version of your app is simple. First, load it up in the simulator as you normally would. Once it's running, click the File menu, then Build For, and select Android, as shown in Figure 11-1.

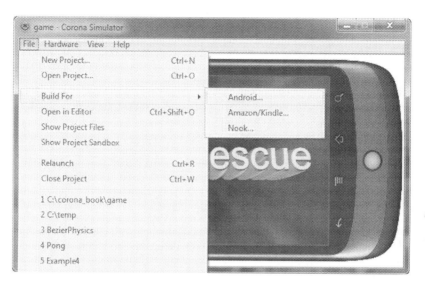

Figure 11-1. Kicking off an Android build

Once you do so, you'll be greeted with the window shown in Figure 11-2. Here, you'll need to fill in a few details, beginning with the Application Name. This can be anything you like, of course (by default, Corona will use the name of the folder your project is in). The Version Code value is an integer value you that must increment every time you update your application. By "update" I mean any time you release a new version into the world as a published application. You **do not** need to change this value every time you do a new build during development and debugging.

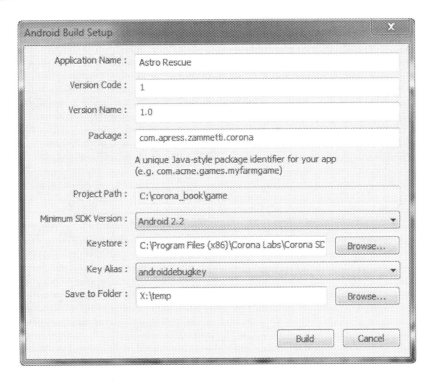

Figure 11-2. *Android build settings*

The Version Name is a more user-friendly version string and can pretty much be anything that makes sense to you.

Perhaps the most important value is Package. Typically, as the note there says, this is in the form of a unique Java-style package identifier, which is normally `tld.company.app`. For example, for Astro Rescue I used `com.apress.zammetti.corona` (com is the top-level domain, or TLD; zammetti is essentially the app name, and corona further breaks it down; you can have as many subdivisions, separated by periods, as you like). If I were publishing this game for real in an app store, I'd probably use something like `com.etherient.astrorescue` instead.

> **Note**   While this Java-style package name is typical, there's no technical reason you have to use that form. In theory, any unique string here would do the trick. However, the Java-style-package naming convention came about as a good way to avoid name collisions, which is the key here. If you try to use `astrorescue` as the package, and another app in the store uses the same string, then that's going to cause problems, most likely for end users who try to install both . . . and since they're the ones paying the bills, they're the last ones you want to aggravate!

Also note that some characters are not valid in a package name. Hyphens, for example, are not allowed and must be converted to underscores (or some other supported character, of course, but an underscore is most typical). Any component of the name (read: a value before or after a period) cannot begin with a number. Last, no component of a package name can use a keyword reserved in Java, such as `static` or `public`.

The Project Path should be filled in for you, so no worries there. The Minimum SDK Version is the minimum version of Android your game will support. Corona supports a minimum of Android 2.2 (using an ARMv7 processor), so at the time of this writing at least that's all you'll find in this dropdown anyway.

The Keystore is next, and for development purposes you'll typically use the keystore supplied by Corona, which should be selected initially for you; otherwise you'll need to browse for it in the Corona directory. The keystore holds the cryptographic keys and certificates Corona needs to sign your APK, or Application Package. An APK is, for all intents and purposes, the executable that Android runs and is the final output that Corona gives you at the end of all of this.

> **Note**   In reality, an APK is actually an archive file (using the ZIP format) that stores your application's code and all the resources it uses, such as artwork and audio files. It also contains a certificate that Android uses to validate your application (hence why you need the keystore to build the APK), and metadata describing important information about your application (which Corona generates for you, and perhaps using some of the values you put in `build.settings`).

The Key Alias field lets you select a certificate stored in the keystore you selected. The Corona-supplied debug keystore only has a single key, androiddebugkey, so make sure that's selected.

Last, in the Save To Folder field, tell Corona where you want the APK to be placed. Once all of that is done, click the Build button and wait a few seconds. While Corona does its thing, you should see a window like that in Figure 11-3.

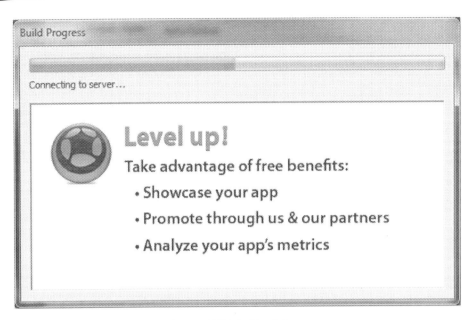

Figure 11-3. *Corona's "twiddling your thumbs while your APK is built" window*

Corona will do a bit of work on your PC and then ship the result off to the Corona build servers to complete the process. What you'll wind up with is an APK file where you told Corona to put it (barring errors or other problems, naturally). This file is ready for you to run either on the Android emulator on your PC, which would require you to first install the Android SDK, or on a real Android device.

RELEASE BUILD SIGNING

Using the debug keystore is great for development, very quick and easy, but at some point you're going to want to release your application to the world, and at that point you'll need your own keystore.

Fortunately, doing so is quite easy. It depends on the JDK you installed earlier. All you need to do is jump out to a command prompt and use this command:

```
keytool -genkey -v -keystore XXX.keystore -alias YYY -keyalg RSA -validity 999999
```

Here, XXX is the name of the keystore (I generally use the name of my application, and I have a separate keystore for each application) and YYY is the alias name of the application. Again, the easiest thing to do is to simply use the same application name.

If you're using a Mac, don't forget that you'll need to sudo to execute this command.

Once you do this, you'll be prompted for some information, starting with a password. It is very important that you do not forget this password! If you do, you will likely not be able to update your application in the future and you'll find yourself having to create a new keystore and essentially a new "branch" of your application. You'll need to enter the password twice to confirm.

You'll also be asked for some identifying information, including first and last name, the name of your organizational unit and organization, city, state, and country. What information you actually enter here isn't terribly important; I'd urge you to use legitimate information, but it's ultimately up to you and shouldn't matter much to anything that might be using the keystore.

Once you do this, you'll be actually prepared to sign and release your application in the Google Play store (which I'll discuss in the "App Store Model of Distribution" section later in this chapter).

Deploying to Android Devices

So, now that you have an APK in hand, how exactly do you get it on a device to play with? Or, on the emulator that comes with the Android SDK? Well, there's actually a number of different ways, but the first is the Android Debug Bridge, or ADB.

ADB is a tool that comes with the Android SDK, so if you don't have that installed you'll either need to visit developer.android.com and install it, or use one of the other methods described.

Assuming you have it installed, then all you need to do is execute this:

```
adb install -r app.apk
```

As long as adb is in your path and app.apk is in the current directory, executing that command will push the APK onto the first device ADB finds attached to your PC. If you have an emulator running, it will be that device. If you have an actual Android phone attached via USB, and assuming USB debugging is enabled on the device as well as allowing third-party (non-market) installations turned on, it will be installed on **that** device.

Another way to get the app onto your device is to simply copy the APK to your device if it's attached in USB mass storage mode. You'll then have to browse to the file on the device with the file system browser of your choice and open it. You should again get the usual installation popup at that point.

A third way, if you have access to a web server, is to copy the APK to that server and then access the APK from the browser on your device. Note, however, that if you encounter a problem where you download a text file instead of triggering an application installation, you will need to add a MIME type to your server's configuration. Assuming it's Apache for example, add the following line to your .htaccess file:

```
AddType application/vnd.android.package-archive .apk
```

A fourth approach, and the technique I personally use most because it is arguably the simplest and, in my mind, definitely the most convenient, is this: I simply create a share to a directory on my PC, ensure the APK is created by the Corona build process in that directory, and then, when the build completes, I use a file system browser like ES File Explorer, Astro, or FX—all of which most relevantly have SMB capabilities—to browse to that share and directly launch the file. This approach is nice because I don't have to bother with USB cables, ensuring drivers are installed, whether ADB sees my device properly, and all that sort of stuff, which can sometimes get sticky with Android development. I also don't have to worry about uploading to a web server (of course, the web server could be running locally, which frankly would make that approach not much different than this one). It's still a two-step process—then again, all of these are, but now it's very straightforward. Plus it's easy when I'm testing on multiple devices, since the same APK is always at the same location and I can browse to it and install it any time I like.

> **Note**   I personally prefer ES File Explorer, but I used Astro early on and FX for a few weeks and they are all quite good. There are also many other choices, which is of course one of the great things about Android generally. Just ensure it has SMB support and you're good to go.

On-Device Debugging with Android

The next question is how to go about debugging your application once it's on a device or the emulator. Here there are a couple of approaches.

First, the Android SDK has some tools specifically for this purpose. One of them, adb, you've already met, and it offers some debugging commands aside from the `install` command. The `logcat` command allows you to view the Android system debug logs. This log contains content from the system as well as from applications. It can be quite helpful, but also can be difficult to wade through. Fortunately, this command also allows you to specify some filtering criteria, such as viewing only fatal error messages. In addition to filtering by priority, you can also filter by tag, which is a string that identifies the component that generated the message. Yes, you can filter it to only see messages generated by your application, but you'll need to find the tag in a message in the log first to know what it is.

> **Tip**   There are `logcat` viewers in the Google Play Store that will let you view the messages on your device. This can be extremely handy when you're debugging away from your PC. Simply search for `logcat` and you'll find many options to choose from. However, by default you'll get an absolute boatload of system messages that come flying in fast and furious, so proper filtering is a must (and this is true whether using an on-device viewer or not). Figure 11-4 shows one such on-device viewer.

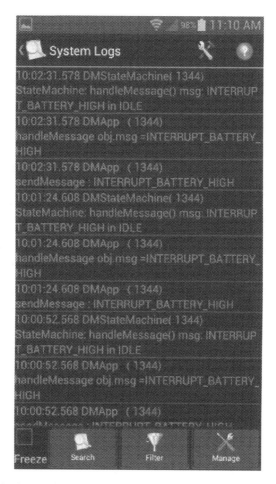

Figure 11-4. The log viewer function in the Android Tuner app

Another `adb` command that can be useful is `pull`. This allows you to grab a specific file from your device. If your application writes its own log file, for example, this is a good way to grab that file to check out on your PC with a proper editor.

If you're a bit more Java-savvy, the `adb jdwp` command might be of some use to you. This prints a list of running JDWP (Java Debug Wire Protocol) processes on the device that you can attach to with a debugger for remote debugging.

The Dalvik Debug Monitor Server, or DDMS, is another option available to you. To use this you'll need to install the Eclipse IDE and the Android Developer Tools extension. Once you do, you'll have access to a powerful tool that provides all sorts of valuable debugging tools, including the ability to take screenshots, viewing heap usage of a process, tracking object allocations, method profiling, network usage analysis, spoofing location information, and more. As a Corona developer, some of this won't be of much use. For example, method profiling isn't likely to provide as much useful information as it does to a native Android developer, since most of the methods you might be interested in are abstracted away from you by Corona itself. Still, you can sometimes gain some insight into your code with it, at least indirectly.

> **Note**   At the time of this writing, DDMS is being deprecated by Google in favor of the Android Device
> Monitor, which is basically the same thing, but with some additional features. You can still use DDMS right
> now, though, and probably will be able to for a while, but you may want to start looking at Android Device
> Monitor, too.

Custom Log File

Don't discount writing out your own log file! Do you remember the utils.lua file and the log()
method that you saw way back in Chapter 3? You could modify that as shown in Listing 11-1 to
easily allow logging to a file.

Listing 11-1. Changing the utils:log( ) Method to Write to a File

```
function utils:log(inFilename, inMessage, inObject)

  if inObject == nil then
    inObject = " ";
  else
    inObject = " - " .. json.encode(inObject);
  end

  local logMessage = inFilename .. " - " .. inMessage .. inObject;
  print(logMessage);

  if logToFile == true then
    if logFile == nil then
      local path = system.pathForFile("log.txt", system.DocumentsDirectory);
      logFile = io.open(path, "w");
      if logFile == nil then
        logFile = io.open(path, "w");
      end
    end
    logFile:write(logMessage .. "\n");
  end

end
```

This version checks the value of the global variable logToFile. If it's true then the logged message
will also be written to the log.txt file. That way, you can leave that variable set to false and only set
it to true when you do a debug build (or vice versa, but that would be a bit dangerous!). You'll have
to close the reference to the opened log file stored in the variable logFile at some point, like when
your app ends, but you get the picture (and I'm sure there are even better ways to do this that you
can write yourself at this point).

Real-Time FPS and Memory Display

Although in no way specific to Android debugging, check out Listing 11-2. This is a handy function that you may well want to add to your own personal `utils.lua` file (which I suggest building up over time with the functions you find generally useful).

Listing 11-2. Showing Real-Time FPS and Memory

```
function utils:showFPSAndMem()

  local prevTime = 0;
  local curTime = 0;
  local dt = 0;
  local fps = 60;
  local mem = 0;
  local frameCount = 0;
  local avg = 0;
  local slowest = 1000;
   underlay = display.newRect(
    0, display.contentHeight - 30, display.contentWidth, 34
  );
  underlay:setReferencePoint(display.TopLeftReferencePoint);
  underlay:setFillColor(0, 0, 0, 128);
   displayInfo = display.newText(
    "FPS: ??, Avg: ?, Slowest: ?, Mem: ????mb", 0, 0, native.systemFontBold, 20
  );
  displayInfo.x = display.contentWidth / 2;
  displayInfo.y = display.contentHeight - 14;
  local function updateText()
    curTime = system.getTimer();
    dt = curTime - prevTime;
    prevTime = curTime;
    fps = math.floor(1000 / dt);
    mem = system.getInfo("textureMemoryUsed") / 1000000;
    if fps > 60 then
      fps = 60
    end
    frameCount = frameCount + 1;
    if frameCount > 150 then
      avg = avg + fps;
      if fps < slowest then
        slowest = fps;
      end
    end
    local a = math.round(avg / (frameCount - 150));
    a = math.floor(a * math.pow(10, 0) + 0.5) / math.pow(10, 0);
    collectgarbage();
    local sysMem = collectgarbage("count") * 0.001;
    sysMem = math.floor(sysMem * 1000) * 0.001;
    displayInfo.text = "FPS: " .. fps .. ", Avg: " .. a ..
      ", Slowest: " .. slowest ..
      ", T-Mem: " .. string.sub(mem, 1, string.len(mem) - 4) .. "mb" ..
      ", S-Mem: " .. sysMem .. "mb";
```

```
    underlay:toFront()
    displayInfo:toFront()
  end
  underlay.isVisible = true;
  displayInfo.isVisible = true;
  Runtime:addEventListener("enterFrame", updateText)

end
```

I'll leave it as an exercise for you to walk through this code and understand it, but the high-level explanation is simple: this will display, in real-time (well, close enough anyway!) the frames per second (FPS) your app is achieving, the average FPS since the app started, the slowest FPS recorded, how much texture memory is in use by your app, and how much total system memory your app is using. This is invaluable information because obviously you want a good frame rate throughout, so if you hit a part in your game where it slows down too much, you'll know exactly where to tune it up. Also, there is a general rule of thumb out there that says you don't want to use more than about 14 MB of texture memory at any given time, lest you run some lower-end devices out of memory and force-close your app.

> **Note**   In reality, there are probably not all that many devices out there anymore where this rule of thumb still matters. However, the underlying point, that texture memory usage should be kept to a minimum, is still valid even on the most high-end devices. Ditto system memory.

Logging Objects

One last function I'd like to toss your way is also very useful when writing your own log file. Listing 11-3 is the dump() function (hey now, no off-color jokes there!).

Listing 11-3. The Unfortunately Named, but Highly Useful, dump( ) Function

```
function utils:dump(inT)

  local print_r_cache = {};

  local function sub_print_r(inT, indent)

    if (print_r_cache[tostring(inT)]) then
      print(indent .. "*" .. tostring(inT));
    else
      print_r_cache[tostring(inT)] = true;
      if (type(inT) == "table") then
        for pos, val in pairs(inT) do
          if (type(val) == "table") then
            print(indent .. "[" .. pos .. "] => " .. tostring(inT) .. " {");
            sub_print_r(val, indent .. string.rep(" ", string.len(pos) + 8));
            print(indent .. string.rep(" ", string.len(pos) + 6) .. "}");
```

```
        elseif (type(val) == "string") then
          print(indent .. "[" .. pos .. '] => "' .. val .. '"');
        else
          print(indent .. "[" .. pos .. "] => " .. tostring(val));
        end
      end
    else
      print(indent .. tostring(inT));
    end
  end
end

if (type(inT) == "table") then
    print(tostring(inT) .. " {");
  sub_print_r(inT, "  ");
  print("}");
else
  sub_print_r(inT, "  ");
end

print();

end
```

This function simply displays a given object passed to it in all its glory. Pass it a table, for example, and it will recursively list every member in that table. This is something that the basic `print()` function can't do, but is something that you wind up needing all the time. Naturally, this is highly useful during development, not just debugging on a real device, but either way it's very useful.

An Apple a Day: Build for iOS

Building your app for iOS isn't really any more difficult than doing so for Android. However, there is one key requirement: you must have a Mac.

You can't build an iOS app on Windows, even though most of the actual build process happens on the Corona Labs servers. This is because Xcode, Apple's IDE and associated tools, and the iOS SDK, are only available on Mac.

> **Tip**   If, like me, you aren't normally a Mac user, and if you don't own one already (or have easy access to one), and if you don't intend to switch to Mac full time, I suggest looking at buying a Mac Mini. Assuming you want to buy new and don't go the eBay route, this is the cheapest way to get a decent enough Mac for iOS development. They are actually very cool little computers and are more than enough for doing some part-time development. There are also services like MacInCloud (www.macincloud.com) that let you essentially rent a virtual Mac over the Internet.

So, I'll assume at this point that you have access to a Mac in some fashion. The next step is to install the Corona SDK, Xcode, and the iOS SDK. You already know where to get Corona of course, and the other two can be downloaded from the Mac version of the App Store. Once that's done, you're ready to build.

Just like under Windows, fire up the Corona Simulator and load your app. Once your app is running, ensure the simulator is the current app and click the File menu, then Build, and finally iOS. This is just like the procedure when building for Android on Windows as previously described; however, the window that results will look a little different, as shown in Figure 11-5.

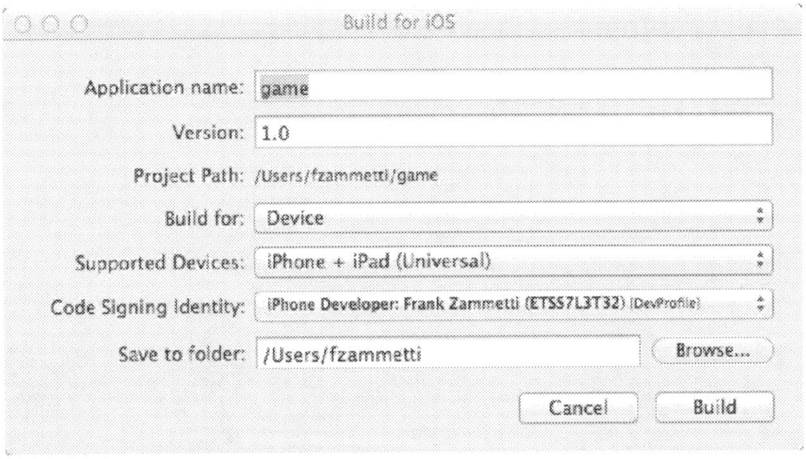

Application name:	game
Version:	1.0
Project Path:	/Users/fzammetti/game
Build for:	Device
Supported Devices:	iPhone + iPad (Universal)
Code Signing Identity:	iPhone Developer: Frank Zammetti (ETSS7L3T32) (DevProfile)
Save to folder:	/Users/fzammetti

Cancel   Build

Figure 11-5. iOS build settings window on Mac

The required information is similar to doing Android builds, but at the same time a little different. Application Name and Version Name are just like when doing an Android build. The Build For drop-down allows you to choose whether you're building for an actual iOS device or for the Xcode simulator. This comes with Xcode/iOS SDK and is similar to the Android emulator, which allows you to test your app on a virtual iOS device. The Supported Devices dropdown allows you to determine whether your app targets iPhone only, iPad only, or is a universal application that is designed to work for either form factor.

The Code Signing Identity is similar to the Keystore/Key Alias fields when building for Android, but in the case of iOS it allows you to select a provisioning profile to build the app. You only need to select a profile if you're building for a real device (not selecting one when building for the simulator is akin to using the Corona-supplied debug certificate when doing an Android build). If you elect to build for the Xcode simulator then at this point you're ready to go—simply click Build and the simulator will launch and run your app once the build process completes. For simulator work, this is the end of the process.

A provisioning profile is required to build for a device, though, and this is what ties your development devices to your team, or allows you to publish to the App Store. Before you can even deal with profiles, however, you'll need to do a few things.

First, you'll need to register as an Apple developer (https://developer.apple.com/programs/register). Once you do that, you need to create a certificate request. To do so you'll launch the Keychain Access tool found in the Utilities folder of your Mac. Next you'll select the Certificate Assistant ➤ Request A Certificate From A Certificate Authority menu. You'll be asked to provide some information such as e-mail address, name, and so on, very much like when creating a certificate for Android builds. Walk through the process as directed until you come to the end, where you'll save the generated key.

> **Note**   Before you can deploy to an actual device and publish to the App Store, you'll need to cough up the $99 annual fee Apple requires to join their iOS developer program. You can sign up for a developer account without paying this fee up front to gain access to iOS development documentation and tools, but until you pay your dues you will only be able to use the Corona and iOS simulators for development, not physical devices.

Next, log on to the iOS Dev Center web site (https://developer.apple.com/devcenter/ios/index.action) and click the link for the iOS Provisioning Portal. Once there, click Devices in the left-hand column and then click the Add Devices button. Add any devices you intend to develop on, including their unique device ID, which you can find in iTunes when your device is connected.

After your devices are added, while still in the provisioning portal, click Certificates on the left and then click Request Certificate. You will then select the keystore file generated in the previous step. In a few seconds, your certificate will be generated and you'll be able to download it. Do so, and then double-click the file in Finder to add the certificate to your computer.

After that, you need to create a new app ID. On the left in the provisioning portal, click App IDs, then click the New App ID button. Fill in the required information (description, bundle identifier, etc.) and click Submit. Your app ID will be created.

At this point you are now ready to create a provisioning profile. This is done from the Provisioning link on the left side of the provisioning portal. Assuming you are doing development, select the Development tab (when you're ready to publish your app, the process is the same, except you'll create a distribution profile via the Distribution tab). Once there, enter the required information, including the app ID you created, select the devices that the profile will work with, and then click Submit.

Now, launch the Xcode Organizer (Figure 11-6) tool on your Mac and click the Devices tab up top. Then, under the Library heading on the left select Provisioning Profiles. Next, click the Refresh button. The profile you just created should appear there. At this point, quit and restart the Corona simulator if it's running, and the profile should now be selectable in the Code Signing Identity drop-down.

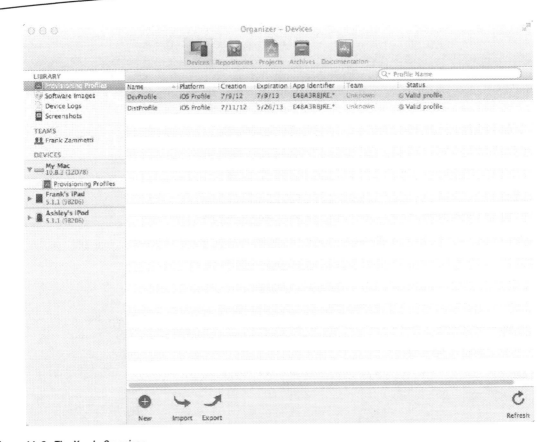

Figure 11-6. The Xcode Organizer

As you can see, the process for getting an iOS build ready for deployment to a device is considerably more involved than for Android. Once all the prerequisites are done, however, the process really boils down to a few simple steps.

Creating an iOS App Store Package

One other step that you'll need to be familiar with at this point is how to create an iOS App Store Package, better known as a .ipa file. You'll need to do this when you're ready to distribute your app to the App Store, or if you're going to use TestFlightApp.com, as described in the TestFlightApp.com section (coming up shortly!).

To create a .ipa file:

- Create a folder named Payload, ensuring you use that specific capitalization, somewhere on your Mac.

- Put the .app file that Corona generated for you into it.

- Zip up the folder in Finder.

- Rename the resultant archive to xxx.ipa where xxx is anything you like.

Yep, that's it! The .ipa file will now be ready to ship off to the App Store (assuming you uses a valid distribution provisioning profile when you built it) or to `TestFlightApp.com`.

Deploying to iOS Devices

Now that you can build an iOS app that is deployable to one of your registered development devices, how do you actually go about getting it onto a device? Here, as with Android, you have a couple of choices.

First, you can use the Xcode Organizer tool. To do this, first connect your device to your Mac. Then launch Xcode Organizer and look for the device name under the Devices header on the left. You should find the device with a green indicator next to it. Next, expand the device menu and select Applications. Click the Add button, navigate to the folder where the .app file that the Corona Simulator generated for you is, and select it. The app should then be installed on the device.

Alternatively, you can use iTunes to install your app. To do this, open iTunes and connect your device. Then, drag the .app file into the Library in the upper left. You should then see the app available for installation in the Apps tab, and you can install it like any other app.

TestFlightApp.com

One third option, which I personally like quite a bit, is a site called `TestFlightApp.com`. This site allows you to distribute your app to beta testers without their needing to do anything special in terms of setting up SDKs or any of that.

The process is simple. First, you sign up for a `TestFlightApp.com` account. Next, you invite users to be part of your testing via tools available on the site. This process will also collect the device IDs of those users. You then add those IDs back on the iOS Provisioning Portal page. Last, you build your app as always and upload it to `https://testflightapp.com`, and that's it! The users will receive notification via e-mail of the app's availability, and will be provided a link to use to install and begin testing it.

This process requires a .ipa file, which was described in the "Creating an iOS App Store Package" section. Other than that, though, the process is very straightforward (oh, and did I mention free?!).

> **Caution**   `TestFlightApp.com` also offers an SDK that allows you to hook in some good telemetry and statistics capturing. Unfortunately, it doesn't seem that you can use that with a Corona-built app, at least not without purchasing an Enterprise license and writing your own plugin in Objective-C, which is a whole other can of worms, as they say. Also, they are currently working on an Android version of their services that, when ready, will help streamline beta testing on that platform as well.

On-Device Debugging with iOS

When working in the iOS simulator, you can view the log by executing the following in a terminal:

```
tail -f /var/log/system.log
```

This is along the lines of using `logcat` to view logs in Android.

When debugging on a real device you can view those same logs from the Xcode Organizer.

> **Note**   Aside from these logs, all the same generic advice given earlier in the "On-Device Debugging with Android" section applies to iOS, too, in terms of extra functions in utils and such. Unfortunately, the native platform tools, whether for Android or iOS, while perhaps helpful in some situations, probably won't be as helpful as you'd like. Logging and perhaps analytics are probably your best bets for the most part.

The App Store Model of Distribution

Sit here at my knee, children, and let me spin you a tale. Time was, I reckon, way back in history, around the year 2000. I remember like it was . . . just 13 years ago!

Microsoft had come out with what I thought was a pretty cool mobile operating system: PocketPC (later renamed to Windows Mobile, and now of course Windows Phone, but I'll stick with PocketPC since that's the timeframe I'm referring to). Back then, when you made an app to sell for PocketPC, you had to do it all yourself. Meaning, you likely created your own web site, as I did, for example, and did your own custom programming to handle purchases and registrations, and all that good stuff. So, you not only had to be an app developer but you had to be a web developer too! You then put your app up there for sale and then went about advertising in whatever way you could.

The plus side to that was complete control and 100% profit. Everything you made went right into your pocket and you could create any sales model that made sense. You could go out and purchase banner ad space that linked back to your site for purchases. You could possibly form a partnership with another developer to include an advertisement for your game when they started up theirs, and vice versa. Whatever you could dream up and make work, it was all up to you.

Now, it didn't take long for people to think to themselves, "Self, there's **got** to be an easier way!"

And before you knew it, there it was: storefront sites started to pop up. These sites would do all the hard work for you: advertising, credit card processing, handling of returns, and so forth. They would do all this in exchange for a percentage of your sales. So, you gave up a little bit off each sale and in return your hassle level went **way** down.

This worked fairly well, but people who wanted apps still had to find out about these sites. They had to go visit them in the relatively primitive web browser on their device, or, as was more common at the time, they would do so on their PC, download the installation file, manually copy it to their device, and then execute it there to be installed.

It wasn't a particularly pleasant experience, truth be told, but by and large it **did** work.

Today, of course, we have what are really the descendants of those storefront sites. Apple's App Store, Google's Play store, Amazon's Appstore for Android: all of these serve the same basic purpose.

They also work in much the same way: for a percentage of each sale, and in some cases some small up-front fees, they will take care of most of the details of selling your apps for you.

In today's world, though, they go a step further (and some **a lot** further). As will be discussed in the remainder of this chapter, these are curated experiences to varying degrees. This means that in contrast to the old days, where the storefront sites would generally sell any app—and of course you could still sell them yourself—the companies that run these new app stores do some degree of quality control on the apps they sell. There are requirements you have to meet, guidelines you have to follow.

But the benefit is great: we very much live in an app-centric world right now. People with their fancy, über-powerful smartphones think of apps when they think of things to do with their devices. As part of that mind-set, they are very much trained to go to the app stores provided to them, and in some cases that's the **only** way they can get apps on to their device (without resorting to nonstandard techniques at least).

These modern-day app stores also absolutely dwarf those old storefront sites, both in terms of the volume of apps available and in terms of your profit potential. Simply put, even if there are other ways you might sell your apps, if you aren't in these modern stores, you are almost certainly giving away money (and if money isn't your motivating factor, then you're giving up exposure, too).

So what are the major app stores out there today, and what does it take to get into them? Well, as I said, that's not a simple, one-size-fits-all answer—it's actually a spectrum. Let's start by discussing the one that most developers generally acknowledge as easiest to deal with in most regards.

Google Play

Google Play (http://play.google.com) is the latest iteration of the store Google has built for its Android platform. While there are a number of other stores out there for Android, Google Play is what you might call the canonical store, and certainly the most popular overall. It also happens to be the one with possibly the lowest barrier to entry.

You can get going with Google Play in just a few minutes! All it takes is a few simple steps:

- Register for a Google Play publisher account (https://accounts.google.com/ServiceLogin?service=androiddeveloper&passive=1209600&continue=https://play.google.com/apps/publish/v2/&followup=https://play.google.com/apps/publish/v2/).

- Pay the $25 registration fee when you sign up.

- Wait approximately 48 hours for your registration to be processed (may be considerably less, but could take this long in some cases).

- If you intend to publish only free apps, then you're done when your registration is processed.

- If you intend to sell apps, you also need to set up a Google Merchant account (https://accounts.google.com/ServiceLogin?service=sierra&ltmpl=seller&continue=https://checkout.google.com/merchantSignInRedirect). You can go ahead and do this while you're waiting for your registration to process.

Once you're alerted via e-mail that your registration is complete, you can log on to the developer console (https://play.google.com/apps/publish) and you can publish an app at your convenience.

> **Tip**   A unique feature of Google Play, and one that is incredibly handy, is the ability to browse for apps on your PC and then automatically install apps to an Android device. As long as your device is known to Google Play, you'll be able to select it from a list when you click the Install button for a given app, and the app will magically be installed in just a few seconds!

Google takes 30% of each sale; 70% goes to you. They handle all the details of sales and refunds for you, and may even do some small degree of advertising on your behalf (although as your only source of advertising it's nothing to count on). You are paid each month via your Google Merchant account, which results in a direct deposit to the checking account you put on file. There are no recurring fees either, just the initial $25. That's quite a low barrier to entry!

Publishing to Google Play

Adding a new application is a simple step-by-step process that the developer console walks you through. Along the way you'll need to enter a host of information, including application title, description, recent changes (if updating an already published app), categories under which your app should appear in Google Play, URLs for your web site, pricing information, and other basic information about the app. You'll also have the opportunity to upload screenshots and even link to demonstration videos of your app in action.

Naturally, you'll have to upload the APK you generated as well, signed with the certificate in the keystore you created as detailed in the "Feed the Robot" section. My experience has been that once you do all this, it should take less than an hour in most cases for your app to appear in Google Play, although it could take 24 to 48 hours when browsing Google Play on your device, because Google Play only shows apps compatible with your device, and it takes some time to populate that list.

Unlike the Apple App Store, which I'll discuss in an upcoming section, Google is **extremely** lenient when it comes to the apps it publishes. There are some automated test tools it runs against your APK to ensure validity and to weed out some obvious malware, but generally you can publish anything you like without a problem.

> **Note**   Some people feel this is too lenient, but it's entirely a matter of opinion. Some people prefer the more stringent Apple curation approach, while others think the Google approach is more open. Certainly it can't be argued that it is easier and faster to get an app published in Google Play, and virtually anyone can do it, but whether that's a good thing or a bad thing is for you as a customer to decide. As an app developer, though, you certainly want to be in as many stores on as many platforms as possible to maximize your earning potential.

Updating your app later is similarly easy: just go back into the developer console, edit your app, upload the new APK (and screenshots if needed), update the meta-information, and click a button. Usually in only a few minutes your new version will be available to the world.

If you are charging for your app, the Google Merchant account you created can be accessed (http://checkout.google.com/sell) to see all the sales you've had, as well as refunds given. You can also get financial reports there for tax purposes.

All in all, there really isn't much to working with Google Play! Once you know how to create an APK using the steps discussed earlier in this chapter, and you have the necessary account(s) set up with Google, it's really just entering some information and clicking a few buttons.

Other App Stores: Amazon Appstore for Android and Barnes & Noble Nook Store

As I mentioned, the Google Play store is the One App Store to Rule Them All™ for Android—or at least, that's probably what Google would want you to think. Strictly speaking, thought, it isn't the only game in town.

With the release of their Kindle device, which is Android based, Amazon has created their own store, pedantically named the Amazon Appstore for Android. However, Amazon's store isn't **just** for Kindle devices: you can install their store app (http://www.amazon.com/mobile-apps/b?ie=UTF8&node=2350149011) on any Android device (as long as you set your device to allow installation of third-party apps from unknown sources; see your device's security settings for these options).

Once you do so, you'll be able to browse their collection of apps. This includes much of what you find on Google Play, but there might be a few other gems unique to the Amazon store to be found. Also, from the first day their store went live, Amazon has given away one app for free daily. As with Android apps in general, if you get an app for free that normally isn't, you'll still "own" the app and can install it later.

> **Tip**   In case it didn't occur to you: even if you don't intend to use Amazon's store, I generally still suggest visiting it daily to get the free app. That way, if you decide down the road you want an app, you may find that you in fact own it already, thanks to Amazon!

Nominally, Amazon charges a $99 annual fee to publish to their store. However, they are "currently" waiving that fee. I use quotes because they have in fact been waiving that fee from the very beginning! They may well stop waiving it at some point, but it seems like a bit of marketing on their part to continue "waiving" it. Like Google, Amazon takes a 30% cut of each sale. However, there's no extra merchant-type account to deal with; the single account you create (https://developer.amazon.com/welcome.html) takes care of all of it in one place. Payment is monthly with Amazon as well, and again is a direct deposit.

Submitting an app is very much like the Google process and requires substantially the same information. The difference, though, is that Amazon does some deeper verification of your app and even does a little bit of quality control (although very little, it seems). There is also a longer waiting period for an app to be initially published, sometimes up to two weeks. Updates tend to be processed much quicker, however.

Barnes & Noble also has a store specific to their Nook devices. Unlike Amazon, however, this store truly is specific to those devices: you cannot access the Nook store from a non–Barnes & Noble device.

Overall, the process is very similar to both Google Play and the Amazon Appstore, and the fees involved are very similar in terms of setting up an account and selling your apps. However, Barnes & Noble is the most stringent of the three when it comes to reviewing your app. In fact, they have been known to reject apps that aren't of "sufficient quality." Other times, you may have to go through review a few times to get all the kinks worked out to their liking before your app is published.

> **Note**   My own experience with Barnes & Noble was like this. My game, Engineer, had to go through review three times before it was accepted. Each time there was something I had missed that didn't meet their app guidelines, which are available to you once you create a developer account with them. I strongly suggest becoming familiar with these guidelines before you begin writing your apps. That will make your life a lot easier down the road, I can tell you from experience!

As I mentioned, it's a good idea to be in as many stores as possible, to reach as large an audience as you can with your apps. Of course, using Corona gives your app the ability to be on many supported platforms, so by choosing Corona you must already be thinking along these lines! None of the Android stores are difficult to get into, nor are they difficult to deal with once you're in them, so I definitely encourage you not to ignore any of them, for the sake of your bank account if nothing else!

The Only Game in Town for iOS: The Apple App Store

You'll need to pay the $99 fee to get into the iOS developer program before you can publish to the App Store. Once you do that, the process isn't very much different than publishing to Google Play. Everything you need is on the Apple Developer Center web site (`https://developer.apple.com/membercenter`).

Getting published is a more difficult experience here than in other stores because Apple takes a much more proactive role in ensuring quality. They do a far more in-depth review of applications and have a much more stringent set of guidelines you'll need to follow. The process also takes considerably longer, sometimes weeks. The result, though, is that apps that make it through the process are all but guaranteed to be of a certain level of quality and to have a certain degree of consistency among them.

The app review guidelines can be found here at `https://developer.apple.com/appstore/guidelines.html` and I highly suggest reviewing them before you submit your app for review. It's not at all unusual to fail review the first (or even second or third!) time through, but the more familiar you are with the guidelines and the more you strive to adhere to them, the better your chances are. It should be noted that if you do fail, subsequent review rounds tend to happen quite a bit faster.

Publishing to the Apple App Store

Figure 11-7 shows what you'll see when you visit the Apple Developer Center site and log in after becoming a member.

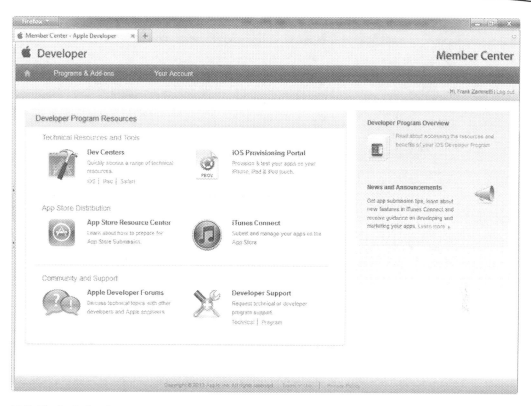

Figure 11-7. The Apple Developer portal page

Once there, you'll use iTunes Connect to begin the process. When you click that link you'll be greeted with the window shown in Figure 11-8.

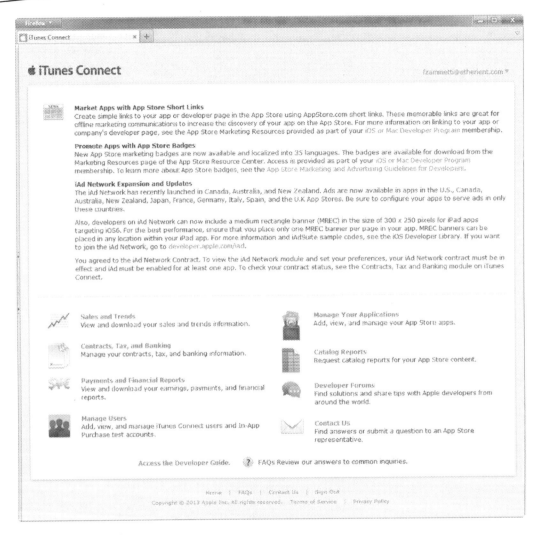

Figure 11-8. iTunes Connect site

Click the Manage Your Applications link and you'll be brought to a page that lists all your existing apps, if any, but the most important feature will be the Add New App button. Once you click that you'll be guided through the process of creating an iTunes Connect app record, which you can think of as the stub of your new application. You'll enter some basic application information as in other stores and eventually, at the end, the record will be created.

You'll be returned to iTunes Connect and will need to select the new link to manage your new application that has been added for you by the system. You will then have to fill out an export compliance questionnaire and then click the Ready to Upload Binary button. The status of the record will then change to Waiting for Upload.

The next step is back on your Mac in the Corona Simulator. Build your app again and this time use a distribution profile that you create. Once you do so you'll be greeted with the message shown in Figure 11-9.

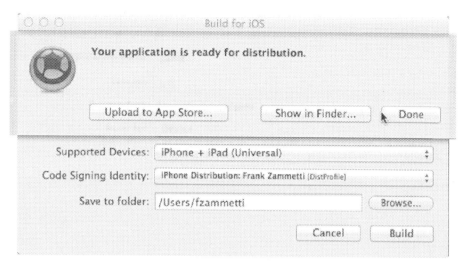

Figure 11-9. *Building for distribution*

Click the Upload to App Store button and the Application Loader (Figure 11-10) will be launched. This tool will walk you through the process of uploading your app in a few simple steps.

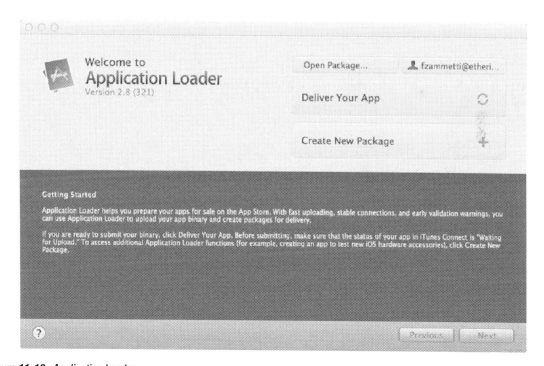

Figure 11-10. *Application Loader*

You simply click the Deliver Your App button and follow the simple directions. Note that you will only be able to do this if the record on the iTunes Connect site is in the Waiting for Upload status, so be sure it is before launching Application Loader or you'll have to start back in the Corona Simulator again.

Once the binary is uploaded your app will be pending review, and then it's just a waiting game (and crossing your fingers hoping it gets through review unscathed!). If you do need to make changes based on the review, you'll follow the same basic steps outlined here and again click the Ready to Upload Binary button in the iTunes Connect site and upload the new version through Application Loader.

Eventually, though, your app will be published and with a little luck you'll be putting your kids through college with money to spare in no time!

Summary

In this chapter, you took the final steps (well, "final" steps in terms of initial development at least—developing a good app almost never stops!) that any application goes through: building and deploying to various real devices for testing.

I also talked about some techniques for debugging on a real device to gather information and deal with real-world issues that don't always arise in the Corona Simulator.

Last, I discussed the app store models of Android and iOS and what it takes to get an app published in those stores.

And with this final chapter, we conclude our journey of exploration in the Corona SDK. I hope you've enjoyed the trip and have learned a lot along the way. I bid you now venture out into the world and produce great games and applications with all you've learned, and it goes without saying: name your next child after me!

Index